THE BULTMANN SCHOOL OF BIBLICAL INTERPRETATION:

NEW DIRECTIONS?

harper ✝ torchbooks

A reference-list of Harper Torchbooks, classified
by subjects, is printed at the end of this volume.

THE BULTMANN SCHOOL OF BIBLICAL INTERPRETATION: NEW DIRECTIONS?

With an Essay Introducing
Journal for Theology and the Church

J. C. B. MOHR (PAUL SIEBECK) TÜBINGEN
HARPER & ROW, PUBLISHERS, INC. NEW YORK
1965

JOURNAL FOR THEOLOGY AND THE CHURCH

Printed in the United States of America

©

1965
J. C. B. Mohr (Paul Siebeck) Tübingen
Harper & Row, Publishers, Inc. New York
First edition: HARPER TORCHBOOKS, published 1965 by
Harper & Row, Publishers, Incorporated
49 East 33rd Street
New York, N. Y. 10016

CONTENTS

AUTHORS

BRAUN, HERBERT, University of Mainz
Friedrich-von-Pfeiffer-Weg 5, Mainz, Germany

DINKLER, ERICH, University of Heidelberg
Karlstraße 4, Heidelberg, Germany

FUCHS, ERNST, University of Marburg
Schückingstraße 15, Marburg/Lahn, Germany

GESE, HARTMUT, University of Tübingen
Wildermuthstraße 36, Tübingen, Germany

HAENCHEN, ERNST, University of Münster
Steveninkstraße 12, Münster/Westfalen, Germany

KÄSEMANN, ERNST, University of Tübingen
Eduard-Haber-Straße 13, Tübingen, Germany

KOESTER, HELMUT, Harvard Divinity School
45 Francis Avenue, Cambridge, Massachusetts

NOTH, MARTIN, University of Bonn
Lennéstraße 24, Bonn, Germany

ROBINSON, JAMES M., Claremont Graduate School
3650 Padua Avenue, Claremont, California

TRANSLATORS

BATDORF, IRVIN W., United Theological Seminary
 Dayton, Ohio

BELLINZONI, ARTHUR, Wells College
 Aurora, New York

BUNGE, WILFRED, Harvard Divinity School
 Cambridge, Massachusetts

CARSE, ALICE F., Drew University
 Madison, New Jersey

KRODEL, GERHARD, Lutheran Theological Seminary
 Philadelphia, Pennsylvania

ROSS, JAMES F., The Theological School, Drew University
 Madison, New Jersey

SANDERS, JACK, Candler School of Theology, Emory University
 Atlanta, Georgia

WILSON, JACK, Tennessee Wesleyan College
 Athens, Tennessee

ABBREVIATIONS

BETh	Beiträge zur Evangelischen Theologie
BHTh	Beiträge zur Historischen Theologie
ExpT	Expository Times
HNT	Handbuch zum Neuen Testament
HTR	Harvard Theological Review
ICC	International Critical Commentary
JR	Journal of Religion
NTS	New Testament Studies
RE	Realencyclopädie für Protestantische Theologie und Kirche
RGG	Die Religion in Geschichte und Gegenwart
ThLZ	Theologische Literaturzeitung
ThR	Theologische Rundschau (NF = Neue Folge)
ThW	Theologisches Wörterbuch zum Neuen Testament
TU	Texte und Untersuchungen zur Geschichte der Altchristlichen Literatur
WA	Martin Luther, Werke: Weimarer Ausgabe
ZAW	Zeitschrift für die Alttestamentliche Wissenschaft
ZDPV	Zeitschrift des Deutschen Palästina-Vereins (NF = Neue Folge)
ZNW	Zeitschrift für die Neutestamentliche Wissenschaft (und die Kunde der Älteren Kirche)
ZThK	Zeitschrift für Theologie und Kirche

FOREWORD

JOURNAL FOR THEOLOGY AND THE CHURCH was conceived in a late night conversation with Gerhard Ebeling during the First Drew Consultation on Hermeneutics in 1962. Looking back on the road that has been traversed since that first talk, now that the first two numbers are ready for the press, it seems short and troublefree indeed. To be sure, many obstacles had to be overcome, but the support and encouragement received by the board helped smooth the way as well as buttress the conviction that the undertaking was worthwhile.

That JOURNAL FOR THEOLOGY AND THE CHURCH 1 and 2 are to appear simultaneously in 1965 is to be credited, above all, to Gerhard Ebeling and the board of ZEITSCHRIFT FÜR THEOLOGIE UND KIRCHE. This distinguished circle agreed, in the course of conversations with members of the *JThC* board, than an English affiliate of *ZThK* would not only serve to broadcast current (in distinction from recent) Continental theology, but to enter into its formulation and testing as well. A sister organ in English, moreover, might be of some benefit to English language theology in and of itself. They were disposed, as a consequence, to lend themselves to the effort of launching a comparable English language journal. They did not propose to help create their own echo, but to help precipitate, if it were desired, a theological dialogue native to the English language world. Such a journal, to be sure, ought to maintain a lively tension with its counterpart in the interests of both Continental and American theology. The board of *JThC* is acutely aware of the trust that has been vested in it by virtue of this invitation to enter into association.

Hans Georg Siebeck, the *Inhaber* of the J. C. B. Mohr *Verlag* and publisher of *ZThK*, was no less sensitive to the possibilities of such a move. He opened the way by agreeing to publish the JOURNAL under his own imprint if necessary. Harper & Row subsequently entered the picture, with the joint result now before the reader. Vindication of the courage of both publishers and of the generosity of the editor and board of *ZThK* now rests with the editorial circle of *JThC* – which will endeavor to merit the attention of all those concerned with theology for the church and for our time – and with the reader – who will perhaps find something in these pages worthy of his sustained consideration.

It should also be said that others gave unstintingly of their time and effort in helping us analyze innumerable problems and proposals. In addition, we should like to acknowledge the special contribution of Professor Raymond P. Morris of the Yale Divinity School, whose keen insight and sound judgment have proved invaluable.

Beyond those who helped bring JOURNAL FOR THEOLOGY AND THE CHURCH into existence, there are those who shared in the production of the first two numbers. For that something extra which makes translation an art rather than a science, thanks are due my colleague, Karlfried Froehlich, who masterfully edited the translations. He is also responsible in part for formal matters. And finally, notice must be taken of the translators who worked industriously and imaginatively at a difficult task. While such quality as has been achieved would not have been easily possible without such assistance, the board and editor must take responsibility for the final form of the material and such blemishes as the JOURNAL may have.

A word is in order regarding format. It may seem odd that a journal should take the form of a paperback book. On the other hand, when one reflects on it, it seems odder still that it is not the rule rather than the exception. The paperback is a more convenient size than the standard journal, comes already bound for the benefit of those who find preserving issues a headache, and is readily available on the bookrack at the local bookseller. Building and maintaining a subscription list, and the expense of mailing, moreover, are formidable overhead items which drive the subscription rates of journals up. The paperback journal, by contrast, is distributed through regular channels, thus making it possible to offer it at a substantially lower price. It is to be hoped that our readers will appreciate this difference and will find it possible to acquire the JOURNAL regularly, either through a local bookseller or by standing order at one of the mail-order houses.

JOURNAL FOR THEOLOGY AND THE CHURCH 1 and 2 reflect the initial stage of the JOURNAL as conceived by the board – one in which we are leaning exclusively or heavily on our affiliate, the *ZThK*. There are two reasons for this. First, we wish to make available some of the significant material published in *ZThK* since it was reorganized under the editorship of Gerhard Ebeling. Early numbers of the JOURNAL will therefore be devoted largely to what has been going on in the pages of *ZThK* between 1950 and the present. And second, the flow of English language contributions will require some time – hopefully no more than a few issues – to develop and to create its own focus. As quickly as the latter materializes, the initial stage will give way to one in which original contributions in English take their place alongside the most significant essays from *ZThK*. For it is the concern of the board of *JThC* to cultivate an indigenous English language theological conversation no less than to foster an international dialogue. In fact, if the former does not emerge, both aims of the JOURNAL will have been frustrated. James M. Robinson has set out this ground plan, together with its underlying rationale, in his introductory essay in the first number.

JOURNAL FOR THEOLOGY AND THE CHURCH 1 presents eight provocative essays from the biblical field, all taken from *ZThK*. In the judgment of the board, each of these essays is significant both for the special discipline from which it emanates and for theology as a whole. It is these two criteria which governed the selection of items to be included. *JThC* 2 offers six stimulating essays in historical, systematic and pastoral theology. These essays likewise reach deep into and far beyond their particular domains. If we have succeeded in forging an inseparable unity between sound scientific scholarship and theological relevance in these numbers, we will have established the character we intend the JOURNAL to have throughout its existence. And we are rash enough to think that English language theologians, theological students, ecclesiastical officials, pastors, and even, or perhaps especially, laymen will welcome the confluence of the two and will profit by it.

Second Sunday in Advent, 1964   ROBERT W. FUNK, Editor
                                             The Theological School
                                             Drew University

For Theology and the Church

by

James M. Robinson

The purpose of this article is to introduce the *Journal for Theology and the Church*. This title contains two overtones audible to the perceptive ear. On the one hand it reflects the title of the German journal, the *Zeitschrift für Theologie und Kirche*, from whose pages some of its contents are drawn. On the other hand it draws into focus the dialectic nature of the cause for which the Journal stands: theology in relation to the church. It is this dialectic relation between theology and the church to which the *Zeitschrift für Theologie und Kirche* has from its beginning been devoted and which has given it its distinctive character throughout its history. It is thus the purpose of this essay to clarify this dialectic and at the same time to provide a survey of the course of the *Zeitschrift für Theologie und Kirche* out of which the *Journal for Theology and the Church* emerges. In this way the issue involved in this dialectic will not remain abstract, nor will the history of the *ZThK* remain immaterial.

The journal in the forefront of German theology since World War II has been the *Zeitschrift für Theologie und Kirche*. On its pages have appeared the programmatic essays leading to most of the new trends characterizing German theology today. "The Problem of the Historical Jesus" was posed anew by Ernst Käsemann in an essay by that title in the *ZThK* in 1954 (Vol. 51, pp. 125–153), and the ensuing movement has continued to center in the *ZThK*, as is indicated e. g. by the supplementary number of 1959 on "The Question about the Historical Jesus" (Vol. 56, *Beiheft* 1). The debate with Heinrich Ott as to the extent to which the philosophy of the later Heidegger shifts the weight of philosophical rapport from the Bultmannian to the Barthian side of theology has been carried on most vigorously in the *ZThK*, as a second supplementary number devoted to that issue indicates (*Beiheft* 2, 1961). The emergence of "the Problem of Hermeneutic" as a focus of contemporary debate was anticipated by Rudolf Bultmann in the first post-war number in an essay by that title (Vol. 47, 1950, pp. 47–69; Eng. tr. in *Essays Philosophical and Theological*, pp. 234–261), a movement carried forward in the *ZThK* in a series of essays by Gerhard Ebeling culminating in his "Word of God and

Hermeneutic" in 1959 (Vol. 56, pp. 224–251; Eng. tr. in *Word and Faith*, pp. 305–332).

This is not to say that no significant movements have emerged in other journals. The current discussion in the field of Old Testament theology calls to mind essays in *Evangelische Theologie* (esp. Vol. 12, Number 1/2, 1952 [largely translated in *Interpretation*, 15, 1961, *passim*] and Vol. 22, Number 1/2, 1962); and the somewhat related movement of younger scholars grouped around Wolfhart Pannenberg presented its programmatic essay in the periodical *Kerygma und Dogma* (Pannenberg's "Heilsgeschichte und Geschichte," Vol. 5, 1959, pp.218–237, 259–288: Eng. tr. of first part in *Essays on Old Testament Hermeneutics*). Nevertheless, the *Zeitschrift für Theologie und Kirche* has played such a dominant role on the German scene as to make the abbreviation *ZThK* a symbol of scholarly perceptiveness and critical relevance for the church of our time.

Various of the new trends that have emerged in the *ZThK* have gradually been introduced into the English speaking community. The series of "Discussions among Continental and American Theologians" appearing under the general title *New Frontiers in Theology* is using material drawn from the *ZThK* as lead essays for the first two volumes. Material from the *ZThK* has also been republished in a number of volumes of collected essays, a literary *genre* that of late has tended to replace the monograph in Germany, and these volumes are gradually being translated into English. For example, Ebeling's *Word and Faith* and Ernst Käsemann's *Essays on New Testament Themes* consist of essays primarily drawn from the *ZThK*. In these ways, the relevance of the *ZThK* to our scene is already well attested.

The *Journal for Theology and the Church*—the *JThC*—proposes to recognize this relevance of the *ZThK* to our scene by presenting its most significant essays in English dress. Initially the *JThC* will incorporate landmarks from as far back as 1950, but the board of the *JThC* will have access to forthcoming essays of the *ZThK* prior to their publication in German and thus will be able to choose, translate and publish the most important ones in English within a year of their appearance in German. In this way two of the main impediments to discussion between the German and English theological communities may be overcome. The time lag between the publication in one language and the translation into the other has in the past often been so great that the debate in the one language had for better or worse been terminated before the theological community dependent upon the other language had entered the discussion. In recent years increasing contacts and language fluency have done much to overcome this time lag; the *JThC* proposes to bring this synchronizing trend one step nearer to simultaneity for a wider theological community.

A second impediment has been that only a relatively few authors or works have been translated, so that the theological matrix out of which their work is to be understood is largely absent. For this reason outstanding works and movements from the other language even when translated seem to float in the air, unrelated to any known reality, coming from nowhere and going to nowhere. This is a glaring instance of the fact that even the best translation does not automatically convey the meaning the work had in the original context. For what may originally have been a really necessary and liberating break-through may in another context come to mean an unnecessary troubling of the waters, a new foreign fad that will soon blow away. Only when one has lived with a theological tradition for a time will a work growing out of it be sensed to have a tie-in with the basic and inescapable task of theology; and only then are its outstanding achievements grasped in their inner necessity and in their relative adequacy for coping with the problems which are addressed. And only then is the theological community of the other language area really in a position to enter into discussion at the deepest level. Thus the *JThC* is not devoted to the narrow interest of any one theological discipline, but rather provides a cross-section of significant German discussion. Over a period of time this could equip the English language theological community to evaluate German theology in a broader and deeper way. In turn theology in the English language will become more urgently relevant to German theologians, who in that way will sense that their problems and proposals have been heard, understood, and taken into account.

It is thus our hope that a two-way discussion will emerge and that the *JThC* can, at an early date, combine translations from the *ZThK* with original English language contributions to the common discussion. If, as has been suggested, the *ZThK* not only has taken the lead in posing theological issues in the last half century and more, but has steadfastly maintained a theological tension with and for the church, the *ZThK* is a natural affiliate for a comparable English language periodical. The initial numbers of the *JThC* will be confined to translations from the *ZThK*, and will serve as an intermediate step in the movement toward a genuine international dialogue on the one hand, and the creation of an indigenous English theological conversation on the other. For if the discussion is to mean the same thing in the English language world as does the *ZThK* on the German scene, it must be carried on among English language theologians as a critique of English language proclamation devoted to making audible what God is saying to us in our situation. Consequently, it is the intention of the board that the *JThC* become, as soon as possible, the medium not only of a lively dialogue between the two theological spheres but also of a robust internal conversation. In this way the aims being set forth here will be brought even closer to fruition.

That the issues of German language theology are not automatically appropriate to the English language world is made evident by noting, for example, that the empirical tradition in English language philosophy provides a different context for scholarship than that of Germany—just as, incidentally, the continuation of German idealism in English language philosophy from Carlyle to Hocking and Kroner is a factor in much of our theology that distinguishes it from contemporary German theology, where a positive correlation with idealism is less typical. Furthermore the American denominations, though largely derived from European confessions and sects, are a different form of church life from either the state church or the sect, as is often most obvious precisely in the comparison of the American branch of a European church with the European "equivalent." European theologians visiting in America are themselves the first to sense the dimensions of the theological translation involved—even where, as in the case of the British, a foreign language barrier is not present.

The focus here given to translation between the German and English language areas is based simply upon the fact that these are the two largest areas of Protestantism. If Germany—or the German language area— has produced a remarkably large share of critical theological thought over the past two centuries, one may recall that at the beginning of that period German theology received its impetus largely from English theology. Whereas e. g. Herder stands at the beginning of the German recognition of the relevance of man's historicness to the hermeneutical task, his precurser was a scholar of New College, Oxford, Robert Lowth. One may compare Lowth's *De Sacra Poesi Hebraeorum Praelectiones Academicae* of 1753—reprinted in Germany in 1758 and 1770, and in German translation in 1815—with Herder's *Vom Geist der hebräischen Poesie* of 1782 ff.

Our choice of a German journal as the basis for the *JThC* thus does not imply any inherent qualification of the German language area for superior theological reflection. The thesis *anima germanica naturaliter christiana*, though emerging in the bitterness of defeat after World War I (*ZThK*, 28, n. s. 1, 1920, p. 5), has long since lost its advocates. On the other hand we are indeed concerned that the translation of the *ZThK* into English eventuate in such a radical translation into our situation that it comes to expression in original English language contributions. Yet this concern does not involve a theological chauvinism that would relate this language area to a preferable revelation of God. Just as the Germans have had enough of theological blood, race, and soil, so have we had enough of "the white man's burden," "manifest destiny," "the American (Southern) way of life," etc., as thinly veiled theologies of national self-interest. As observers from Kierkegaard to the so-called non-Christian nations agree in pointing out, Christendom and what is Christian do not coincide. The hermeneutical objective of translating fully into a culture so that God's word speaks in the language of the culture should not be identified with the assumption that the culture is inherently Christian or that this hermeneutical procedure harmonizes Christian faith and the culture. It is within the language of a given culture that God's word can best carry through its critical task with regard to that culture. For here too the hermeneutical circle is at work. The language used to convey the meaning is itself subject to criticism in terms of that meaning, and, just as every translation is imperfect, the continuing task of translation is itself a heuristic aid in identifying those areas in a culture in which such criticism is most needed.

We are also aware that the English language world of theological discourse into which the *ZThK* is being translated is not simply the area across the channel and the North Atlantic, but also the vast areas beyond, for which English is the *lingua franca* of theological discourse. To be sure these areas will have a further task of translation, as the theological discussion here translated into and carried on within the English language world of discourse is translated into indigenous languages and cultures. For with regard to the younger churches the hermeneutical task has become clear even to those who remain blind to it in their own cultures: the difficulty of preserving meaning in a language with completely different thought patterns and associations—and yet the necessity of radical translation, if the message is to mean Christian faith and not simply Western imperialism.

In view of the linguistic gulf over which the translation must be made in many such cases, it is true that the dimensions of the translation task between German and English should not be exaggerated. The German contribution to the American population—from Hessian deserters via Nineteenth Century famines to GI-brides—is second only to the British component. And this has been true specifically of American theology. William Sanday, in tracing the history of the exegesis of Romans, states: "At a time when biblical exegesis was not being very actively prosecuted in Great Britain two works of solid merit were produced in America. One of these was by Moses Stuart, who did much to naturalize German methods. ... Like Moses Stuart, Dr. (Charles) Hodge also owed much of his philological equipment to Germany where he had studied" (*ICC, Romans,* pp. cvi-cvii); and Burton Scott Easton designated the Swiss born and German trained Philip Schaff the "father" of New Testament scholarship in America (*ExpT*, March, 1931; cf. Alexander C. Purdy, *ThR*, n.F. 3, 1931, 377). Not only did the Nineteenth Century include the Mercersburg school related more directly to the German part of the population, but in the Twentieth Century the theologians of nation-wide significance have been primarily those with explicit German ties: Rauschenbusch, the Niebuhrs, and Tillich—not to speak of such influential imports as Brunnerite, Barthian, and Bultmannian theology. And just as American isolationism in the Mid-West often involved pro-German sympathies on the part of the immigrant population, the Chicago school of theology—which in that period seemed most genuinely American—was built upon such scholars as Edgar Goodspeed and Shirley Jackson Case, whose roots were deep in German as well as American scholarship.

Indicative of the tradition of German-American theological ties only temporarily interrupted by the period of the two world wars is the fact that a journal was published in German in the United States for thirty-seven years, from 1879 through 1916, under the title *Deutsch-Amerika-nische Zeitschrift für Theologie und Kirche*. This inter-denominational organ for German-speaking Protestantism in America, though betraying theological proclivities that were often more oriented to Erlangen than to Marburg, did mediate to the German immigrant population not only German theology, but probably the only English language theology (in book reviews and translations) to which most of its readers had access. It pooled the resources of the various German language theological seminaries in America, such as the Baptist seminary at Rochester, New York (with Walter Rauschenbusch at one time on the Editorial Board of the Journal), the Presbyterian seminary at Bloomfield, New Jersey, and the Methodist Nast Theological Seminary of Berea, Ohio, whose faculty edited the "dritte Folge" of the journal until its abrupt termination in the throes of the first World War.

Meanwhile the *Zeitschrift für Theologie und Kirche* was founded in 1891 in Germany, as a result of the conviction that the relation of theology and the church is not what it should be. The theology of relevance to the church is sometimes regarded as being at a less scholarly (and "more practical") level than that carried on at the university. It is especially the role of critical scholarship within a church that understands itself as *ecclesia semper reformanda* which is often obscured. Sometimes such evaluations within church circles are taken at face value in scholarly circles, with the result that a science of religion emerges whose claim to scholarly excellence is coupled with explicit withdrawal from participation in the concerns of the church. Thus the critical role of theological scholarship in and for the church tends on both sides to be obscured.

Julius Kaftan began the *ZThK* with a programmatic essay that expressed this concern as follows: "Theology and the church mutually condition and influence each other. It was to serve the church that theology arose in Christianity. It must execute this service in its way and with its means, i.e. as a science and with intellectual means. But the task is and remains service to the church. Conversely the church most decidedly cannot dispense with such service on the part of theology. Christianity as an intellectual religion has to stand for a universal truth. Furthermore it arose in the civilized world and has found its abode among civilized nations. Hence the church can not preserve and spread Christianity without making use, among other things, of the services of science, indeed without calling into being and cultivating a science peculiar to itself, namely theology."

The editorial board of the *ZThK* included Adolf Harnack and Wilhelm Herrmann, so that the *ZThK* was clearly the "organ of the Ritschlian School" (*PRE*, 3rd ed., XXIV, 1913, p. 684; *RGG*, 2nd ed., II, 1928, col. 1404). Main editorial responsibility was vested in Julius Gottschick, one of Ritschl's most faithful pupils, who had already published in 1890 a work entitled "The Churchliness of the So-called Churchly Theology Tested," followed in 1893 by a work on "The Significance of the Critical Historical Study of Scripture for the Evangelical Church"—a title to be echoed more than half a century later when Gerhard Ebeling re-opened the journal in 1950 with an essay on "The Significance of the Critical Historical Method for Church and Theology in Protestantism" (Vol. 47, pp. 1–46; Eng. tr. in *Word and Faith*, pp. 17–61). Thus the *ZThK* has from the first been committed to the standpoint that critical scholarship stands in a positive relationship to the church—both in the sense that critical scholars should understand their work as a service for and in the church, and in the sense that the church should understand critical scholarship in the same way. It was this thesis that Kaftan worked out for his day in his lead essay, and that has received a series of restatements as the *ZThK* has translated itself into a series of new generations and altered situations.

Although Kaftan's statement at every step betrays, as it should, the language of his day, its material position is remarkably similar to the hermeneutic of Ebeling's lead essay of 1950. Although "Christianity" is always "experienced as the same," the "forms in which it expresses itself" are "inseparable from the change of times and things" (p. 3). It is in this hermeneutical context that the basic material influence of theology upon the church and the church upon theology is seen. When e.g. "in place of the near kingdom of the consummation that would bring the returning Lord there emerged (the concept of) future deification causally rooted in the incarnation of the Son of God who had come," this shift was not an arbitrary move on theology's part, but rather a necessary step, if Christianity was to "plant itself firmly in the intellectual world of antiquity" (p. 4). Conversely, the inevitable influence of the church upon theology is illustrated by the influence of the legal institutionism in the Western church upon the doctrine of the atonement, as is evidenced by the rapid and continuing prevalence of Anselm's theory of legal satisfaction in the theology of the West, but not in that of the East.

Such positive interaction between theology and the church is as it should be, and need cause no basic tension. Kaftan sensed such a tension in his day, manifesting itself in an attempt on the part of the church to limit theology's freedom. This situation Kaftan traced back to a reticence on the church's part to carry through its hermeneutical task. Romanticism and idealism had rightly reacted against the rationalism of the enlightenment, introducing at the opening of the Nineteenth Century a "new theology" that was necessary. But by Kaftan's time that theology had perpetuated itself as a power-invested establishment in a situation for which it was no longer adequate. "But especially the inner stance of the participants had inevitably become another one with the change of generations and times" (p. 10). The earlier idealist theologians had known themselves to be standing "in union with the emerging powers of their time" (p. 10), whereas in a period dominated by the natural sciences and detailed historical research such a theology does not take place "in awareness of harmony with the intellectual forces of the present" (p. 11). Rather it is compelled to insist upon its authority and upon the tradition in order to maintain itself in a situation to which it no longer really speaks. That is to say, the same theology in a different situation has come to mean something quite different.

Over against this theology of the ecclesiastical hierarchy there had emerged at the university a theology that had been compelled to go its own way if it was to fulfill its hermeneutical task of addressing the day and age in which it found itself. This theology had replaced the philosophical speculation characteristic of the first half of the Nineteenth Century with the historical research characteristic of the second half. Thus the hermeneutical tension between church and theology had in practice its focus in the differing role accorded to the critical historical method. "The churchly renewal still clings even in the present to the theological forms in which it originally arose—forms that rest, in what concerns Scripture and dogma, upon erroneous presuppositions. But on the other hand theology is working out more accurate historical knowledge that does not fail to indicate different directions for the theological undertaking as a whole" (p. 12). Kaftan argues that this theology, not that of the ecclesiastical hierarchy, is the truly churchly theology. "That which decides here as to what is churchly and what really advances the church is *faith* and only faith, namely the faith that bases itself upon God's word as it must be understood according to its own meaning, faith that corresponds to the intention of the Reformation; and this decides against those dominant ecclesiastical tendencies" (p. 18). "We want first of all to see with a *free eye* what the *real* Holy Scripture really is and really contains—not a loss but a gain for faith" (p. 21).

If the method of historical criticism is the particular mode of thinking into which theology at the end of the Nineteenth Century is to be translated, it is, conversely, the active force compelling recognition of such translation as the basic task of theology. For historical criticism had so altered the understanding of the individual theological disciplines as to necessitate a new understanding of the whole theological enterprise. OT scholarship had replaced "a picture that itself first arose as a product of later religious reflection" with "the understanding of the revelation as a *historical development*" (p. 22). The NT in turn is not the work of dogmaticians and philosophers of religion, but is rather "a living organism of historical revelation of God. Not theories but facts, real historical facts, not dogmatically constructed facts, comprise the content of the NT proclamation" (p. 22). This understanding of the Bible based upon historical criticism means conversely for the understanding of the history of doctrine "that the most important affirmations of ecclesiastical doctrine are not as they are formulated derived from Holy Scripture, but rather are the *product of ecclesiastical doctrinal construction*" (p. 23). The recognition that these constructions are often not the expression of faith but rather of divergent forms of piety prevalent at various times relativizes the authority of dogma for the believer and leads to a new understanding of the function of doctrinal theology: Its task is not to complete the systems of the past but to restate Christian meaning for today. Systematic theology becomes contemporary theology.

It was thus historical criticism, in disengaging the sharp contours within biblical and historical theology, that dramatized the fundamental necessity for envisaging theology as a whole in terms of the hermeneutical problem. This understanding of historical criticism in its hermeneutical implications and hence in its direct relevance for theology and the church is the specific scope of the *ZThK*. "Of course it is an urgent need to advocate this historical knowledge of Scripture over against the aftereffects of the old method, and to make intelligible its churchly significance, *its significance for faith*. To share in this work is one of the tasks that our Journal poses for itself. Detailed research and discussions relevant only within one discipline remain outside its scope. There is hardly a need for creating a new medium for collecting works of this kind. In any case that is not the intention here. Our concern is theological work in the service of the church" (p. 23).

To be sure there is much in Kaftan's presentation that would call for criticism today, such as the naive identification of the results of positivistic historiography with the subject matter of theology, an identification against which Barth so violently protested in his famous debate with Harnack; the equally naive assumption that having rejected idealism meant having freed oneself from philosophical influence as a whole, whereas one had merely taken over the positivism implicit in the natural sciences of the day; the unclear mingling of the hermeneutical task of translating into the language of the culture with "conforming to and making oneself at home in" a culture in the sense of the *Kulturprotestan-*

tismus that tended to deify the culture rather than confronting it critically with God's word; the assumption that the task of translation was still incomplete merely because Protestantism had not completed its task, rather than recognizing that the hermeneutical task is unending. Indeed Kaftan had not yet grasped the position he advocated in terms of hermeneutic as such, for it was only with the renewal of the *ZThK* in 1950 that the position characteristic of the *ZThK* was identified by Ebeling as the hermeneutical position.

The second period in the life of the *ZThK* began in 1907, when at the death of Gottschick the editorship passed into the hands of Wilhelm Herrmann and Martin Rade. Herrmann had lectured at the University of Chicago in 1904 (*ZThK*, 15, 1905, 1–26), and Rade participated in the International Congress of Religious Liberals in Boston in 1907. Thus both editors were in personal contact with American theology in its home grounds—a policy resumed in 1962 and 1963 with the visits of Gerhard Ebeling to America. Under Herrmann and Rade the *ZThK* shifted its emphasis from a primary orientation upon the historical disciplines in their theological relevance to a priority of doctrinal theology, as was indicated by a new sub-title, "Organ for Systematic and Principle Theology." This was explained in a prospectus that read as follows:

"Our intention is to make the journal more than ever into a working organ for *principle, systematic theology*. Dogmatics and ethics are to be especially cultivated, and, in addition, what from the fields of Old and New Testament scholarship, doctrinal, ecclesiastical, and religious history, and practical theology is relevant to the discussion of the religious contents, the correct methods, and the mutual relations between theology and the church. All these disciplines have at their disposal departmental periodicals that tend increasingly to lose themselves in practical matters or in technical interests of relevance only within the given field. Over against this tendency we wish to seek after a more rigorous *concentration of the whole theological undertaking* and to draw together the fragmented achievement of the disciplines under the idea of the one truth and the one goal.

"There are at hand indications enough to the effect that it is desirable to move beyond one-sided critical historical work to *lay hold of the connections and ideas*. We would like to serve this need for basic consideration of the total situation of our religious knowledge and for energetic utilization of what historiography has achieved for faith and living.

"There are already enough periodicals, and there will emerge still more, that reach out into the breadth of modern intellectual life, to prove their Christianity in an intellectual give and take. We in our journal would like to provide a place where theology can hold communion with itself and reflect upon its most inner nature and task, so as to collect new insight and strength for the discussion with minds outside.

"Thus the *Zeitschrift für Theologie und Kirche* addresses itself simply and confidently to the *theologians*, more precisely to all those who, aware that much work must be done within the theological scholarly enterprise that does not ask '*Cui bono?*' nonetheless realize that above it all there must stand the recognition: *Theology* is to serve the *church* and conversely lives from the *service of the church*."

A new feature of the *ZThK* introduced with the new management was a section of "Theses and Antitheses," an open forum much like the "Letters to the Editor" section in our magazines. In the first issue as co-editor Martin Rade replied to a complaint about the impracticality of theological education with remarks revelatory of the new editors' concept of the journal: "Why are we talking about all this today and in this place? Because no doubt should arise that our Journal, in the moment when it would like to become a special organ for the department of dogmatics and ethics, intends at the same time and by that very means nothing other than to *serve church practice*. This is intended not at all in the sense that we want to enshroud with a practical mantle what we say and do... There can be no question in our dogmatic and ethical discussions of rushing impatiently to draw the moral from the story. That has all too often meant to pluck the fruit before it is ripe, or even to send invitations to the harvest festival when the tree has yet to bloom. But the *Zeitschrift für Theologie und Kirche* would not be an organ for systematic theology if it did not derive its material, the mass of problems it confronts, again and again from life, in order to give them back to life" (*ZThK*, 17, 1907, 68f.).

If Martin Rade, seasoned editor of the *Christliche Welt*, assumed responsibility for the technical process of editing the *ZThK*, it was his co-editor Wilhelm Herrmann whose theological position provided its focal center. Herrmann had been on the editorial board since the beginning, and had been indeed the first contributor ("The Penance of the Evangelical Christian," *ZThK*, 1, 1891, 28–81). The last volume to appear during World War I was a *Festschrift* for Herrmann's seventieth birthday (Vol. 27, 1917), and the first issue to appear after the war opened with an essay whose sub-title was "A War-time Testimony to Wilhelm Herrmann's Religion" (*ZThK*, 28, n.s. 1, 1920, 3–13). Indeed Herrmann was "the most important adviser" at the reorganization after World War I, according to Horst Stephan, successor to Herrmann and Rade as editor, in his obituary at Herrmann's death (*ZThK*, 30, n.s. 3, 1922, 1). Herrmann's position continued to be represented after the termination of his editorship e.g. in the essay of his pupil F. W. Schmidt on "The Relation of Christology to the Quest of the Historical Jesus" (*ZThK*, 28, n.s. 1, 1920, 249–276, 323–353). And when the *ZThK* came to be reorganized after World War II, Ebeling named Herrmann in first place among the "manifold lines of communication" between contemporary theology and Nineteenth Century

theology—a remark whose significance for the future as well as for the
past has become increasingly evident in the *ZThK*, in Ebeling's own
appropriation of Herrmann's interpretation of Jesus as the "ground of
faith." One may compare in this regard Herrmann's essay "The Historic
Christ the Ground of our Faith" (*ZThK*, 2, 1892, 232–273) with Ebeling's
essay "Jesus and Faith" (*ZThK*, 55, 1958, 64–110; Eng. tr. in *Word and
Faith*, pp. 201–246). Indicative of the relevance of Herrmann for the
discussion now taking place in the *ZThK* is the republication in 1960
(Vol. 57, 231–237) of Herrmann's review, originally published in 1912
(*ThLZ*, 37, 245–249), of Troeltsch's pamphlet of 1911 on "The Significance of the Historicity of Jesus for Faith."

The revival of Herrmann's theology in Germany today is primarily due
to Herrmann's basic recognition of the hermeneutical importance of the
modern secular world in which the church finds itself. "For the people of
our time Christ is initially not a fact unquestionably certain to them.
Hence pointing to him does not bring them upon the path of self-examin-
ation which the reformers walked... Hence we must rather, if we want to
show what is universally valid about religion, think only of that which
must be visible to the man who is able and willing to become clearer about
himself. Only thus do we create for ancient Christianity a basis for its
effectiveness also in our time" (*ZThK*, 17, 1907, 194f.). The task of
translation can hardly be grasped more radically than in such statements—
which have great relevance for our situation, analyzed by Dietrich Bon-
hoeffer as a secularized, post-Christian world that has come of age and
outgrown religion.

Herrmann identified in the modern concern for ethics the path that
leads to Christian faith. He opened his editorship of the *ZThK* with a
programmatic essay calling upon the church to recognize this approach as
the truly churchly theology, rather than the doctrinal systems preferred
by the ecclesiastical hierarchy ("The Situation and Task of Evangelical
Dogmatics in the Present," *ZThK*, 17, 1907, 1–33, 172–201, 315–351).
This approach to theology of relevance in a secular world has been renewed
half a century later by Gerhard Ebeling, in an essay on "Theology and the
Evidentness of the Ethical" (*ZThK*, 57, 1960, 318–356), that, appropriately
enough, is presented in the second number of the *JThC*. Neither for Herrmann
nor for Ebeling is it a matter of providing an ethical proof for Christian
faith, as has been suggested by Wolfhart Pannenberg in his critical response,
"Theology and the Crisis of Ethics" (*ThLZ*, 87, 1962, 7–16). Rather, the
argument of Herrmann and Ebeling is that faith is the ground of ethics. If
the summons of ethics is "universally valid" (Herrmann), "evident" (Ebeling), but can be adequately met only on the basis of Christian faith, then the
indispensibility of faith is itself evident in an age for which Christian faith
would otherwise seem superfluous. Herrmann states this view as follows:

"The need met by religion and the possibility of understanding it grow out of an activity of the ethical will in a certain direction. All occupation with what one regards as an appearance of religion in history is worthless, so long as one has not recognized this insight and thereby attained the means for distinguishing religion from fantasies that lame man inwardly" (p. 189). It is in this regard that Ebeling can speak of "Herrmann's view of the hermeneutical significance of ethics for theology" (p. 325, n. 1, i.e. *JThC*, no.2, p.102, n.6). For two ingredients are involved in the ethical problem, which Ebeling describes as the "summons to man himself" and the "summons to works"—"the radical demand and the limited demands" (p. 331, i.e. *JThC*, no. 2, p.107). The summons to man himself is met only by faith, and only when it is met can the summons to works be adequately answered. It is in this correlation that the point of faith becomes intelligible to modern man, as is illustrated by no other than Karl Barth, in his concession that is was only on reading Herrmann's *Ethik* that he came to understand what theology is all about (*Theology and Church*, 1962, p. 238, at the opening of a lecture of 1925 on Herrmann).

Herrmann describes this religious problem inherent in ethics as the question of the inner vitality of the will, the question as to whether one has actually become a self. "We are then struck by the question as to whether the concept of a life of our own, a concept we have and make use of, is true, or whether our feeling of selfhood is not rather just the pretense of being a self, i.e. something non-existent" (*ZThK*, 17, 1907, 191). Rather than seeking this authenticity of selfhood in mystic inwardness, Herrmann has recognized man's historicness and hence grapples with the problem of authentic selfhood in view of acknowledging man's finitude and dependence. "Our life feeling is only true when in the reality determining our existence we no longer need to see something foreign to us whose power turns into a deception the concept of a life of our own" (p. 318). At first glance this may seem to be asking the impossible, and indeed to be a contradiction of terms. But on second glance one recognizes that Herrmann has defined, in terms of the historicness of existence, the basic question as to God. If, on conceding our finitude and dependence, life has no authenticity or reality, this is equivalent to saying there is no hope of God in human life. If on the other hand one has encountered a reality upon which one is dependent and which yet brings one to authentic selfhood, then life in history is not a tale told by an idiot signifying nothing; rather the world is a stage where meaningful reality takes place, a world "created by God."

According to Herrmann such an issue cannot be settled scientifically, and indeed such a sophisticated attempt as Troeltsch's philosophy of religion was regarded by Herrmann as sharing with the "positive" ecclesiastical theology the vestiges of the medieval understanding of religion as consisting of ideas one has to believe. According to Herrmann the issue must be settled experientially: Only he who has encountered such a reality that necessitates his submission, and yet does so in a way that actualizes man's selfhood rather than eliminating it, can acknowledge that such is in fact the ultimate nature of reality, i.e. that the world is God's creation.

"We must meet with a reality from which we would be dependent not in the sense of losing thereby the unity of self, but rather in the sense that being determined by that reality would give this inner unity or authentic life" (p. 195). "We are able to give ourselves fully only to the power in whose control over us our will to freedom is carried out. We can experience this only in the power of the good, when we see it intervene in our existence as a power saving us" (p. 319). Thus Herrmann's position is that the only conceivable reality to which one could yield oneself under these conditions is "the power of the good will that accepts us" (p. 196)—or, stated in a play on words (*das Gute, die Güte*), the "good" that we experience as "kindness" toward us (p. 319). "Here alone is complete subjection possible for the human individual for whom it is as impossible to surrender his self as it is to escape the force of the ethical requirement. We can close ourselves inwardly against everything else. In our sense of guilt we feel separated from the power of good when it stands alone, and from all friendliness that is shown us we are separated by the realization that only the good has the right to rule us. Only the union of both forces breaks all resistance in us" (p. 196). When we encounter such a power over us in our own lives, we have encountered God and arrived at religion; our yielding to that power is our faith, which is not our work but God's work upon us.

The crucial question for Herrmann is whether "in the sphere of our own existence" we encounter such a reality in which the reality of our own selfhood can be grounded. When a person experiences self-sacrificial love directed toward him, he catches sight of "another reality" than that which "makes him subservient and splits up his existence," a reality that necessitates his trust. This is the discovery of history in distinction from nature, and this in turn "creates history." "To be sure this lingering at the beginning of historic life in one's own existence is not yet religion, but it is the sole way to it" (p. 320). For Herrmann this historicness of existence finds its solid ground in the encounter with Jesus. "That mighty thing that creates in us the life power of pure surrender, i.e. faith," is "the experienced fact of a wonderful man," Jesus (p. 197).

To be sure the Jesus with whom Herrmann is concerned is in a sense not the "historical Jesus," insofar as that term designates the results of the historian's research. Indeed Herrmann had long since anticipated the Barthian-Bultmannian recognition that the main contribution of historical research to faith is that it "removes false props"; it cannot produce a "biography" of Jesus (*ZThK*, 2, 1892, 251 f.). To those who would associate Herrmann with the quest of the historical Jesus he replied: "I regard the criticism of Th. Kaftan, Grützmacher, Beth, etc., as quite insignificant when they assert: 'He who calls as we do for the full freedom of historical criticism that makes all historical facts problematic should not desire to ground faith on the unquestionableness of a historical fact.' Of course he should not. But we too know our faith created not through a fact that could be historically proved. Of course that would be meaningless. We owe our faith to a fact that each of us experiences for himself in a particular way from the same tradition. We intend indeed to show how religion bound to the biblical tradition can know itself to be independent of the shifts of historical research. If the original tendency toward religion resides in a person's question as to the truth of his individual life, then if we thus seek God we will hear a gospel by seeing ourselves placed, in the Jesus the NT lets us find, before the wonderful appearance of the spirit to which we willingly submit" (*ZThK*, 17, 1907, 347).

Already in his declining days Herrmann came to realize that Jesus' historicity or at least his own view of Jesus was not an indisputable part of concrete reality (cf. the scattered allusions collected on pp. 68 ff. of my dissertation *Das Problem des Heiligen Geistes bei Wilhelm Herrmann*, 1952). And when Herrmann had argued that only what belongs to my reality can ground my faith, Martin Kähler had answered with his famous play on words to the effect that only that is "real" (*wirklich*) which "works" (*wirkt*): "It is after all obvious that initially the historic Jesus belongs to my reality because he works as a historic fact up to my time— through the church; but in the church primarily through the proclamation, the word, which Herrmann does not at all wish to deny to be God's word" (*Der sogenannte historische Jesus und der geschichtliche, biblische Christus*, 2nd ed., 1896, reprint ed. by Ernst Wolf, 2nd ed., 1956, p. 57). It was hardly surprising that Herrmann's position led in his two outstanding pupils to a Barthian theology of the word and a Bultmannian theology of the kerygma, both of which combined the recognition that we cannot know Jesus' inner life as Herrmann initially assumed we could with the recognition that God is not encountered as a reality in direct continuity with reality as we otherwise know it, but only dialectically (Barth, *Theology and Church*, pp. 238 ff.; Bultmann, *Glauben und Verstehen*, I, 9 ff.). Only with the clarification of the continuity between the existentialist interpretation of Jesus' language as itself speaking on the one hand and the normative proclamation of the church on the other, a clarification worked out in terms of the "word event" in the new hermeneutic of Fuchs and Ebeling, has a positive renewal of Herrmann's position become possible.

Although the last issue of the *ZThK* in 1914 closed with the remark

by the publisher and the editors that "the first issue of the next volume
will probably be published only after the war," the journal continued to
publish through 1917 (Vol. 27). The revival of the *ZThK* in 1920 was
designated a "new series," with the awkward numbering system "Volume
1, 1920 (Volume 28 of the whole series)." This "new series" involved a
thorough reorganization of the journal. Horst Stephan became editor,
aided by an editorial board composed of Karl Bornhausen, Karl Heim, and
Theophil Steinmann. The very listing of these names, even if by a *via
negativa*, indicates that the "new series" was not as new as it should have
been. And it was precisely the failure of the *ZThK* to translate into the
period between the wars as radically as the situation called for that accounts
for the decline in relevance for the *ZThK* during that period. For in a
period of sharp reaction against liberalism articles such as Hans Hinrich
Wendt's on "Albrecht Ritschl's Theological Significance" (*ZThK*, 30, n.s.
3, 1922, 3–48) or Karl Bornhausen's on "The Significance of Wilhelm
Herrmann's Theology for the Present" (*ZThK*, 30, n.s. 3, 1922, 161–179)
seemed more involved in preserving a great tradition than in moving into
a new future.

To be sure Stephan's pledge in his obituary to Herrmann on his death
was not really carried out: "We want to remain true to him in all the
alterations of the situation and of the problems that have come and are yet
to come upon us in a new way" (*ZThK*, 30, n.s. 3, 1922, 2). For Herrmann's "Organ for Systematic and Principle Theology" was now referred
to in the sub-title as an "Organ for the Systematic Questions of the Science
of Religion and Spiritual Culture"—a designation more suggestive of the
religionsgeschichtliche Schule and Troeltsch's philosophy of religion than
of the Ritschlian School and Herrmann's ethics. This is confirmed in the
little there is of concrete theological profile in the two-page introductory
statement of the editors in the first number: "We wish to help to think
through in the spirit of evangelical piety everything that the religious
development, historical theology, the science of culture, and philosophy
offer by way of fruitful materials." The limited extent to which the
editors recognized the amount of theological translation called for by the
new situation in which the church found itself is revealed in the phrase-
ology with which they do acknowledge the new situation: "[Our church
and theology] have become in the experiences of the past years more
mature than otherwise would have taken place over a period of decades.
Much that we see gives courage to such hope: The longing of the church
for inner reflection, of Christianity for forming the world, of the culture
for soul, of the whole times for renewal of the spirit" (*ZThK*, 28, n.s. 1, 1).
One does not in fact hear in such a formulation the tones that were to
characterize the theological and churchly renewal in the period between
the wars.

The presence of the theologians who were to dominate the period between the wars was very peripheral in the "new series" of the *ZThK*, although Friedrich Gogarten did publish an article on "Revelation and Time" (3, 1922, 347–367), Paul Tillich one on "The Idea of Revelation" (8, 1927, 403–412), and Rudolf Bultmann one entitled "The Historicness of Existence and Faith. Answer to Gerhardt Kuhlmann" (11, 1930, 339–364). But the emerging dialectic theology was to create its own organs, such as *Zwischen den Zeiten*, *Theologische Existenz heute*, *Evangelische Theologie*, *Theologische Blätter*, and *Theologische Studien*. Under the Third Reich the subscription to the "new series" dwindled until the journal discontinued publication in 1938 (n. s. 14, Vol. 46 of the whole series).

In the year 1950 the *ZThK* was completely reorganized, with a return to the original numeration and an omission of the term "new series," which, like the omission of the subtitle, may be of more than purely technical significance. An editorial board consisting of Erich Dinkler, Robert Frick (†), Ernst Käsemann, Martin Noth (succeeded by Hartmut Gese), Gerhard Rosenkranz, Hanns Rückert and Ernst Steinbach, was organized under the distinguished editorship of Gerhard Ebeling. This concentration of critical scholarship is broader than any one school, although the focus of the new *ZThK* has been Bultmannian. Yet from the beginning ingredients have been present that in retrospect can be identified as leading to the post-Bultmannian position of the present. The lead essay by Gerhard Ebeling on "The Significance of the Critical Historical Method for Church and Theology in Protestantism" (*ZThK*, 47, 1950, 1–46; Eng. tr. in *Word and Faith*, pp. 17–61), although speaking concretely in terms of the situation of 1950, sensed the hermeneutical relevance of the critical historical method and of the Herrmannian position dominating the first two periods of the *ZThK*, as theology between the wars had not. "Twentieth Century theology" has come to be recognized as the theology merely of the first half of the century.

The new beginning in 1950 was accompanied by a prospectus summarizing in profile Ebeling's essay:

"For three decades theological work has been standing under this sign of a determined rejection of Neo-Protestantism and a return to Reformation theology. The *Kirchenkampf* of the 'Thirties strengthened this tendency that found confessional expression in the theological declaration of Barmen. The present situation in theology and the church calls for keeping pure the attained and unrelinquishable insights and experiences by seeing and opposing the dangers that have become evident in the process.

"These dangers threaten us in various forms. Theology can become positivistic in a dogmatic or a biblicistic sense. It can degenerate into traditionalistic confessionalism. It can become clericalistic or sacramentalistic. It is especially in danger of simplifying in an inappropriate way the theological questions in general. Such tendencies are rooted in a search for securities intended to provide for theology—but also for the church—protection from the encounter with the world, in some sacral enclosure free of temptation and trial. But to give ground to such tendencies would mean to withdraw from the critical significance of the Pauline doctrine of justification and to obscure the assurance of salvation that, according to the view of the Reformation, rests upon the *sola fide*.

"The widespread distrust and dislike today of the critical historical method derives from the same root. To be sure the chronological distance of the Reformation from the emergence of the critical historical method in modern times makes it difficult to see the hidden inner material relation in which both, the Reformation doctrine of justification and the critical historical method, stand to each other. Instead people are inclined without carefully differentiating, to regard as anti-Christian the shift into the modern period in our intellectual history. Correspondingly the critical historical method is either falsely rendered harmless as merely a formal technique, or, where its connection with certain intellectual presuppositions of modern times is recognized, it is rejected as unsuited for theological work. The development of Protestant theology especially in the Nineteenth Century seems to vindicate this last judgment and to make the fundamentally anti-modernistic stand of the Roman church worthy of imitation.

"Yet this only proves that the relation between historical criticism and Reformation theology has not yet been basically thought through to the point of their convergence within the gospel itself. The situation that by and large critical historical research on the one hand and systematic theology and the preaching of the church on the other by-pass each other is the problem the Nineteenth Century left unsolved. It cannot be gotten rid of by dodging it or no longer even seeing it. This danger is a present threat. It is to be opposed not only for the sake of the scholarly character of theology, but also—and this is not something different, but rather ultimately identical with the first—for the sake of the service, correctly understood, that theology is to perform for the church of the Reformation.

"In view of the importance of this task it seems to us, in spite of all contrary considerations, that it is necessary to create an organ that makes the issues sketched above, which we hold to be absolutely decisive, in their inclusive theological and ecclesiastical significance the objective of a common enterprise. It is not only systematic theology that should come to expression here. Rather everything hangs on the individual theological disciplines in turn contributing to the clarification of the total problem in terms of their tasks and approaches. The editorial board that draws together around the *Zeitschrift für Theologie und Kirche* in this new series understands its objective not to be a reaction against the theological and ecclesiastical development since the end of World War I. It does not propose to revive outdated and quite rightly eliminated fronts. Its concern is rather to keep the genuine critical function of theology alert."

It is thus the constancy of purpose and of direction within a changing cultural and theological world which has characterized the *ZThK* in the series of renewals and reorganizations through which it has thus far gone. Indeed in changing circumstances it had to change if it was to perform the same task and maintain the same relative position in an altered situation. For the continuity of meaning had to be translated, carried, from one situation and its world of thought into another, there to be spoken anew, and that means differently, in a different situation and its world of thought. It is the success of the *ZThK* in this central hermeneutical task which has given it its continuing focal relevance in German theology for over 70 years. And it is this same hermeneutical task to which the *Journal for Theology and the Church* is dedicated. It proposes to translate the outstanding characteristic of the *Zeitschrift für Theologie und Kirche*, the service of critical scholarship to the church, into our language, our world of discourse, our culture, and our church life. It is our purpose thus to carry through the "word event," as Ebeling puts it, which is the hermeneutical work of theology and the church.

God, King, People in the Old Testament

A Methodological Debate With a Contemporary School of Thought*

by

Martin Noth

Translated by Alice F. Carse

That the Old Testament itself is and should remain the basis for an "understanding" of the Old Testament will have to be maintained under all circumstances. One may be convinced that the subject matter at stake in the Old Testament leads beyond the Old Testament writings and reaches over into the New Testament. However, even then, this conviction can only be substantiated if both, the Old and the New Testament, are allowed to speak and to be heard each in its own right. Without question, both the Old Testament as well as the New Testament are entitled to such a hearing inasmuch as they are entities handed down to us as part of the tradition.

It is obvious that the "understanding" of the Old Testament has to take into account the historicality of this literary complex, and that the difficulties connected with our efforts of understanding are at least partially inherent in the very fact of this historicality. The fundamental questions of understanding constantly recur, and their urgency as well as the fact that they have not yet been definitely answered have become more clearly manifest today than was the case in previous generations. This may well be considered the characteristic element of contemporary Old Testament scholarship. The comprehensive historical-critical approach to the Old Testament has shed light on its subject matter from a wide range of perspectives and has led to irreversible results, not only with regard to numerous details but especially with regard to the fundamentals. Historical-critical studies have greatly advanced the philological understanding of the words and concepts and have created the critical and historical presuppositions for an exegesis which is scientifically sound and well-founded. However, beyond the establishment of the exact reading of a text whose date can be ascertained with more or less assurance, whose his|torical context may be relatively well-known, and the occasion on which it was spoken or written might be surmised, there arise even deeper questions of "under-

* "Gott, König, Volk im Alten Testament: Eine methodologische Auseinandersetzung mit einer gegenwärtigen Forschungsrichtung," ZThK, 47, 1950, pp. 157–191. – The manuscript of this essay was presented to Professor OTTO EISSFELDT on the occasion of his sixtieth birthday on September 1, 1947.

standing" which are not answered by these factors alone. They emerge whenever it is a problem not merely of taking notice of a given set of historical circumstances, but when the validity of a word is at stake.

Is real "understanding" in this deeper sense possible at all in view of the fact that the Old Testament originated in a realm of human history which is not only temporally and spatially remote from us, but at closer observation reveals conceptual modes and presuppositions of thought which are altogether different from those familiar to us? Or, in order for us to attain this "understanding," is it necessary that we enter into these different conceptual modes and presuppositions of thought to such a degree that, in the end, we no longer remain ourselves? Henry J. Cadbury recently addressed himself to this latter question in an article entitled "The Peril of Archaizing Ourselves" in the American journal *Interpretation*, vol. 3, 1949, pp. 331ff., which, as the name indicates, gives special attention to the questions concerning the "understanding" of the Bible, of the Old Testament as well as of the New Testament. Cadbury allows the validity of the task of scientific empathy with the thought world of the Old and New Testament; however, he sees a "peril" in the acceptance of this world if our involvement goes beyond the mere observation of a scientific investigator. In an article, "The Problem of Archaizing Ourselves," G. Ernest Wright answered Cadbury in the same journal, vol. 3, 1949, pp. 450ff. He points to the fact that the unbroken Christian tradition unites us with the world of the Bible; and that the substantive content of the Bible is not bound to conceptual modes or thought patterns which are always subject to change in human history, and which today have as little validity as they had in past centuries and millenia. He contends that grasping what has been expressed in the forms of another conceptual world is not merely something permissible, and not merely a matter of scientific interest, but rather a part of our essential task. We need not decide at this point whether this is possible to a full extent or to a limited extent only, at least with regard to many details of what has been said. The ability of sharing in the world of concepts and thoughts of another person is a | presupposition for any "understanding" between men, although for such understanding it is not necessary that one give up his own being. This ability is based on the fact that between man and man there exists an ultimate common denominator which lies deeper than the variable modes of conception and thought. The same is probably true with regard to the understanding which spans vast periods of time. In any case, one must make an effort to penetrate into the world of that other person who is to be understood.

Therefore the task of Old Testament studies remains the illumination of the thought world in which the scriptures of the Old Testament originated and were formulated, insofar as this is possible. This is not only a matter of academic interest, but also a task which is of essential current significance.

There are many sources which nowadays familiarize us with the totality of the ancient Near East, and we know that the Old Testament originated in this realm. At the same time it has become clear that such a general statement says relatively little since the ancient Near East was such a comprehensive phenomenon with such a long and fluctuating history that the locus of the Old Testament within this totality must be established much more precisely before the material connections between the Old Testament and the ancient Near East can be examined in greater detail. It may very well be possible that certain views and ideas were common throughout the ancient Near East and therefore could be expected to function as presuppositions of the Old Testament as well. However, this demands further substantiation, and our present knowledge of the ancient Near East is ample and specific enough that it is no longer permissible to use the term "ancient Near Eastern" without a more explicit definition, nor to regard everything belonging to the "Near East" as part of the historical and ideological background of the Old Testament without further ado.

It is not so easy to ascertain the conceptual postulates and intellectual presuppositions of a world which is remote from us. For in the nature of the case these presuppositions are not explicitly transmitted. They lie at the root of what the spoken or written word expresses or of what is portrayed in the arts; and because they are taken for granted they are neither defined nor formulated. Indeed, they are not even consciously known to be something distinctive, for in their own world they are simply accepted as valid. Only another world which in turn has its own and different presuppositions regards them as something special and not universal. They | can therefore be inferred and scientifically apprehended only from the totality of life-expressions. They cannot be as precisely and easily identified as, for example, isolated facts which one can establish on the basis of a tradition. Therefore, what is needed is scholarly intuition, which is certainly indispensable to all scholarly work seeking to establish new knowledge, but which is, in this particular instance, of special importance since the task is to uncover from a multiplicity of phenomena the essentials of the underlying and unexpressed ideas and conceptions. Obviously the danger of a subjective and incorrect approach is especially great here; any such approach must prove itself by making more intelligible a large number of the traditional facts and by presenting them convincingly in a new light.

In the following discussion we shall try to examine such an intuitive approach to the thought world of the ancient Near East and of the Old Testament which has come to play an important role in contemporary scholarship. On the one hand we shall consider this view for its own sake as a conspicuous phenomenon; but then, on the other hand, we shall consider it because there are several essential factors emerging from a dialogue with this view, factors which have to do with the question of the relationship of the Old Testament to the religious world of the ancient Near East, and therefore with the appropriate exegesis of the Old Testament as a whole. This view has emerged chiefly in the work of English and Scandinavian scholars. Especially in Scandinavia it is connected with a rejection of, or at least an express aversion towards, the literary-critical study of the Old Testament. This is no accident; for, on the whole, this approach is a reaction against a methodology which, like all others, has had its one-sidedness. For this reason alone it is important and worthy of attention. Without questioning the necessity and relevance of literary criticism, one must indeed state that literary critics have seen the Old Testament, like many other things, far too exclusively with the eyes of an age which is accustomed to literary forms, and from the point of view of an overly intellectual mode of life; insufficient account has been taken of the depths of human life and their effects on conceptualization and thinking. To be sure, awareness of the limitations of literary criticism in biblical scholarship is not new. And the new school of thought to be discussed here is by no means the first nor perhaps even the first significant reaction to those | studies; rather, it must be seen in the wider context of a particular development in scholarship which has long since been underway. Since this essay is not in the field of the history of scholarship, it is not essential here to enumerate all its points of departure and its antecedents and thus exactly to determine its locus within the structure of scholarship. We simply have to focus on this school of thought as it presents itself today.

In 1933 a collection of essays appeared in England bearing the title *Myth and Ritual*. It was edited by the London Old Testament scholar S. H. Hooke, who himself contributed the first article on "The Myth and Ritual Pattern of the Ancient East"; various other experts dealt with the subject "Myth and Ritual" with reference to individual areas of the ancient Near East. Another collection, also edited by S. H. Hooke and entitled: *The Labyrinth: Further Studies in the Relation Between Myth and Ritual in the Ancient World*, followed in 1935. It was a group of loosely connected essays by various British scholars, all of whom again considered the subject of "Myth and Ritual." The editor himself contributed an article on "The Myth and Ritual Pattern in Jewish and Christian Apocalyptic." And finally, in 1938, Hooke published his Schweich Lectures of 1935, entitled: *The Origins of Early Semitic Ritual*.

These titles already indicate what is at stake. They intend to clarify not only the self-evident fact that throughout the ancient Near East we can trace the belief in effective cultic action, and the equally undisputed fact that the myth belongs to this cultic action, having grown out of it as its liturgical rubric. They intend furthermore to point out that cult and myth decisively determined living, conceptualizing and thinking as a whole.

But they also assert that throughout the entire ancient Near East there existed a specific "myth and ritual pattern" with its basic content being restricted to relatively few details everywhere. This basic content has essentially to do with the annually repeated renewal of life, acted out liturgically on New Year's Day; i. e. with the cultic-mythical theme of the so-called dying and rising God. This has long been known, and there is no doubt that in the ancient Near East this cult was not only widespread but that it also significantly influenced the life and thought of the people. Insofar as this cult combined with the annual re-enactment of the renewal of life | the idea of a constant repetition of creation, it constituted an important element of what is commonly called "cyclical thinking" in the ancient Near East, in which the course of things was conceived as a constant repetition of the same event. The dying and rising was enacted in the New Year's ritual of the renewal of life in a manner to be discussed below. Connected with it was the ritual enactment of the "holy marriage" (ἱερὸς γάμος) by which the newly created world was blessed and made fertile. The spread and significance of this ritual act has long been known from various sources.

Now, the characteristic feature of the "myth and ritual school" is its consideration of the entire cultic-mythical reality of the ancient Near East as being concentrated essentially in this *one* festival of the New Year with its various celebrations, and, as far as I can see, its assumption that certain cultic acts were secondarily separated from this total complex and became independent cultic festivals. It is further implied that there was the same original cultic-mythical "pattern" throughout the entire world of the ancient Near East, and that the actual content of this pattern did not develop significant variations in the different areas of that world, so that its main elements are still to be found in later history, even though it eventually underwent a certain "disintegration." Israel also participated in this common ancient Near Eastern heritage. And according to S. H. Hooke (*The Origins of Early Semitic Ritual*, p. ix), only "the great prophetic movement" of the eighth century B. C. severed the connection with the religious environment and pointed out for Israel new ways of her own. We shall come back to this more explicitly below. The characteristic feature of the "myth and ritual school" lies finally and chiefly in the fact that it attributes to the *king* a central and decisive role in the cultic action. The king in his person is both the embodiment of all of his subjects and, at the same time, is himself God. In identity with the dying and rising God he himself re-enacts in the ritual of the New Year festival the universal renewal of life; and in the celebration of the "holy marriage" he assures life and fertility for the new beginning of the annual cycle. He himself is both the true priest and, at the same time, the deity at work in the cult. The annual death and resurrection of the | God-King may have been acted out in various ways, starting possibly with the actual slaughter of the present king, then later moving on to all kinds of symbolic actions of the king, and finally to the use of various sorts of substitutes for the king.[1] In all cases, we have in principle to do with the death and resurrection of the God-King himself. The God-King consummated the "holy marriage" with the queen, who was likewise conceived in divine-priestly categories. Thus this "divine kingship" was the actual and essential foundation of life as a whole. And this meaning of the divine kingship within the context of the annual renewal of life was the same throughout the ancient Near East. In this respect Israel also was part of the vast world of the ancient Near East.[2]

The conception of the "myth and ritual school" was subsequently adopted by a number of Scandinavian scholars and developed further, especially with regard to the idea of "divine kingship." Since we are not concerned here with a bibliographical survey, but rather with the discussion of a specific history-of-religion view, it may suffice to mention several important publications. In *Uppsala Universitets Årsskrift* of 1941 Geo Widengren, a historian of religions, published a study of *Psalm 110 och det sakrala kungadömet i Israel*, in which, on the basis of the pre-Israelite Jerusalem tradition, the Davidic dynasty in Jerusalem is viewed in the light of the above-mentioned God-King ideology.[3] And then, in 1943, the Old Testament scholar Ivan Engnell of Uppsala published his detailed *Studies in Divine Kingship*. Drawing on an extensive body of textual materials, he tries in a comprehensive way to prove the thesis that in cultic-mythical actions and conceptions the "divine kingship" had indeed the central and vital significance throughout the entire ancient Near East which is claimed by the "myth and ritual school." Engnell gives a detailed account of kingship in Egypt and in Mesopotamia, and then treats the God-King ideology in the Canaanite area (Syria-Palestine). In accordance with the situation in contemporary scholarship, he refers – as did S. H. Hooke before him –[4] primarily to the newly discovered texts of *Ras Shamra*, | ancient Ugarit. At present, these constitute the only original, ancient religious documents of any length from Syria-Palestine, that is, specifically from the time immediately before the conquest of the Israelite tribes (14th century B. C.). These texts are doubtlessly very important, but unfortunately also very difficult and obscure, and are still not explained in detail in spite of the

---

[1] For details see S. H. HOOKE, "The Myth and Ritual Pattern," in: Myth and Ritual. Essays on the Myth and Ritual of the Hebrews in Relation to the Culture Pattern of the Ancient East, ed. by S. H. HOOKE, London, 1933, pp. 10 ff.

[2] Cf. A. R. JOHNSON, "The Rôle of the King in the Jerusalem Cultus," in: The Labyrinth. Further Studies in the Relation Between Myth and Ritual in the Ancient World, ed. S. H. HOOKE, London, 1935, pp. 71–111.

[3] See G. WIDENGREN, Sakrales Königtum im Alten Testament und im Judentum, Stuttgart, 1955. Cf. Evangelische Theologie, 16, 1956, p. 345, note 30.

[4] Cf. especially HOOKE's book: The Origins of Early Semitic Ritual, London, 1938, pp. 28 ff.

many scientific efforts to this end. Engnell devoted a great amount of independent research and study to making them intelligible in light of the "divine kingship pattern." The KRT text from *Ras Shamra*, an extensive but still fragmentary piece, was especially important to his thesis. In the center of this text we have a figure by the name of KRT. Engnell dealt with this text in a special article, "The Text II K from Ras Shamra" *(Horae Soederblomianae*, I, Uppsala, 1944, pp. 1 ff.), after a second tablet of the text, not yet published when he wrote his *Studies in Divine Kingship*, had come to his attention. One gets the impression that Engnell has made an important and quite noteworthy contribution to the interpretation of the texts from *Ras Shamra*, both as a whole and with regard to numerous details. We have yet to see the extent to which his explanations will prove to be correct during the course of the philological and historical studies of these texts now fully underway.

However, in this particular context, we are concerned neither with the texts of *Ras Shamra* in particular, nor directly with the phenomena of ancient Near Eastern religion in general, but with the Old Testament. And, in fact, the works which we have just cited are also basically interested in the consequences for Old Testament studies. Even the English contributions to the "myth and ritual" theme really aim at a new understanding of the Old Testament; and Engnell is even more concerned with the Old Testament in his researches. His *Studies in Divine Kingship* set forth an extensive preliminary study for a fresh comprehension of the fundamental contents of the Old Testament from the point of view of the "God-King ideology." Engnell reserved the detailed proof of his thesis that the God-King ideology of the ancient Near East was also of decisive significance for the Old Testament for a future independent inquiry which has not yet been published. However, on pp. 174–177 of his *Studies* he briefly summarized the results of his inquiry for the | Old Testament. From this summary it appears that the consequences will be extraordinarily extensive and radical. He holds that the idea of divine kingship was indeed of central significance for Israel, and thus for the Old Testament, but that this ideology has been obscured by the later and secondary Jerusalem redaction of the Old Testament canon, although it is still clearly visible in numerous traces. He maintains that this idea even influenced the original traditions of the primeval and patriarchal history and, of course, the tradition of the Davidic monarchy which later lived on in the institution of the high priestly office in Jerusalem. The "divine king" is said to have stood in a special relationship to the (dying and rising) fertility god, and was therefore always considered as a life-giving bringer of salvation, i. e. as "Messiah." Therefore, "messianism" was the central "motif" of the entire Old Testament. Above all, this God-King ideology is still visible in the psalms. All of the psalms are said to be cultic – i. e. they are to be interpreted from the point of view of the God-King ritual; and almost all psalms are said to be pre-exilic.[5] Since the king is conceived as a God who ritually dies and rises again, even the psalms of lament must be royal psalms; they reflect the situation of the king's deliverance to the power of death which occurred in the annual New Year's ritual (however this was specifically enacted) and from the power of which he annually emerged again, re-animated and giving new life. Thus, for instance, the well-known Psalm 22 was a royal psalm, and – in view of the "messianic" nature of kingship – a messianic psalm.

In addition, there exist a number of special studies in which Engnell and others draw the consequences of the general idea of the God-King ideology in the ancient Near East for the Old Testament. In an essay on the "Servant of God" in Deutero-Isaiah[6] Engnell interpreted the servant figure "messianically" on the basis of this general idea, and emphatically pronounced this interpretation | to be the only possible one. The "servant of God," he asserted, could only be the divine king from the house of David; and the uniqueness of the servant songs in Deutero-Isaiah was that the God-King, as the embodiment of the whole, was viewed primarily under the aspect of expiating and suffering – analogous to the dying and rising God *Tammuz* – even though he was simultaneously conceived as triumphant in the end. The conviction that the "messianic" proclamation was the essential and central element of Old Testament prophecy is in the background of Engnell's study of *The Call of Isaiah*,[7] in which he undertakes a thorough exegesis of Isaiah 6. In connection with the examination of the God-King ideology an interesting study by Harald Riesenfeld[8] tried to show that even Ezekiel's famous vision of the resurrection of the dry bones (Ezek. 37) is to be interpreted in terms of the New Year's ritual in which dying and rising are ritually enacted by the divine king. The consequences of this conception penetrate directly into the New Testament, as can clearly be seen in the extensive and extraordinarily learned book by the same H. Riesenfeld on the *Transfiguration of Jesus* to which we shall refer below (see pp.47f.).The views of this school have also left their traces beyond the narrower circle of

---

[5] The one exception is Ps. 137, probably the only psalm which can be dated with certainty. ENGNELL, Studies in Divine Kingship, p. 172 note 2, regards it as the only psalm which is not of pre-exilic origin, and thus as the latest psalm of all. Conversely, those who used to advocate a postexilic date for the psalms in general had to exclude Ps. 137 and consider it as the oldest psalm (cf. B. DUHM, Die Psalmen, Freiburg-Tübingen-Leipzig, 1899, p. XIX).

[6] This study appeared first in Swedish: Svensk Exegetisk Årsbok, 10, 1945, pp. 31–65, then in English translation under the title "The Ebed Yahweh Songs and the Suffering Messiah in 'Deutero-Isaiah,'" Bulletin of the John Rylands Library, 31, 1948, pp. 3–42.

[7] I. ENGNELL, The Call of Isaiah. An Exegetical and Comparative Study, Uppsala-Leipzig, 1949 (Uppsala Universitets Årsskrift, 1949, no. 4).

[8] H. RIESENFELD, The Resurrection in Ezekiel xxxvii and in the Dura-Europos Paintings, Uppsala-Leipzig, 1948 (Uppsala Universitets Årsskrift, 1948, no. 11).

the actual advocates of the God-King ideology in the ancient Near East and in the Old Testament. One example is a monograph by Aage Bentzen, *King and Messiah in the Old Testament*.[9] In spite of his many reservations concerning the theses of the "Uppsala school," Bentzen generally agrees with them regarding the relation of the psalms, including the psalms of lament, to the king, and the "messianic" interpretation of the "servant of God" in Deutero-Isaiah. There is also agreement in the identification of the king acting ritually as the embodiment of the whole with the Primal Man, an identification already suggested by Engnell.[10] And yet at the same time, because of these reservations, Bentzen's study shows elements of ambiguity and imprecision.

To many it may be attractive that in this "school" opinions suddenly reappear as almost self-evident which historical-critical studies and especially literary | criticism had rendered problematical. We have in mind such things as the emphasis on "messianism" as a central theme of the entire Old Testament, the "messianic" understanding of the "servant of God" in Deutero-Isaiah, the reference of Psalm 22 to the "messianic king," and others. However, one must be clearly aware of the fact that "messianic" is by no means understood in the traditional Christian sense, nor does it initially refer to the future. Rather it designates the bearer of a divine kingship which has its place in a timeless world-order, as the bringer of salvation (Savior) who acts effectively each year in the ritual of the New Year. This is to say, the Messiah is understood here within the framework of a "cyclical" thinking which is definitely opposed to a *final historical fulfillment* of messianic expectation. However, what is ultimately at stake is not the question as to whether this or that understanding is acceptable or unacceptable for one reason or another, but rather the quite sober and rigorous question as to whether the conception is correct and tenable; in other words, whether we are able to test its correctness and tenability. We must now tackle this question in as unprejudiced a manner as possible.

In the "myth and ritual" theory we have an intuitive view of the presuppositions underlying the conceptions and thought patterns in the whole ancient Near East, including the Old Testament. This view, if it is correct, must be of fundamental significance for the "understanding" of the traditions of that particular world. We have to do with a conception which, on an impressively large scale, attempts to draw together the abundance of phenomena into one pattern of conceptions and thoughts, a pattern of rather surprising simplicity. This conception has obviously not been fabricated from nothing, but is supported on the basis of a large number of methodologically sound textual interpretations. The above sur-

---

[9] A. BENTZEN, King and Messiah in the Old Testament, London, 1955. The German original appeared in 1948.

[10] Cf. ENGNELL, "The Ebed Yahweh Songs," pp. 40f.

vey of the publications pertaining to this research indicated only the rough outlines, without presenting the details of the argumentation or showing the manifold connections said to exist between the many religious phenomena and the presupposed pattern. At the same time we are dealing here with a conception which cannot be simply derived from the available traditions, but which has to be deduced from an overall interpretation of data in the tradition which at first glance seem to be quite diverse. The pursuit of the question concerning the tenability of this view could start with an examination of the individual arguments. This is not possible in this context; moreover it is not the only, and | perhaps not even the truly appropriate, method. For there may be various opinions in the interpretation of many texts, since these are often ambiguous. Such variation of opinion would not yet determine anything essential about the total view, since the total view was prior to its specific manifestations, and could conceivably continue even if many details were to be regarded differently. One must attempt both to focus on the whole and to examine the general principles on which it rests.

The following discussion will deal primarily with the Old Testament and the question of the *religionsgeschichtliche* connection of the Old Testament with the world of the ancient Near East, a question which this intuitive school of thought regards in a very distinctive way. That is to say, we shall examine more closely the concrete question concerning "divine kingship" which is of decisive importance in the "myth and ritual pattern." The Old Testament tradition, it seems to me, allows us to make very definite remarks about this question. However, for this purpose we must first of all consider some very general questions; for only in this way will we do justice to the comprehensive scope of the "myth and ritual school."

It is beyond question that in the ancient Near East there existed the idea of the divine king who embodied the totality (within the given historical context) and, through his ritual actions, was the bearer of the life of this totality. The classical instance of this is Egypt. In the ancient Near Eastern period Egypt led an essentially self-contained life which changed strikingly little during thousands of years of history, even while assimilating immigrating foreigners. Here the Pharaoh was in fact the incarnate deity and at the same time *the* true priest. He was the sun and the life of his land. Thus Engnell quite properly opens his *Studies in Divine Kingship* with a description of Egyptian kingship. Nor was the idea of the divine king unfamiliar in Mesopotamia, the other large river oasis within the realm of the ancient Near East. It too was a region of very ancient settlements with a very ancient culture. In this instance, however, it is already doubtful that the conception of the divine king was generally known. The evidence is not very strong. The history of this land was full of change, saw many migrations of peoples and shifts of rulers and witnessed many different political systems. Thus it first would have to be demonstrated that one can speak of *the* king|ship in Mesopotamia at all. Further it would also have to be demonstrated that in the old Sumerian city-states at the lower course of the Tigris and the Euphrates the conception of the nature of kingship was identical with that held by the ruling class out of which emerged, among others, the first dynasty of Babylon, or with the conception prevalent in the warrior-state of Assyria, not to mention the foreign powers who periodically came out of the Iranian mountains as conquerors. It could indeed be the case that here too an original, indigenous conception of divine kingship prevailed through all historical change. However, this is not self-evident. It is also possible that, even if a rather unified opinion concerning the nature of kingship remained alive in Mesopotamia throughout its history in spite of the diversity of its inhabitants and political systems, this opinion might not have been identical with that of Egypt. In any case, H. Frankfort, in his comprehensive book, *Kingship and the Gods*, 1948, arrived at the conclusion, based on an extensive evaluation of the available traditions, that the Egyptian conception of the Pharaoh as the incarnate God was antithetical to the entirely different conception of the king as the "chosen servant" of the deity prevailing in Mesopotamia. [11] We do not need to pursue this question in greater detail at this point. It must be stated, however, that the general validity of the "divine kingship scheme" is at least doubtful in the case of the large and important culture of Mesopotamia, if this area can be considered a unity at all.

Syria-Palestine, the bridge between these cultures and the world into which the Israelite tribes entered and where they settled, is of more immediate significance for the Old Testament than the ancient cultures on the Nile and the Tigris and Euphrates. If we ask about the concept of the nature of kingship in pre-Israelite Syria-Palestine, i.e., the Syria-Palestine of the Bronze Age, we can say on the one hand that insofar as we can look back into history at all, many small kingdoms existed in this area. However, during the second millenium B. C., about which we now have more precise information, many different migrations swept through the land, so that one must again ask whether the different elements in the population and the various systems of government in this area all | conceived their kingship in the same way. At different times Syria-Palestine was under the strong influence of Egypt or Mesopotamia. The extent of this influence cannot be assessed in detail, of course. And it is not absolutely certain that the prevailing conceptions of those cultures were generally held throughout Syria-Palestine as well. It is also more than doubtful that the same conceptions would have prevailed throughout the ancient Near East because of a

---

[11] Similarly, C. J. GADD, Ideas of Divine Rule in the Ancient East, London, 1948, p. 34.

common *Urzeit*. The notion "early Semitic" used in the "myth and ritual school," especially by its head, S. H. Hooke, to designate Mesopotamia *and* Syria-Palestine is no longer applicable due to our present knowledge of the various migrations of peoples during the oldest times known to us. In Mesopotamia the non-Semitic Sumerians exercised a lasting and far-reaching influence, and there were continuous non-Semitic immigrations from the Iranian mountains; in Syria-Palestine we find, in the time of which the extant documents allow a more certain knowledge, that many non-Semitic elements of the population had long since begun to play a role which was not at all insignificant. In neither of the regions can we single out with certainty what is "early Semitic" (in the sense of "primitive Semitic"). Even the much more modest concept of the "north-western Semitic religion," [12] which is meant to designate the entire cultic complex of Syria-Palestine during the Bronze Age, can be used only with great reservations in view of the variegated population of Syria-Palestine in the second millenium B. C.

Nevertheless, we do have 14th century sources from Syria-Palestine which give some clues as to the concept of kingship. These sources originated in the time of the Egyptian rule over Syria-Palestine, which raises the question whether the idea of divine kingship expressed in them is that of the Egyptians. This applies especially to the *Amarna* tablets. In these tablets the smaller vassals of the land address their royal sovereign, the Pharaoh, as the divine sun, the universal giver of life, the omnipresent Lord, etc. [13] Engnell (p. 206) wants to consider these formulae primarily as expressions of an indigenous God-King ideology in Syria-Palestine. However, a careful weighing of the evidence compels us to regard these addresses to | the Pharaoh by the city-rulers within his domain rather as Egyptian "court-etiquette" and therefore representative of the *Egyptian* conception of kingship. Nevertheless, we have here the evidence that during the Late Bronze Age in Syria-Palestine the notion of a divine king was well-known in the numerous city-states scattered across the land; if it did not refer to the native rulers, it was at least used with reference to the Egyptian sovereign. The texts of *Ras Shamra*, which are roughly contemporary with the *Amarna* tablets, lead even further. They too were written during the Egyptian rule; but it is quite probable that their content leads back to older, and perhaps even very old, traditions. Thus one might assume that some aspects of the indigenous Syro-Palestinian concepts become visible in them. Notwithstanding the uncertainty of interpretation, it can be said that the dying and rising fertility god is of essential importance in these texts; and Engnell's thorough examination, especially of the so-called KRT text,

---

[12] ENGNELL, Studies in Divine Kingship, p. 71.

[13] ENGNELL has compiled the pertinent data: Studies in Divine Kingship, pp. 84 ff.; especially pp. 91 ff.

shows that one must indeed take into account the idea that this deity was incarnate in the king. Just how much this says concerning the totality of Syria-Palestine remains completely undecided, however. It is probable that in the 14th century there existed in the city of Ugarit, whose ruins are preserved in *Ras Shamra*, a very strong non-Semitic, Hurrian ruling class.[14] The name of the king during whose reign the texts were written down was presumably non-Semitic.[15] However, it is probably true that the substance of the *Ras Shamra* texts dates from an indigenous Canaanite tradition which was familiar in Syria-Palestine to an indeterminable degree. We might therefore conclude that, even though we know very little of the details as to the spread and development of a God-King ideology, this conception was very likely familiar in the Syro-Palestinian world into which the Israelite tribes entered soon after the 14th century. This may have been due to earlier indigenous traditions or to the direct influence of Egyptian rule.

How then is the Old Testament related to this ancient Near Eastern and Canaanite heritage? The "divine kingship school" presupposes quite simply that Israel as a part of the world of the ancient Near East participated in this heritage from the beginning, and that clear | traces of this are found in the Old Testament tradition. The only qualification is that in Israel – as elsewhere – this heritage had reached the stage of "disintegration" and "democratization," and that within the framework of the Old Testament faith, certain objections against this heritage made themselves felt. Before we consider the question as to whether something like "divine kingship" existed in ancient Israel, and thus look into certain details of the Old Testament background, we must make a few more general observations.

The Israelite tribes carried out their conquest within the framework of a larger movement which introduced into Syria-Palestine the neighboring Edomites, Moabites and Ammonites, and in addition to these, all those ethnic elements included under the designation "Aramaeans." This extensive conquest is simultaneous with a break in the history of Syria-Palestine, namely the transition from the culture of the Bronze Age to the culture of the Iron Age. In their new place of residence the newcomers developed a life which differed in many respects from the urban culture of the Bronze Age. The ancient cultural traditions of Syria-Palestine, which had absorbed a variety of influences from Egypt and Mesopotamia, certainly exerted a decisive influence on these "younger nations" (if we may use this general term). Yet, however certain this influence may be, it is neither self-evident nor obvious that all the institutions and ideas of older Syria-Palestine were

---

[14] Cf. M. Noth, Zeitschrift des Deutschen Palästina-Vereins, 65, 1942, pp. 58 ff. and 147 ff., and M. Noth, The History of Israel, London, 1958, pp. 24 f.

[15] Cf. Noth, Zeitschrift des Deutschen Palästina-Vereins, 65, 1942, pp. 161 ff.

accepted by the younger nations. And it is even less self-evident that before they settled in the land, these younger nations shared the conceptions which in the old civilizations can be traced far back. It would first have to be proved that they were familiar with the institution of a divine king who acted in the New Year ritual as a life-giver. Unfortunately we know almost nothing about their cultic life. The few inscriptions from their sphere do not amount to very much. K. F. Euler once examined "Kingship and Gods in the Old Aramaic Inscriptions of Northern Syria."[16] He found that these inscriptions say nothing about a divine origin of the king nor about his posthumous deification, nor even about the king's position as a representative of the deity (p. 296); and he concludes that the | king appears here rather as a servant of the deity. To be sure, Engnell may not be altogether wrong when, on p. 205 of his *Studies*, he points out that the evidence adduced from the inscriptions is too scanty to permit far-reaching conclusions. But what is more important is that these inscriptions contain not a single positive allusion to the idea of divine kingship; the existence of such an idea in the "younger nations" would yet have to be proved. The newly discovered inscription of King *Bar-Hadad* I (Old Testament: *Ben Hadad*) of Damascus, also supports Euler's result. In this inscription the king calls the god *Melkart* his "lord," to whom he has promised a stele since *Melkart* had "listened to his voice," (i.e., his prayers of petition).[17] The Aramaic name of the king *Bar-Hadad* (Son of the God Hadad) cannot be cited as evidence, since the father-son relationship between deity and king can be interpreted in different ways. We will have to discuss this matter further when considering the Old Testament evidence. Finally, the only Moabite inscription of a king which has been preserved, the well-known *Mesha* inscription, does not furnish a single reference to such a God-King ideology.[18] If one intends to stay within the area of unprejudiced factual research, he will have to admit, until proof to the contrary is forthcoming, that at least the "younger nations" who settled in Syria-Palestine at the turn of the Iron Age knew nothing of a divine kingship, even though a "divine kingship pattern" may have been known in Syria-Palestine in connection with the ancient civilizations on the Nile and the Tigris and Euphrates.

---

[16] K. F. Euler, "Königtum und Götterwelt in den altaramäischen Inschriften Nordsyriens," ZAW, N. F. 15, 1938, pp. 272–313.

[17] See M. Noth, History of Israel, pp. 239f.

[18] In his Studies in Divine Kingship, p. 80, Engnell strangely enough says that Mesha, in the first line of his inscription, calls himself "Son of (the god) Kemos," when in fact there is a textual omission after the name "Kemos." In this case, one must rather assume that this was not the name of the god Kemos but a personal name, the name of the human father of King Mesha, whose name had as its first element the name of the god.

Israel was one of these "younger nations." And in the case of Israel we do not have to depend upon an *argumentum e silentio* which always remains uncertain. For in the Old Testament we have such a multiplicity of traditions concerning Israel, and especially concerning the history of kingship in Israel, that henceforth we are on firmer ground. To be sure, those who advocate the thesis of the divine kingship also appeal extensively to the Old Testament, and try to prove from Old Testament passages that at least the oldest, or older, Israel was familiar with a God-King acting in the ritual, along with the entire ancient Near East. Before we take up these arguments | we must first emphasize a general methodological principle. If one intends to make statements concerning kingship in Israel, he cannot start from detached, ambiguous allusions, as found primarily in the psalms, and then pass by the whole body of historical traditions of the Old Testament about the kingship and its various manifestations. First of all, the distinct and unequivocal circumstances must have their say. And only then can the attempt be made to interpret that which is questionable and problematical. A reverse course can hardly be called proper procedure. Such a course cannot be justified by the thesis that original material is chiefly preserved in the liturgical texts of the psalms, while the narrative historical tradition had been so "purged" and distorted through later redactions that the idea of "divine kingship" was suppressed in favor of a later tendency which strictly separated the divine and the human spheres. It is certainly correct that original materials are usually preserved more tenaciously within established cultic forms, and that the narrative sections of the Old Testament have gone through secondary redactions. This does not mean, however, that the validity of historical sources can be denied wholesale in the content of the Old Testament narratives without examination. On the contrary, the thorough literary and critical studies of the Old Testament not only performed the destructive task of calling into question the traditional assertions concerning the origin of the Old Testament scriptures, but also tried to extricate the old traditions from the later redactional revisions and frameworks. And indeed this did lead to results which may stand as wellfounded. Thus it is no longer left to subjective judgment to consider materials within the Old Testament tradition as old and original or young and secondary merely in light of a definite presupposed theory as to what may *seem* old or young.

The most striking historical fact concerning kingship in Israel is that Israel established this institution at a rather late date. According to the Old Testament tradition this cannot be disputed. For at least | two centuries Israel lived without a king in a country which had known numerous city kingdoms ever since the Bronze Age, as a neighbor of those "younger nations" who belonged to the same group and who had established kingdoms rather quickly after their settlement. This does not convey the

impression that the idea of the vital significance of divine kingship had
been alive in early Israel, much less that Israel had brought this notion
with her from the period before the conquest. Rather it suggests that
Israel resisted the establishment of a monarchy. And it is altogether possible that her reservations were due precisely to the fact that in Syro-
Palestinian civilization the political institution of kingship was coupled with
the cultic-ritual function of the divine king, a notion which would not have
been acceptable to Israel. A. Bentzen[19] suggests that the "Divine King"
idea was derived from the more inclusive figure of a divine "Primal Man"
who would embody the totality and could have appeared concretely as
chieftain or king, priest or prophet. This thesis, however, is also inappli-
cable for early Israel. For before the monarchy we know of no figure in
Israel who could have represented the totality in cult and ritual. To attribute this fact merely to the insufficiency of the data transmitted to us,
would indeed be nothing but a *petitio principii* which could hardly be
substantiated. The occasional charismatic leaders of the premonarchic
period, the so-called "great judges," were important only within the limits
of individual tribes or groups of tribes, and never represented or embodied
the totality of Israel, as the earliest primary tradition clearly shows. Only
a later revision, probably during the period of the monarchy, grouped them
together as significant for Israel as a whole.[20] The individual tribes did not
have a single "chieftain" but were represented by a group of elders; this is
even more obvious for the twelve-tribe league as a whole. To be sure, the
old Israelite amphictyony had a cultic center and a common cult. But apart
from the tradition of Aaron and the sons of Aaron, which is almost certainly post-exilic, we find in the genuine old tradition no clear trace of a continuous or even hereditary priesthood at this central sanctuary. During the
pre-monarchic period we know of only one continuous office for the whole
of Israel, the office of the "judge of Israel" which appears in the seemingly
insignificant tradition of the so-called "minor | judges" (Judges 10:1–5;
12:7–15).[21] Even though we can only conjecture that the significance of
this office consisted in the task of preserving and interpreting the "law of
God," which was binding for Israel, the tradition certainly gives no support
to the view that this office had a cultic-ritualistic function in the sense of a
God-King ideology. And since the "patriarchs" do not qualify because
originally their importance as recipients of the promise was clearly local,

---

[19] BENTZEN, King and Messiah, pp. 43ff., 64.

[20] Still later, in the deuteronomistic work, where the conception has changed to
that of a permanent office, each one of these leaders is given special importance
for Israel as a whole.

[21] Cf. M. NOTH, "Das Amt des 'Richters Israels,'" in: Festschrift, A. BERTHOLET
zum 80. Geburtstag, ed. by W. BAUMGARTNER *et. al.*, Tübingen, 1950, pp. 404–417.
Joshua himself may have been connected with this group of "minor judges."

there remains at best the figure of Moses who indeed seems to stand in a mediatory position between God and the entire nation and is given extensive responsibilities. However, at this point the difficult question arises as to how much of the Moses narrative was gradually added to the original core, and whether Moses' universal significance for the history of his time, as attributed to him in the final form of the Pentateuch tradition, is not secondary. Whatever the case may be, if the traditional image of Moses in the Pentateuch tradition is to be retained, Moses would be such a unique and isolated figure in history, without predecessor or successor, that the burden of the thesis of a "divine kingship pattern" in early Israel could not be carried by him alone. It seems safe, therefore, to assert that premonarchic Israel did not know any bearer of a possible "God-King ideology" and thus, that this ideology cannot have been part of Israel's original and early heritage of concepts and thoughts.

After living without a king for centuries, much longer than her neighbors, Israel finally established a state and adopted kingship. We have in the Old Testament such detailed and reliable early accounts concerning the formation of the state in Israel that it is impossible to speak about the nature of her kingship without using these traditions as our main source. Moreover, their content has been so thoroughly examined both historically and in terms of tradition history[22] that one cannot possibly ignore the result of these investigations. In this case we are immediately impressed how clearly it is stated that the monarchy was created by human actions in a specific histor|ical situation. When Saul, seized by the "spirit of God" like one of the charismatic leaders from the "period of the judges," had conquered the Ammonites east of the Jordan, all the people went to Gilgal and "made Saul king" in the sanctuary there (I Sam. 11:15). Naturally the "making" of the king was a sacral act and took place in the sanctuary "before Yahweh." It is notable, however, that the subject of this "king-making" is still "the people."[23] After Saul had fallen, "the men of Judah" came to David in Hebron and "there they anointed David king over the house of Judah" (II Sam. 2:4a).[24] And after the murder of Saul's son, Esh-baal, who had been "made king" by Abner, the commander of the army (II Sam. 2:9), "all the elders of Israel came to the king [David] at Hebron, and King David made a covenant with them at Hebron before Yahweh, and they

---

[22] Cf. the various Histories of Israel, and particularly: A. Alt, "Die Staatenbildung der Israeliten in Palästina," (Leipziger Reformationsprogramm, 1930), in: Kleine Schriften zur Geschichte des Volkes Israel, II, München, 1953, pp. 1 f.

[23] Samuel's role is not completely clear. According to I Sam. 11:14, he summoned "the people" to Gilgal. In any case, even he could not do more than prompt "the people" to "make Saul king."

[24] We probably have here an abridged expression. It is certain that the anointment was carried out by priests; the actual subject of the entire procedure was, however, "the men of Judah."

anointed David king over Israel" (II Sam. 5:3). In this last case a "covenant," a contract is expressly mentioned which, to be sure, was probably implied in the first case as well. It could hardly be said more distinctly that the kingship of David was based upon human agreements with the "elders" as representatives of the Israelite tribes. Solomon was made king and successor of David by a human decision of his father instigated by influential circles at court, as is vividly and extensively described in I Kings 1:11ff. After Solomon's death "all Israel" gathered in Shechem "to make Rehoboam (the son of Solomon) king" (I Kings 12:1). When the negotiations with Rehoboam failed, Israel separated from the Davidic dynasty, brought Jeroboam "and made him king over all Israel" (I Kings 12:20). These data of the tradition which are well known and whose meaning is quite clear, cannot be left aside in the question concerning the nature of kingship in Israel. In fact, what is important here is not only that these are most reliable data for the actual process of the formation of the state, but also that those events were recorded at all and formed part of Israel's continuous tradition. After several revisions, | the information about Saul, David, Solomon, etc. finally came to be included in the great deuteronomistic work. Even though the circles in which the historical traditions about the first kings were cultivated and passed on are no longer precisely known, it is nonetheless clear that the knowledge of the historical process of the formation of the state *was* preserved in Israel, and with it the knowledge that the institution of kingship was not an original part of Israel's existence but developed at a late and advanced stage of Israel's history, and in fact, through the initiative of "the people" or their elders. This knowledge scarcely can be said to permit a conception which regards kingship as an element of a timeless, divine world-order, as is necessarily presupposed by the God-King ideology. In addition to this we have the fact that the institution of kingship was very short-lived in Israel. As early as two and an half centuries after the formation of the state of David, i. e. after a period which was scarcely longer than the preceding period of Israel's living in Canaan without a king, most of the Israelite tribes had lost their independent kingship. The kingship over the smaller circle of the Southern tribes which continued for another century and a half had deteriorated into a vassal kingship within the framework of the hegemony of a foreign power. After the end of this small vassal kingship there were again nearly 500 years without a king, a time of subjection to the ruler of a foreign empire. To be sure, even after the Davidic kingship had come to an end, Ezekiel, in his program for the future (Ezek. 40–48), regarded the cultic responsibilities of the king to be so important that he provided for a future "prince" to carry out these very responsibilities. But such a "prince" never came; and these cultic responsibilities passed on in part to the high priest of the post-exilic period. The fact is, however, that this high priest was not really a king.

These well-known facts force us to the conclusion that, after Israel had existed for a long time without a king and a God-King ideology, the events leading to the formation of the state as well as the living remembrance of these events, and furthermore the actual history of kingship, did not provide very favorable conditions for an acceptance of the ancient Near Eastern ideology even at a later time. It is therefore not surprising that the Old Testament tradition in general indicates the "secular" character of kingship even in places where it does not take an explicitly negative | attitude toward it; [25] and the bearers of this office are regarded as men who stand under the obligation of obedience toward their God. C. R. North, in his study of "The Religious Aspects of Hebrew Kingship," reaches this conclusion; [26] and H. Frankfort also stresses the secular nature of kingship in Israel in the short "epilogue" to his previously mentioned book *Kingship and the Gods*. The relationship of God and people constitutes the basis of the Pentateuchal tradition which is substantially pre-monarchic. This relationship means that Israel was bound to her God within the framework of the divine plan of salvation and did not need the mediating role of a cultic-ritual divine king.

But this is not all that has to be said. The "divine-kingship school" can quote Old Testament passages which point to a divine character of kingship. The most obvious examples are found in Psalm 45:7 where, according to the transmitted text which cannot so easily be changed, the king is addressed as "god," and then in II Sam. 7:14; Psalm 2:7 (perhaps also Psalm 110:3) where the Davidic king is called "son" of God. Even after it has been established that originally Israel herself neither had nor knew a "divine king," these statements have to be seriously considered. It can hardly be disputed that after the conquest Israel did assimilate elements from the vast reservoir of the indigenous cultural tradition of Canaan. We know that this occurred primarily in the area of the cult though not blindly and indiscriminately. Israel celebrated the cultic-agricultural festivals of the new land which were so intimately connected with the rhythm of life in the land. It was in the context of these festivals that the "cyclical thinking" of the ancient Near East was introduced into Israel, especially at the point where these festivals developed beyond their immediate connection with the annually recurrent activities of the harvest and the ingathering of grain and fruit into ever recurring representations of unique |

---

[25] A literary polemic against kingship is not found but at a relatively late stage in the Old Testament, even though it may be assumed that the negative attitude toward kingship is much older. The fact that this attitude – not against individual kings but toward the very institution of kingship – could develop at all and could express itself, speaks against divine kingship in Israel as a universal or even widespread conception.

[26] ZAW, N. F. 9, 1932, pp. 8ff., especially pp. 36ff.

historical events. [27] According to what is said in Deuteronomy 16 and Leviticus 23, it is not a matter of an annual repetition of a cultic-ritualistic new creation as we know it from the ancient Near Eastern New Year's festival, but rather a "remembrance" (Deut. 16:3, 12) of the mighty and fundamental divine act of the exodus. However, the deuteronomic term of "remembrance" may already signify a weakening and rationalization of a more original cultic realism for which these festivals were not only days of remembrance but an ever new and present realization of the fundamental event of salvation. Thus, due to the lack of truly conclusive evidence one may be skeptical of the widespread opinion that a New Year's and coronation festival showing the general form and meaning of such festivals in the ancient Near East has been assimilated by the old Israelite cult. Nevertheless, in the well-attested connection of cultic annual festivals with a unique and basic historical event in Israel, an influence of ancient Near Eastern cyclical thinking has to be recognized. And such an influence was certainly mediated through the traditions of the Syro-Palestinian culture; but in the framework of these traditions the specifically Israelite reference to the exodus from Egypt now took the place of the ancient Near Eastern reference to the creation of the world. Through the Israelite calendar of festivals ancient Near Eastern concepts and thoughts exercised their influence even as late as the formation of the Christian church year.

The above-discussed phenomenon seems to me to be of great importance. The theme of the assimilation on the part of the Israelite tribes of the cultic traditions of Canaan and of the concomitant ideas and concepts could be discussed in great detail. This is not necessary here, nor is it possible; for it would require an extensive discussion of the complicated relationship between Israel's resistance and openness toward the Canaanite heritage. It is sufficient to note that it is by no means excluded as a matter of course that elements of an ideology connected with the institution of kingship in the new land might possibly have been taken over by Israel. The important thing would be to prove this concretely.

In this connection we must first point out that in Israel one cannot even talk about *the* kingship as such. The Old Testament tradition shows quite clearly that we have in Israel several kingships which were not only separated in space but were also different in kind. Recent research has made this abundantly | clear. [28] Whoever makes any assertion about the nature of *the* kingship in Israel must not overlook this fact. And any inquiry into Israel's possible adoption of the ancient Near Eastern God-King ideology will have to determine the point at which such an adoption may have occurred.

---

[27] Cf. M. Noth, "The 'Re-Presentation' of the Old Testament in Proclamation," in: Essays in Old Testament Hermeneutics, ed. by C. Westermann, Richmond, Va., 1963, pp. 76–88.

[28] Cf. especially the study by A. Alt mentioned above (footnote 22).

After the short episode of Saul's military kingship over the twelve tribes we have, starting with David, primarily two kingships over the two states of Israel and Judah, which existed concurrently. The subsequent history of kingship in northern Israel shows that in this part the prevailing idea was that only a person whom the prophet had previously designated as one called by Yahweh could be made king by the people or their elders.[29] This had already been the case with Saul. And even when Israel gave way to the natural tendency of forming a dynasty in those cases where there was no such designated person, still from time to time some new charismatic leader would rise up and take over the kingship.[30] In all of this there was hardly a point of entrance for Canaanite conceptions of the kingship. This kingship over a large number of tribes had no indigenous tradition; and there was no established locus for it, e. g., in an old Canaanite city.[31] It rested basically on the consent of the people or their elders. The divine calling, similar to that of the so-called "(great) judges" of the pre-monarchic period, did not confer upon the king a divine character, but meant a commissioning.

Beginning with David there existed simultaneously another kingship in the state of Judah over the southern tribes of Israel. It differed from the kingship of northern Israel primarily in the fact that here the house of David continued to rule. But here, too, kingship originated from the will of the people. The "men of Judah" had once "anointed David king" (cf. above p. 36). After the fall of Athaliah who, | as a usurper, was the only one to interrupt the Davidic line on the throne of Judah, the people gathered[32] to "proclaim" Joash, the only Davidic survivor, "king and they anointed him,[33] and they clapped their hands and said: 'Long live the King!'" (II Kgs. 11:12) Occasionally the *'am ha-aretz*, i.e., all full citizens of Judah,[34] stood up to ascertain the legitimate succession within the house of David (II Kgs. 21:24) and to "anoint and proclaim as king" the legitimate successor (II Kgs. 23:30). This kingship over the southern tribes was not connected with any indigenous tradition of the new land. To be sure, the old royal city of Hebron had once been a Canaanite city state. But even at the time of the conquest it had already been seized by the Calebites and

---

[29] For example, in the story of how Jeroboam I was made king, according to I Kgs. 11:29–39 and 12:1 ff.

[30] Cf. I Kgs. 16:2, and particularly II Kgs. 9:1 ff.

[31] The most likely place would have been the city of Shechem. There Jeroboam I had in fact lived initially (I Kgs. 12:25). But he soon gave up this residence and the Israelite kings never returned to Shechem.

[32] This subject is not explicitly mentioned, but the indefinite third person plural can hardly be understood otherwise.

[33] Cf. above, footnote 24.

[34] Cf. E. WÜRTHWEIN, Der 'amm ha- 'aretz im Alten Testament, Stuttgart, 1936 (Beiträge zur Wissenschaft vom Alten und Neuen Testament, 4. Folge 17).

thus the tradition of Canaanite kingship no longer existed; nor were the remaining tribes in the Judean mountains under a Canaanite kingship. Thus fundamentally the same must be said of this kingship as was said of the kingship in northern Israel.

There was still another kind of kingship in the realm of Israel, that is, the Davidic kingship in the city state of Jerusalem. David, with his personal military retinue, had conquered this city, which until that time had been Canaanite. He made it his royal residence. In this capacity, it was part neither of the state of Israel nor of the state of Judah. David chose it as a "neutral" city *in between* the territories of both these states, so that the city kingship over Jerusalem was an independent institution alongside the kingships of Israel and Judah. This city kingship of Jerusalem did have a direct Canaanite tradition. With the conquest of the city David became the successor of the previous Canaanite city king. Thus it was natural for him to take over the cultic-ritual function of the latter within the local cult of Jerusalem. We do not know much about the earlier Canaanite history of the Jerusalem kingship. The six letters from the city king *Abdi-ḫepa* of Jerusalem to the Egyptian Pharaoh which are preserved in the archives of *Tell-el-Amarna* [35] do not contribute much to the question which is of interest here. In one place *Abdi-ḫepa* writes to his Egyptian overlord that "he had inscribed his name | at the rise and at the setting of the sun." [36] However, this merely says something about the *Egyptian* king, probably referring to the idea of the incarnation of the sun god; it indicates nothing about the kingship of Jerusalem. [37] But from the Old Testament tradition we know the figure of Melchizedek. He was evidently a Canaanite city king of Jerusalem [38] who lived on in the Jerusalem tradition. The main point

[35] Cf. J. A. KNUDTZON, Die El-Amarna-Tafeln, Leipzig, 1915 (Vorderasiatische Bibliothek, Band II), nos. 285–290; see also: Ancient Near Eastern Texts, ed. by J. B. PRITCHARD, 2nd ed., Princeton, 1955, pp. 487 ff. (= ANET).

[36] KNUTDZON, no. 288, 5–7 (ANET, p. 488).

[37] See above, pp. 31 f. *Abdi-ḫepa* repeatedly designates himself with an Egyptian word as a *u-e-u* of the king (KNUDTZON, no. 285 ,6; 287, 69; 288, 10; ANET, p. 488). ENGNELL, Studies in Divine Kingship, p. 86, regards this word as an Egyptian title for the priest and considers it to be evidence for the sacral function of the city-king of Jerusalem. However, this assumption is probably incorrect since what we have here is the Egyptian term *w'w* which designates an officer of lower rank. In the context at hand it served as an expression of subservience of the city-lord of Jerusalem to the Egyptian sovereign. In spite of ENGNELL's confidence (p. 86, note 7), the meaning of the word *ruhi* which occurs in this context (KNUDTZON, no. 288, 11; ANET, p. 488) does not seem certain to me. However, even if it were to be the Canaanite word for "shepherd," one can hardly draw far-reaching conclusions from this fact. The figurative expression, "I am a shepherd of the king," could be interpreted in various ways.

[38] The name "Salem" which occurs in Gen. 14:18 is usually and, as I think, correctly taken as a reference to Jerusalem (cf. Ps. 110).

about him is that he combined priesthood with kingship in the Jerusalem cult (Gen. 14:18; Ps. 110:4). This combination must have been Jerusalem tradition but probably did not signify anything unusual and may have been customary in other Canaanite city states. It was only in the eyes of the Israelite tribes that this combination seems to have been peculiar. At least the solemn statement in Ps. 110:4 would indicate this; here the example of the Canaanite king Melchizedek of Jerusalem is invoked for the combination of priestly functions with the kingship. These priestly functions are by no means a proof for the "divine" nature of the king, however. At any rate, the Davidic kings of Jerusalem seem to have participated in these priestly functions. And, in fact, the priestly activities of kings in the Old Testament are primarily restricted to the Davidic rulers in Jerusalem.

For our problem it would be important to know whether or not the Canaanite city kingship of Jerusalem was based on a God-King ideology in the sense of a "myth-ritual pattern." We indicated earlier (on p. 32) that this cannot simply be assumed as self-evident in the case of any Syro-Palestinian city kingship. And we lack the resources to prove it for Jerusalem. If, for a moment, we assume that this proof can be | established, then we must ask what this must have meant for the Israelite tribes as well as for the Davidic kings of Jerusalem, who were simultaneously members of "Israel." We could say that for the Israelites it was of little consequence since there existed only an indirect political link of the tribes with the city state of Jerusalem and its institutions through the person of the Davidic ruler. They could let him decide whether or not, as city king of Jerusalem, he deemed it appropriate to assume the role of a "divine king" – which was out of question for him as king of Israel or Judah. It is of course questionable whether the Davidic king really was in a position to assume in Jerusalem a role which ran counter to Israelite tradition. For another reason, however, the nature of the Jerusalem kingship did take on significance for the Israelite tribes. The holy ark of the covenant, which had been and continued to be the ancient cultic center for the tribes, and which David had brought to his city of Jerusalem, was located in the royal sanctuary. It was by no means a matter of indifference for "Israel" whether or not the king, standing before the ark, acted in the ritual as the incarnate God. Besides this, the union between the city state of Jerusalem and the state of Judah, at least under Davidic rulership, lasted so long that in time the cultic position of the king of Jerusalem would necessarily have become normative for the kingship in Judah also.

As we have seen, it is at the point of the Davidic kingship in Jerusalem that the ancient Near Eastern God-King ideology in its Syro-Palestinian form could have entered the sphere of Israel. And, in spite of the special position of this city kingship, the role of the royal sanctuary in Jerusalem, as the cultic center of the tribes, could in fact have mediated such an ideology to the wider circle of the tribes. Thus the whole matter really depends upon whether it is possible to prove the assimilation of elements of a God-King ideology in the Old Testament. As we have previously shown, the emphatic, unequivocal tradition about the historical limitations of kingship does not exactly support this. And in addition it must be remarked, that precisely the important historiographical accounts about David which clearly state that David "was made king" by the representatives of the tribes both in Judah and Israel, and that the conquest of Jerusalem was a military operation and not some sacred action, very probably originated in Davidic-Solomonic court circles in Jerusalem and were probably | also transmitted in Jerusalem. In this case the divine character of kingship was obviously not regarded as self-evident in the court of Jerusalem. If we turn to the positive arguments for the "divine kingship" thesis, all those instances merely stating something about priestly functions of the king must be eliminated. For even though these do refer for the most part to Jerusalem because we have here a pre-Israelite practice, and as far as we know the kings of Israel and of Judah rarely acted as priests, [39] these instances are in no way proof for the divinity of kingship nor for the embodiment and incorporation of the totality in the person of the king. They only indicate that in the realm of the sacred, too, the king was the head of his subjects.

The designation of the king as "son of God" is a different matter. It refers to the Davidic ruler as king of Jerusalem and is based chiefly on Ps. 2:7; originally it may also have appeared in Ps. 110:3, where the text is obviously corrupt. In Ps. 2:7, and presumably Ps. 110:3, we have an adoptionist formula. This is an important detail since it means that the king was not by nature "son" of God, nor did he enter the sphere of divinity as a natural concomitant of his accession to the throne. But when he assumed the office of the king he was *declared* "son" by an act of will on the part of the God of Israel. Nevertheless, the Davidic king thereby entered into a close relationship with the realm of the divine. And here in all probability we do have the impact of the ancient Near Eastern God-King ideology. This

---

[39] King Jeroboam I of Israel indeed once appears in a priestly function in his new royal sanctuary at Bethel (I Kgs. 12:33). However, this instance is only recorded in the late post-Josiah legend of I Kgs. 12:32–13:32 and II Kgs. 23:16–18, whose historical value is rather dubious. Moreover, we would have here a mere imitation of the role of the Davidic kings in Jerusalem. There is also no sure evidence that Saul performed priestly functions. The verse, I Sam. 14:35, hardly furnishes a specific indication in this direction, and the passage, I Sam. 13:7–15a, which constitutes a later insertion, cannot be used as a historical source. It is based on the assumption that the exercise of priestly activities was in fact *not* incumbent upon the king and intends to give a secondary explanation of the dissent between Saul and Samuel. According to this explanation, Saul once sacrificed without being authorized and with a bad conscience. It is improbable that this secondary text is based upon an old historical tradition which held that Saul carried out sacrifices.

may lead indirectly to the conclusion that the Canaanite tradition of the
Jerusalem king knew the idea of the divinity of the king's person. For
only in this way can we | understand the unusual statements about the
Davidic king in Jerusalem which are so different from the ideas about the
nature of kingship in the states of Israel and Judah. Of course, we face
here a decisive and characteristic *modification* of the traditional God-King
ideology if we concede that such existed in pre-Davidic Jerusalem at all.
This variation would indicate that the Davidic line even as kings of Jerusalem did not blindly take over the royal tradition of Jerusalem. The use of the
adoptionist formula shows that the Davidic king in Jerusalem is not the incarnate God; he is not of divine origin or of divine nature, but is declared
"son" by a gracious act of God. Thus, this modification is not so much
evidence for a Davidic God-kingship in Jerusalem as it is a reference to the
rejection of genuine God-King ideology, although a certain concession *is*
made to a kingship tradition already present in Jerusalem. The ambiguous
phrase of Ps. 110:1, "sit at my right hand," must be interpreted accordingly. This formula may have been derived from a pre-Davidic royal
ritual of Jerusalem, or at least be dependent upon such a ritual. But in the
context of Ps. 110 it can be understood only in the sense of a special honor
bestowed on the king by his god, not in the sense of an equality of the
king with God.

The adoptionist formula is also found in II Sam. 7:14, though in a form
different from Psalm 2:7. To be sure, this particular verse is probably not
an original part of the so-called prophecy of Nathan in II Sam. 7.[40] But it
has not been improperly included in the later expansion of this passage,
for Nathan's prophecy, too, presupposes specifically the Jerusalem Davidic
kingship. In II Sam. 12:1ff., but especially in II Sam. 12:25, and I Kgs.
1:8, 10, 11ff., we meet the prophet Nathan at the court of Jerusalem
in the closer environment of David. In Nathan's original prophecy David
is promised that Yahweh would "build him a house," i.e., establish a
dynasty (v. 11b), and that this house would stand "forever" and the
kingship of David would abide "forever" (v. 16). The range of the Davidic
kingship meant here is not exactly stated. It seems certain that it did
encompass the vast | Davidic state in its entirety, yet seen from the Jerusalem
perspective. The author of the comprehensive historiographic account of
the succession of David reported this prophecy of Nathan and used it as his
starting point because it clarified the burning question of the successor, at
least to the extent that the succession was restricted to one of David's sons.
Nathan's prophecy itself hardly focused on this very practical question; but

---

[40] Cf. the literary analysis presented by L. Rost, Die Überlieferung von der
Thronnachfolge Davids, Stuttgart, 1926, pp. 47ff. (Beiträge zur Wissenschaft vom
Alten und Neuen Testament, 3. Folge 6). – Psalm 89:27ff. could be dependent
upon II Sam. 7:14.

as the wording shows, it dealt with the institution of the Davidic kingship as a whole and with the long-range view of its future. The prophecy contains the promise that this kingship shall be everlasting – a promise which in view of the historical, human circumstances of the establishment of this kingship seems almost outrageous. Is it too much to suspect this to be again a *modification* of a notion of divine kingship, as it might have corresponded to the kingship tradition of Jerusalem? In this case the kingship would not have been divine, nor would the king have been an incarnate God. But the promise of an unending reign would have lifted the institution of kingship out of the contingency of human history and would have brought it closer to the divine sphere. Thus, here again the assimilation of a pre-Davidic king ideology in Jerusalem would appear to be rejected, though exerting at least an indirect influence.

We know that the content of Nathan's promise had strong after-effects. The messianic expectation ties onto it. As we said before, this messianic expectation certainly had its starting point in the Davidic kingship in Jerusalem, but it was really conceived in terms of the vast entirety of David's reign. The messianic proclamations also understood it in this latter sense. That such proclamations are found exclusively in the prophets of *Judah* is due to the fact that after the death of Solomon only Judah continued to be connected with the Davidic dynasty which resided in Jerusalem. The content of the messianic proclamations retained an "all-Israelite" orientation, however; and the connection of the ark, the ancient sanctuary of the tribes, with the royal city of David may well have directed the attention of the tribes even outside the state of Judah to the house of David and the promise given to it. It would have to be asked how the promises and expectations associated with the house of David on the basis of the kingship in Jerusalem squared with the older all-Israelite tradition. L. Rost once touched upon this whole array of questions in an article entitled "*Sinaibund und Davidsbund*" and | rightly pointed out the problem with which we are faced here.[41] He concludes that for a time "Sinai covenant" and "Davidic covenant" existed side by side, their validity corresponding to the two states of Israel and Judah. In view of the fact that the ark was localized in the city of David, this solution is perhaps too simple. We will rather have to say that within the all-Israelite tradition the expectations in connection with the promises made to the house of David, whenever they were assimilated by the various tribes, became part of the traditional "God-People" pattern as a special element which pointed more and more to the future. We shall not pursue these questions in detail here. The reference to them was necessary, however, because the circumstances out of which they

---

[41] "Sinaibund und Davidsbund," Theologische Literaturzeitung, 72, 1947, cols. 129–134.

arise go back to the Davidic kingship in Jerusalem and to the specific position and honor promised to this kingship in particular.

Thus it will have to be maintained that a divine character was never imputed to the kingship even of Jerusalem, let alone the kingships of the states of Israel and Judah. This assertion also implies that in Psalm 45:6 the king cannot be assumed to be addressed as "god," even though we have here, in the middle of a psalm which addresses the king in the first half, a sentence which would most simply be translated: "Your throne, O God, endures for ever and ever." Yet in this form it is a completely isolated statement in the entire Old Testament and it must be questioned whether the phrase is to be understood this way. [42] There exists a very plausible possibility for a textual change which various exegetes have recommended. But one is of course hesitant to make such a change since it is not very likely that such an unusual and objectionable statement should have slipped into the text later through carelessness. It might well be asked, however, whether this is not an abbreviated form of expression to which counterparts can be found in the Old Testament; [43] in this case the phrase could be interpreted as follows: "Your throne is (as) that of God, namely enduring for ever and ever." Then we would have here the promise of the everlasting kingship familiar to us from the prophecy of Nathan. And accordingly one also would consider Psalm 45 as referring to the Davidic kingship in Jerusalem. Psalm 45:6a alone can under no circumstances bear the entire burden of | the thesis of a divine kingship in Israel. The fact that with reference to the Jerusalem kingship we probably find in the Old Testament modifications and adaptations of the concepts of a God-King ideology rather supports the notion that this ideology itself was *not* appropriated in Israel and that it *could* not be appropriated under the presuppositions of the Old Testament faith. This makes superfluous the thesis that in the ritual the king specifically embodies the dying and rising god and that he effectively enacts death and new life, and therefore, that the lamentations in the Old Testament Psalms are to be understood as songs of the king presupposing the situation of the king's being ritually delivered to the power of death. The text of the lamentations itself does not provide any substantial reason for such a reference to the king.

It is therefore well-advised not to use the thesis of the divine character of kingship throughout the entire ancient Near East, including Israel, as a self-evident presupposition for the exegesis of Old Testament texts. On the contrary, it seems that we have here an area in which the Old Testament did not assimilate conceptions which, though not universally prevalent, were familiar in the great cultures of the ancient Near East. This resistance

---

[42] A thorough discussion of this passage is found in C. R. NORTH's article, "The Religious Aspects of Hebrew Kingship," ZAW, N. F. 9, 1932, pp. 27 ff.

[43] Cf. NORTH, p. 30.

may have to be seen as part of the total context of those "younger nations" who immigrated into Syria-Palestine at the beginning of the Iron Age, but it may also have to do with the specific presuppositions of the Old Testament. Thus the further question will have to be pursued as to why this was so. Again, the chief task here will be to make the right distinctions. The vast world of the ancient Near East shared certain general presuppositions in conception and thought which for us today are no longer as self-evident as they were in that world. This means that we first must try to determine these presuppositions scientifically if we are to understand the life-manifestations of that world. But as certain as this is, it appears just as unlikely, in view of the historical variegations of human life, that a developed cultic-ritual pattern as postulated by the "myth and ritual school" would have been spread throughout the entire Near East over so many centuries. Thus, even for the special inquiry into the nature of kingship, it would seem less promising to look for a unified and homogeneous pattern instead of dealing with the specific manifestations of the phenomenon of kingship. | In this way only can we do justice to the Old Testament within the world of the ancient Near East.

In conclusion we must allude to one further question which neither will nor can be answered here. This question grows out of the subject under discussion and would deserve a thorough examination in its own context. H. Riesenfeld's formidable book, *Jésus Transfiguré* (Acta Seminarii Neo-testamentici Upsaliensis, XVI, 1947), interprets Christ's transfiguration messianically against the background of an ancient Near Eastern God-King ideology. In reading this book one is extremely impressed by the almost overwhelming amount of material from post-canonical Jewish and Rabbinic literature which the author is able to adduce in support of his thesis. He holds that this literature, in its dealing with worship and in its basic orientation of conceptions and thoughts, knows and presupposes the whole cultic-ritual complex of that ideology. For the author it is self-understood that in all this only those elements live on which Israel has always known and held in common with the entire ancient Near East. He thus rejects the idea of a secondary intrusion of this heritage into the post-canonical literature from the environment. He might be considered correct, at least insofar as there is in fact little in favor of assuming that foreign ideas have been mechanically appropriated; undoubtedly certain points of departure must be presupposed from which an appropriation of foreign concepts and customs could have arisen. However, those who do not believe that ideas attested only in later sources can be dated as early as one wishes without clear evidence, and especially those who are unable to discover in the Old Testament the conception of a divine kingship with all its functions and relationships, will not be able to accept Riesenfeld's argumentation. Above all, they will have to call into question the assertion that the late Jewish references and modes of expression are based on a consistent pattern of concepts and thoughts, or that we deal here with "disintegrated" elements of an older consistent pattern. Of course, they will in that case then have to find an explanation for the late emergence of numerous and in part quite substantial customs and views. They will recall in this connection the occurrence of other rather archaic conceptions which can be found elsewhere in the post-canonical Jewish literature, but are still unknown to the Old Testament, as, for example, in the area of angelology and demonology. Obviously these are not simply later developments but rather adaptations and trans|formations of older materials from the wider realm of the ancient Near Eastern world[44]. Are these perhaps elements of a rich world of popular beliefs which existed in Israel but were officially rejected by the group of the Israelite tribes until they finally entered post-canonic Judaism? And do we perhaps have to assume that the attitude of ancient Israel toward the Near Eastern world of ideas, on the basis of her faith, was that of resistance and that this attitude relaxed at a time of decadence? Or, could it be that as time passed, the Old Testament faith felt so confident and sure of itself due to its canonical literature that it could become more tolerant towards many popular conceptions? Or, must we rather assume that the ancient, homogeneous Israel of the twelve tribes knew how to protect her unique position and her individuality, and that the appropriation of current popular notions of the ancient Near Eastern world was initiated only with the disintegration of that ancient Israel and the rise of a widely diffused diaspora?[45]

We must leave these questions open here. The attempt to answer them would require a comprehensive study. Perhaps an unequivocal and uniform answer is altogether impossible since historical life is always multiform and complicated. The importance of these questions is quite obvious, however, unless one relies upon a general and pre-established pattern of conceptions and thoughts which remained essentially the same and which Israel is thought to have shared with the entire ancient Near Eastern world.

The above discussion is a brief attempt to demonstrate that such a pattern cannot be assumed. In light of the given Old Testament materials, even the appeal to the post-canonical literature cannot really salvage the assumption that a God-King ideology was current in Israel from the very beginning.

---

[44] A. BENTZEN, King and Messiah, p. 79, refers to this phenomenon as a "renaissance of mythology" in later Judaism. This expression implies, of course, a certain interpretation of the phenomenon which, lacking more specific proof, remains open to question.

[45] One would have to take into account here that these conceptions were not appropriated without alterations. H. RIESENFELD (Jésus Transfiguré, p. 239 f.) certainly is not wrong when he speaks about a spiritualization and eschatologization of ancient cultic-ritual "motifs" in late Judaism.

The Idea of History in the Ancient Near East
and the Old Testament [*]

by

Hartmut Gese

Translated by James F. Ross

Ever since the discovery of ancient Near Eastern sources comparable
with the Old Testament, both biblical exegetes and students of ancient
history have frequently pointed out the unique way in which the Old
Testament, in its view of history, differs from the ancient Near East. [1] It
has been emphasized that in the Near East as a whole historical thought,
and thus the writing of history, developed only in Israel. But even if the
observations about the Old Testament used to justify this conclusion are
correct, the theological significance of this thesis urgently demands a basic
comparison between the literary evidence from ancient Near Eastern
cultures having to do with what we call historical experience or historical
thought, and corresponding Old Testament documents. No matter how
often it is repeated, a reference to the entanglement of the ancient Near
East in an a-historical nature-myth of the eternal cycle of all events is
meaningless in light of the fact that such a mythology simply does not ·
exist in the historiographic documents of the ancient, i. e., pre-Persian,
Near East. [2] |

Naturally in the brief space allowed me here it is impossible to make an
extensive comparison. Therefore I must limit the relevant material both
historically and geographically. I think it sufficient to follow the development of historical thought in the ancient Near East up to the middle of
the first millenium B. C., thus to the beginning of the Persian Empire. The
pre-exilic history of Israel ends during this time span, and thus important

---

[*] "Geschichtliches Denken im Alten Orient und im Alten Testament," ZThK,
55, 1958, pp. 127–145. – Inaugural address delivered in Tübingen on July 14, 1958.

[1] We may cite only three examples from the vast literature: E. MEYER, Geschichte des Altertums, II, 2, 3rd ed., 1953, p. 285; W. EICHRODT, "Offenbarung und
Geschichte im Alten Testament," Theologische Zeitschrift, 4, 1948, pp. 322, 329;
G. VON RAD, "Theologische Geschichtsschreibung im Alten Testament," Theologische Zeitschrift, 4, 1948, p. 161.

[2] The mention of the *adē nannar* (phases of the moon?) in a text of Sargon II
(Keilinschriftliche Bibliothek A, II, p. 66) is not sufficient proof. Cf. J. HEMPEL,
Altes Testament und Geschichte, (Studien des apologetischen Seminars, ed. by
C. STANGE, XXVII), Gütersloh, 1930, p. 36.

evidence for the Old Testament view of history is given. The establishment of the Persian Empire meant a basic change in the ancient Near Eastern world. And furthermore Herodotus, who is generally called the Father of History, lived in the fifth century. This historical pause may therefore justify our limitations. However, we shall leave Egypt completely out of account, since at first glance the Egyptian evidence seems to be quite irrelevant to our question. [3]

At the beginning of this inquiry I purposefully avoid giving a definition of history or historical thought which would serve as a criterion for the question when and where historical thought occurs. Such a procedure, which may well be largely responsible for the unfruitfulness of modern studies in the field of the philosophy of history for the historian of the ancient Near East, [4] seems especially misleading to me since we cannot make a simple division between historical and a-historical thought. Clearly there were several quite different forms of thought which one must characterize as resting upon the conception of time as a course of history. This will become clearer in the ensuing discussion.

Before we turn to the area of ancient Mesopotamian culture, we must point out two characteristics of that culture which were important for the development of the forms of its historical thought. The area defined by the Tigris and Euphrates rivers was dominated by a culture which was by and large unified in terms of history, language, and race, in spite of the variety of its peoples. This cultural unity may be attributed to the system of writing developed by this civilization, namely cuneiform, as well as to the two languages, Sumerian and Akkadian, which coexisted without much tension, | and thus to the unity of literature embodying the religious and political traditions. We can speak of *the* typical ancient Mesopotamian. Of course the various political units (Ashur, Babylon) should not be underestimated, but in spite of this, Mesopotamian man was given his character by the unified culture, the derivation from *one* Sumer, from *one* Akkad – a phenomenon wellknown to the historian. It is a mark of this unified culture that it preserved ancient cultural elements (e. g., literary forms) for a long period of time, although there was further development and eventually, because of the transformation in the intellectual climate, these elements lost their real reason for existence. As a second characteristic this

---

[3] Cf. the summary judgment of the egyptologist L. BULL, "Ancient Egypt," (in: The Idea of History in the Ancient Near East, by R. H. BAINTON, *et al.*, New Haven, 1955), p. 32.

[4] Compare, e. g., the rejection of R. COLLINGWOOD, The Idea of History, Oxford, 1946, by orientalists: W. A. IRWIN, "The Orientalist as Historian," Journal of Near Eastern Studies, 7, 1949, pp. 303 f.; E. A. SPEISER, "Ancient Mesopotamia," (in: The Idea of History in the Ancient Near East, by R. H. BAINTON, *et al.*, 1955), p. 39 n. 6; pp. 55 f. n. 50.

cultural unity gives rise to the trans-racial, almost "cosmopolitan" attitude of the Mesopotamian.[5] The conditions for the development of certain forms of historical thought are given by this stance within a trans-racial tradition complex.

In Mesopotamia statements about the past are primarily found in connection with cultic life.[6] Thus in inscriptions in temples or on cultic objects we have not only a report of the recently completed erection of the building or statue, but also references to the previous history of the cult object. For example, the Assyrian King Shalmaneser I reports that a temple in Ashur was originally built by Ushpia; reconstructed by Irishum I; 159 years later renovated by Shamshi-adad; and finally erected again, after 580 years, by himself, Shalmaneser. Furthermore Esarhaddon reports that he reconstructed the very same temple 580 years after the reconstruction by Shalmaneser I. Or Ashurbanipal reports that after the capture of Susa he was able to find the cultic image of the goddess Nana, which had been purloined by the Elamite Kudur-Naḫundi from Uruk 1635 years earlier. How are we to explain these references to the history of a cultic object, which seem to be quite exact, although they may not always agree with the results of historical-critical research? They are to be explained from the cultic function, the cultic purpose of these objects. A cult is not merely a human invention, but a divine institution. This divine institution must be legally documented, and the temple must be legitimately devoted to the divinity. If a temple | is changed in any way or even reconstructed, this change must also be legally documented and, in particular, it must be linked up with the tradition of the original founding. We may refer to the legal practice of declaring pieces of land and houses to be the property of a certain person by inserting a nail. The same procedure could be used in validating judicial sentences. This leads to the custom of erecting a large clay nail (sikkatu) with an appropriate inscription as a dedication document in the temple.[7] A sikkatu must not be carried away. Thus the above-mentioned Irishum I writes, "If the house of the god falls into disrepair, and a king, standing in my place, desires to rebuild the house, let him not disturb the sikkatu which I have put into place; let him put it in its place again."[8] Later the clay nail was replaced by an inscribed cornerstone (temennu or narū). The original founding of the temple must remain legally documented

[5] Cf. SPEISER, "Ancient Mesopotamia," pp. 41–43.

[6] In connection with this paragraph see particularly Section III, "Nature of the Source Material," in SPEISER, "Ancient Mesopotamia," pp. 45–49, from which the examples are taken. Further examples of historical reviews in B. MEISSNER, Babylonien und Assyrien, Heidelberg, II, 1925, p. 363.

[7] B. LANDSBERGER and K. BALKAN, "Die Inschrift des assyrischen Königs Irişum, gefunden in Kültepe 1948," Türk Tarih Kurumu Belleten, 14, 1950, pp. 252ff., particulary pp. 255f.

[8] Lines 19–23 of the inscription published by Landsberger.

for all subsequent times, since the functioning of the cult is dependent upon it. For by means of the foundation a pact, a *covenant*, is concluded with the deity, and it must be upheld and preserved.[9] Since the famous sanctuaries of Mesopotamia reach back into prehistoric time, it is not surprising that the founding of the covenant is cast back into the primeval period. Thus the Anunnaki founded the temple Esagila for Marduk after his battle against the chaos dragon, which brought about the creation of the world.[10] The same is said of the temple Esharra in Ashur.[11] This retrojection into a primeval period will be examined further in the following discussion. At the moment we must be content with the fact that historical documentation is found in the cultic sphere and that it has its source in the derivation of the cult from a pact or covenant with the deity. In this connection it may be of interest to note that all historical inscriptions of Mesopotamia[12] have developed from the literary | form of the dedicatory or building inscription.[13]

In the examination of the Old Testament idea of history it will be of importance to note that the covenant idea itself demands a historical consciousness. But we cannot derive the structure of historical thought in Mesopotamia from the fact of historical documentation in the cultic sphere. To learn more about it we must turn to the area of Mesopotamian science. Mesopotamian science has been given the characterizing name "list science."[14] Already in the ancient Sumerian period lists of all terrestrial phenomena, including the gods, were gathered for the purpose of naming and thus ordering them: all plants, all animals, all objects made out of wood, out of stone, etc. In this way the system of writing could also be learned; in later times, when the lists appear as Sumero-Akkadian vocabularies, one could learn the Sumerian language, which was necessary for the cult and for the writing system. But the chief purpose was to recognize and realize order in the world. This purpose was also served by the forma-

---

[9] Observe how many sanctuary legends, ἱεροὶ λόγοι, are transmitted to us in the Old Testament, or how important every change in the Jerusalem temple appears to the deuteronomistic historians.

[10] Enuma Elish, VI, 34ff. (Ancient Near Eastern Texts Relating to the Old Testament, ed. by J. B. PRITCHARD (= ANET), Princeton, 1950, pp. 68f.); cf. W. ZIMMERLI, "Promise and Fulfillment" (in: Essays in Old Testament Hermeneutics, ed. by C. WESTERMANN, Richmond, Va., 1963), pp. 95f.

[11] H. GRESSMANN (ed.), Altorientalische Texte zum Alten Testament, 2nd ed., Berlin, 1926, p. 132; cf. W. ZIMMERLI, "Promise and Fulfillment," p. 96.

[12] To be sure there are some peculiarities in Assyrian annals beginning in the fourteenth century B. C.; see below p. 58.

[13] Cf. S. MOWINCKEL, "Die vorderasiatischen Königs- und Fürsteninschriften," (in: Eucharisterion, Festschrift für Hermann Gunkel, ed. by H. SCHMIDT, Göttingen, I, 1923), pp. 278ff.

[14] Cf. W. VON SODEN, "Leistung und Grenze sumerischer und babylonischer Wissenschaft," (in: Die Welt als Geschichte, II, 1936), pp. 411ff. and 509ff.

tion and collection of proverbs, which were intended to demonstrate the structural laws of human life.[15] This "ordering science,"[16] if I may call it that, also turned to historical phenomena. At times it took the form of a so-called sign (= omen) science, on which we have extensive information from the omina lists. In this science one proceeded from the presupposition that there was a finite, although large, number of distinct "times" which could be defined in terms of certain phenomena. Such symptomatic phenomena are, e. g., the shapes of the liver of a sheep which was sacrificed at a specific time. The variety of liver forms permitted the arrangement of the "times" in that the liver forms were connected with the historical events taking place after the sacrifice. Then if the same omen occurred again, if it was thus the same "time," the corresponding events would necessarily transpire. This combination of liver forms and kinds of time, established by empirical observation, [17] | came to be used in divining the present or the immediate future.[18] E.g., "when the liver is formed in such and such a fashion (a detailed description follows), this is an omen of the man of Apishal (the king of Apishal), whom Naram-sin took captive when he tried to break through the wall of his city."[19] For it was recorded that the liver was formed in such and such a way at that time; if this omen should occur again, the Mesopotamians will be careful not to attempt an escape from their besieged city. We have here the following idea of history, if we may call it that: Every situation or kind of time has already existed once in the incomprehensible sequence of situations; every one comes back again, although the sequence as such cannot be determined; the symptoms can only help us to determine which situation is about ready to appear again. We have here no thought of the development of one condition out of another in the course of time, let alone the idea that history has a goal and purpose, although the "times," or situations, were set in order and arranged in lists. In the indeterminable character of the course of time as such, and in the unfathomable sequence even of past times, the basic and profound insecurity of Sumerian man is reflected, over against the un-

---

[15] Cf. H. Gese, Lehre und Wirklichkeit in der alten Weisheit, Tübingen, 1958, pp. 66–68.

[16] The expression "science" may be allowed to stand although we are not concerned, like the Greeks, with ἀρχή, or principium; on "empiric-gnomic apperception" see G. von Rad, "Die ältere Weisheit Israels," Kerygma und Dogma, 2, 1956, pp. 56, 60.

[17] Undoubtedly the deductive method also existed, in which one judged the character of the "times" from the form of the liver as a model; cf. H. Gese, Lehre und Wirklichkeit, p. 48 n. 1.

[18] Cf. A. Goetze, "Historical Allusions in Old Babylonian Texts," Journal of Cuneiform Studies, 1, 1947, pp. 253 ff.

[19] A. Goetze (ed.), Old Babylonian Omen Texts (Yale Oriental Series, Babylonian Texts, V, 10, 1947), 24, 9; cf. A. Goetze, "Historical Allusions . . .," pp. 257 f.

fathomable and capricious will of the gods. Nevertheless even in subsequent periods, when the intellectual presuppositions were different, omina-science, once established, was maintained in its original form.

But this "list science" approached the phenomena of history in still another way: the year was felt to be a unity and this was of course deduced from the cycle of the seasons and astronomical phenomena. One could arrange the years according to an important event that took place in each. This is at least the case in Babylon; in Assyria the process was somewhat different. [20] In this way lists of years were prepared which served chrono-logical purposes for the most part. [21] But a year is too short a unit for histori-cal periods. A more suitable means | was developed for arranging the times. They were divided into times of good fortune and times of doom, and this rigid schematization was carried to the point where times of good fortune were broadly portrayed as periods of blessing from the gods, whereas times of doom were generally pictured as times of curse. This schematization of history is found in the "Sumerian historical literature," of which the more important known exemplars concern the Akkadian rulers Sargon and Naram-sin, who elsewhere play a prominent role in Mesopotamian literature. [22] The supposition that the extant exemplars of the Sumerian historical literature once formed parts of an extensive historical work beginning with the creation of the world[23] has not been confirmed. It is possible that the reigns of Sargon and Naram-sin were chosen because to a certain extent they could be used as paradigms for the change from the time of good fortune to the time of doom, or, and this is even more likely, because this change is obvious in terms of the historical significance of Sargon and Naram-sin. It is important, however, that the times of good fortune and doom are not simply divided between the two rulers. Naram-sin has a time of good fortune, a time of doom, and another time of good fortune. The sudden appearance of the time of doom is caused by nothing other than the displeasure of the goddess Inanna. [24] It is interesting to note that we have no reference to a motivation in terms of Naram-sin's deeds to which the goddess would have reacted with "anger."[25] Such a conception not only corresponds to that which we have learned from the omina literature, but is also well known elsewhere in Sumerian literature.

---

[20] Cf. A. UNGNAD, in: Reallexikon der Assyriologie, II, pp. 412 ff., s.v. "Eponym."

[21] Cf. ANET, pp. 269 ff.

[22] On the "Sumerian historical literature" cf. H.-G. GÜTERBOCK, "Die histori-sche Tradition und ihre literarische Gestaltung bei Babyloniern und Hethitern bis 1200," Zeitschrift für Assyriologie, 42, 1934, pp. 24 ff.

[23] E. CHIERA, Sumerian Religious Texts, Upland, Pa., 1924.

[24] GÜTERBOCK, "Die historische Tradition," p. 27 (31) line A 55 (B 21).

[25] Lines 55 ff. contain only a description of the actions of Inanna which bring the doom. There is no trace of a reason for this action; note that line 55 follows line 54 without any transition (against H.-G. GÜTERBOCK, p. 54).

In ancient times Sumerian religion knows only the will of the gods, which is naturally bound up with a rigid hierarchy of the gods, and this will is beyond human comprehension. But man is not thereby abandoned to the chaotic caprice of the gods; one's personal protective deity can provide help against the evil actions of the other gods. Nevertheless in all this man remains completely passive. In the course of events the gods act according to their own principles. [26] The fact that the outbreak of a time of doom cannot be plotted in advance prevents us from seeking a cyclical | view of history in the change from a time of good fortune to a time of doom. Also the extent of the times of good fortune and doom shows quite a variety and is therefore undefinable. There is no scheme of periods which could serve as a basis for the view of history.

From this concept of history, documented in the "ordering science," namely history as an indefinable sequence of times, repeating themselves arbitrarily according to the will of the gods, and capable of being characterized as times of good fortune and doom, the Sumerian scientists were nevertheless able to write a kind of world history; it is a history of the sequence of city states and their temples. [27] Kingship migrated from one city state to another. The kings and their reigns are enumerated and then it is remarked that this particular city state was defeated in battle, whereupon kingship was transferred to another city state. Furthermore the total of the years of reign in a certain city state is given. The shepherd Etana stands at the beginning of this sequence of times; it is he who has established the order of all lands and has made it possible for kingship, which is the active power in terrestrial history, to migrate from king to king and from city to city. But Etana was able to do this only because he had succeeded in ascending to heaven and descending to earth again. Naturally this material was later expanded with all sorts of legendary motifs and developed into an epic which we have in an Old Babylonian, a Middle and a New Assyrian recension. [28] According to these recensions Etana brought down from heaven a plant enabling a royal heir to be born to him. In his trip to heaven he used an eagle whom he had freed from the power of a serpent. However, the Sumerian chronicle only briefly mentions the trip to heaven. Thus the establishment of kingship as an ordering institution appears at the beginning of history. But according to the Sumerian chronicle, this is not the beginning of the world. Sumerian scientists claimed that all social order on earth is merely a reflection of the heavenly order, and that it never completely corresponds to the "idea" of that order. Thus before beginning history with Etana they construct a history of the primeval period. This primeval period is characterized not only by enormously long reigns, but

---

[26] Cf. H. GESE, Lehre und Wirklichkeit, p. 65, and the literature cited there.
[27] Cf. T. JACOBSEN, The Sumerian King List, (Assyriological Studies, 11), Chicago, 1939.   [28] ANET, pp. 114 ff.

also by the fact that there were no wars to cause the migration of kingship from one city state to another in the course of | time. But this primeval history corresponds to later history like a prototype to a copy. This primeval period ends in the flood of chaotic waters, in which the world returns to the condition prior to the creation. Thus Sumerian tradition has a myth about the destruction of the primeval order preceding the chronicle of time sequences. At a later time this outline of world history came to be of considerable importance for Israelite history writing, although it underwent significant changes.

The concept of history developed in Sumerian "ordering science," namely, a mere sequence of times, is to be radically distinguished from a later view, first found in the Babylonian chronicles. Here we have a decisive juncture in the development of human thought: the recognition of a connection between act and consequence. [29] No longer is history merely a sequence of times of good fortune and doom according to the unfathomable decision of the gods; history is no longer sequence, but rather *consequence*, a consequence of human actions and deeds. Naturally the recognition of a connection between man's actions and man's condition does not yet mean the discovery of the principle of causality. In ancient Near Eastern thought there is no "principle," no $\dot{\alpha}\varrho\chi\acute{\eta}$. Rather, act and consequence are so closely connected that they appear as a unity. The Babylonian word ordinarily translated "sin" *(arnu* or *annu)* means two things: the evil which a man does *and* the misfortune which he suffers for it. [30] This idea of a connection between man's conduct and man's condition [31] or the so-called synthetic view of life [32] is also found frequently in the Old Testament: רעה is the evil which someone does, and also the misfortune which befalls him. This way of thinking can be demonstrated in the semantic analysis of many Hebrew words, and elsewhere as well. [33] The transition from the conception

---

[29] Cf. H. GESE, Lehre und Wirklichkeit, pp. 42ff., 65ff.

[30] Cf. W. VON SODEN, "Religion und Sittlichkeit nach den Anschauungen der Babylonier," Zeitschrift der Deutschen Morgenländischen Gesellschaft, 89, 1935, p. 160 n. 1.

[31] Or "the conception of a sphere of actions bringing about a certain fate": K. KOCH, "Gibt es ein Vergeltungsdogma im Alten Testament?" ZThK, 52, 1955, p. 31 and elsewhere.

[32] K. H. FAHLGREN, Ṣᵉdāqâ nahestehende und entgegengesetzte Begriffe im Alten Testament, Uppsala, 1932.

[33] E.g., רשע Hiph.: 1. make oneself guilty, 2. declare someone to be guilty, bring misfortune to a guilty person; אשם: 1. become guilty, 2. atone for guilt. There are many further examples of such extensions in Hebrew as compared with modern languages; e. g., פקד means both "to miss something" and "to pursue, search for it"; then both "to discover the fault or the ones at fault" and "to eliminate the fault, or call the ones at fault to account," i. e., to restore the *status quo*. Thus one is concerned not with a *situation*, but with a *process*. This gives rise to the difficulty of using semantics in a study of thought structures; a single word can gather various

of sequence to that of | consequence can be studied in Mesopotamia in a quite unparalleled way. In this connection we cannot go into the question of the source of this transition, nor the time and place of its origin.[34] It should only be emphasized that this change in Mesopotamia is not to be traced back merely to the Babylonians, but had already arisen among the Sumerians themselves, even though the major shift in historiography comes between Sumerian and Babylonian historiography. This is to be explained from the fact that Sumerian historiographic texts are a part of canonical, official literature, which can only work with the official concept of history.

The first Babylonian chronicle available to us, the so-called Weidner Chronicle,[35] is a classic textbook for the conception of history as the consequence of human action. Beginning with the first dynasty after the primeval flood, the chronicle relates the history of the land and sees that the doom which befalls a given ruler is brought on because of his offence against the cult of the central sanctuary in Babylon, Esagila, the temple of Marduk. There is a considerable variety of offences, but they are always directed against the Esagila cult. Thus we have here a conception of history as consequence, specified, as it were, according to a definite criterion, in terms of which human conduct is judged. But it is interesting to note that in this theory of history the consequences of human actions are not limited to the responsible individual, but rather spread out to the whole dynasty. So, for example, Sargon commits an offence, but suffers only a certain amount of disquietude; only with Naram-sin, who also commits an offence, does complete doom result. This judgment is perhaps influenced by the fact that, prior to his offence, Sargon had performed many useful services for Esagila. But there is no explicit appeal to these; furthermore, the beneficial effects of this service had long since been exhausted. In the introduction to this historical work there is a general remark that anyone who transgresses against the gods of this city, Babylon, *(ša ana ilī ali šāšu uqallalū)* will perish. This technical term, *qullulu*, "transgress," occurs again and again in the later historiographic texts, and they always have a conception of history as consequence; naturally it is no | longer confined only to a transgression against the central sanctuary of Babylon. Besides *qullulu* we find the technical terms, *mamīta etēqu*,[36] "fail in the oath of office," or *itē ili etēqu*, literally "transgress the bounds of the god," i. e., transgress the bounds which were established for the king by his protective deity, ὑβρίζειν.

---

concepts about itself. A typical case is the secondary differentiation of the Hiph. of נוח, in which the semantic differentiation is accounted for in the development of the forms.   [34] See above, note 29.

[35] GÜTERBOCK, "Die historische Tradition . . .," pp. 47 ff.

[36] LANDSBERGER-BALKAN (see above n. 7), p. 263; cf. E. A. SPEISER, "Ancient Mesopotamia," pp. 56 f.

All later historical and historiographic literature works with these terms. Further investigation of this literature is unnecessary at this point; the concept of history implied in it remains by and large the same: history is the consequence of human actions; doom comes by necessity to any one who transgresses against the divine order, or to one who breaks the covenant implied by his oath of office.

We should also mention, however, a marginal phenomenon in Mesopotamian historiography: the writing of history as didactics. Indeed when history is viewed as the consequence of human actions and deeds it is immediately obvious that the writing of history can serve a didactic purpose. This didactic literature consists of fictitious royal inscriptions in the form of historical documentation. Accordingly it has been given the name *narū* literature.[37] But in contrast to the genuine royal inscription, where we find an exhortation to preserve the inscription forever and not to change it (the so-called curse formula), we have here an exhortation to take to heart the teaching contained in this historical report. In other words, one should "draw the moral of the story."

Finally, I would like to refer to an oft-repeated judgment on Mesopotamian historiography. It is said that historical understanding could not have developed very extensively in Mesopotamia since the numerous Assyrian royal inscriptions and annals which have been preserved contain so many uncritical exaggerations of the deeds of Assyrian kings, and since the inscriptions are written in such a bombastic style, that any critical assessment of their deeds is impossible. Rather it is said that historical reality is falsified for the sake of a royal desire for power and glory. Such a judgment overlooks the origin of the form of these inscriptions. On the basis of the Mari texts it can now be shown that the ancient form of the letter to a god has influenced the Assyrian royal inscriptions, which in and of themselves are basically a development of the dedicatory inscription.[38] These royal inscriptions are to be understood as letters to the god Ashur, as reports on the way in which the king | was able to extend the honor and power of the god Ashur and to expand his (the god's) kingdom to the ends of the earth. Indeed the Assyrian kings were filled with this idea of mission for Ashur. One lengthy inscription even has a more extensive duplicate in the form of a stylized letter.[39] On the other hand an inscription of Ashurbanipal has the colophon "Message of Ashurbanipal to Ashur . . ."[40]

The historiography of the Mesopotamians is far surpassed by that of the

[37] GÜTERBOCK, "Die historische Tradition . . .," pp. 19, 62 ff.

[38] References in SPEISER, "Ancient Mesopotamia," pp. 63 ff.

[39] F. THUREAU-DANGIN, Une relation de la huitième campagne de Sargon, Paris, 1912; SPEISER, "Ancient Mesopotamia," p. 65 n. 80.

[40] Cuneiform Texts from the Babylonian Tablets . . . in the British Museum, vol. 35, nos. 44 f., verso 23 f.; SPEISER, "Ancient Mesopotamia," p. 66 n. 81.

Hittites. [41] They developed the gift of historical observation to the highest degree. The art of narration is now further refined; situations can be described in a penetrating way, and extensive summaries and reviews of past events can be given from particular points of view. The religious purpose so characteristic of the Mesopotamian historical documents recedes into the background. In form the Hittite annals are royal edicts [42] and do not degenerate into a whitewashing of political events. At the beginning of international treaties the Hittites usually give an extensive historical review in which the political relationships up to the time of the treaty are analyzed. But in spite of this historiographic refinement the concept of history is largely the same: history is thought to be the consequence of human deeds. A breach of the divine ordinances, e. g., the breaking of an oath or the violation of an international treaty, leads automatically to doom. The famous plague prayers of Mursilis [43] are characteristic for this view of history. A pestilence had raged in the land of the Hittites for twenty years. A consultation of the oracles gave two replies: (1) the sacrifices for the river Mala had been discontinued for a long period, and (2) in his war with the Egyptians Mursilis' father had broken their mutual treaty established when the inhabitants of Kurustama were sent to Egypt. The whole affair is extensively described in a historical review. In the name of his people King Mursilis confesses his sins: "I | have confessed it before the Hittite Storm-God, my lord, and the gods, my lords: It is true, we have sinned."

Let me mention here a document from the first half of the thirteenth century B. C. which impresses me as a high point of Hittite historical writing: the so-called apology of Hattusilis. [44] It is actually an autobiography in the form of a royal edict. (Autobiographies always have a somewhat apologetic character!) The introduction to this biography, following the formula of a royal edict, defines its purpose: the power of a goddess is to be proclaimed. Unfortunately we do not know her Hittite name, but in the cuneiform text the sign for Ishtar occurs. So for the sake of simplicity we refer to her as Ishtar. The document begins with the words, "I will proclaim the divine power of Ishtar. And in the future Ishtar shall be especially honored among the gods of my majesty, among those of the son, among those of the grandson, among those of the descendents of my

---

[41] A. GOETZE, Kleinasien (Handbuch der Altertumswissenschaft III, 1, 3, vol. 3, 1), 1933, pp. 161 ff.; *idem*, Hethiter, Churriter und Assyrer (Instituttet for Sammenlignende Kulturforskning A 17), Oslo, 1936, pp. 73 f.; H.-G. GÜTERBOCK, "Die historische Tradition . . .," pp. 45 ff.

[42] GÜTERBOCK, "Die historische Tradition . . .," p. 94

[43] ANET, pp. 394 ff.

[44] A. GOETZE, "Ḫattušiliš, der Bericht über seine Thronbesteigung nebst den Paralleltexten: Hethitische Texte in Umschrift I" (Mitteilungen der Vorderasiatischen Gesellschaft, Berlin, 29, 3, 1925).

majesty."[45] At this point Hattusilis begins to tell the story of his life, which has been guided and protected by Ishtar from his youth up. His successful reign as a governor arouses the jealousy of others, who seek to bring him misfortune; his brother, the Hittite king Muwatallis, brings him to trial. "But," says Hattusilis, "my lady Ishtar appeared to me in a dream, and by means of a dream she said to me, 'Would I give you into the power of some hostile deity? Fear not!'"[46] And so even in this trial (most likely a duel of some sort) he is not handed over to the hostile deity. Hattusilis says, "Since the goddess, my lady, held me by the hand, she did not give me into the power of the hostile deity, the hostile judgment. The weapons of my enemy did not conquer me. My lady Ishtar always rescued me."[47] The whole eventful life of Hattusilis is related in this style, leading finally to the Hittite throne. Again and again it is Ishtar who rescues him from all dangers or gives him orders concerning wise decisions.

In this biography of Hattusilis there are two features of special significance: (1) The concept of history as the consequence of human action is constantly upheld. This is particularly clear in one passage of the biography: Muwatallis, Hattusilis' brother, is succeeded on the Hittite | throne by his son, Urhi-tessub, and the latter begins to persecute Hattusilis unjustly. The resulting war between the two leads to victory for Hattusilis. The fault is clearly on the side of Urhi-tessub, and is set forth in great detail. The text reads literally, "Would the gods overthrow any great king who deals justly with a little king?"[48] Enough is said in this rhetorical question.

(2) History is understood as election and guidance by a personal protective deity. Nevertheless the presentation is in no way unhistorical. There are no reports of marvelous wonders and miracles; rather the events are simply described. Yet this history is interpreted as guidance by the deity. This gives fresh nuances to the idea of history. But this protection by a personal deity is a widespread and wellknown idea in the ancient Near East.[49] Thus one cannot speak here of a basic change in the idea of history. Ishtar remains only a protective deity and must bring good fortune only in the framework of the divine hierarchy. In spite of the heavy emphasis upon the good fortune which Ishtar has brought to Hattusilis there is no rejection or renunciation of other gods. The biography's formula for the declaration of war against Urhi-tessub is characteristic here. It reads, "Come! Ishtar of Samuha and the Weather-God of Nerik shall decide the case!"[50] The Weather-God of Nerik plays a most decisive role among the Hittite national deities; furthermore, Hattusilis was a priest of this god.[51]

---

[45] 1, 5–8.   [46] 1, 36–38.   [47] 1, 39–43.
[48] 3, 78.

[49] Cf. T. JACOBSEN, "Mesopotamia" (in: H. FRANKFORT et al., The Intellectual Adventure of Ancient Man, Chicago 1946), pp. 202 ff. (= Before Philosophy [Pelican], pp. 137 ff.).   [50] 3, 71–72.   [51] 3, 60.

Let us now turn to the *Old Testament*. Israel, as a combination of Yahweh-worshiping tribes, appears at a relatively late date in the course of history, namely at the end of the Bronze Age. In one important point she differs from the other peoples who had settled down in the ancient Near East: Israel does not become assimilated to the culture of the settled area, but lives in constant tension with it. Thus the mutual relations are here exactly reversed from those of "cosmopolitan" Mesopotamia, in which various peoples at various times become part of *one* great culture. On the one hand Israel, because of her late appearance in the course of history, presupposes the cultural development of the past, | including that of the idea of history;[52] on the other hand, however, Israel firmly maintains her uniqueness. According to the witness of the Old Testament this uniqueness is the covenant with Yahweh.

Yahweh is the God of Israel and Israel is the people of Yahweh; there are no other gods to whom Israel can belong. Yahweh showed himself to be the God of Israel when he led Israel out of Egypt. This leading out of Egypt by Yahweh is the primal confession of Israel – the traditio-historical analyses of the last few decades have made this sufficiently clear.[53] Yahweh shows himself to be the God of Israel by his leading the people in the wilderness, by his leading them into the cultured land, where he plants Israel as the people of his heritage. On Sinai Yahweh establishes the covenant with Israel: Israel, as a holy people, belongs to him alone.

From this may be derived two theses: (1) By means of the exodus from Egypt the covenant has become a historical event. The establishment of the covenant does not occur in some mythological, timeless primeval era, but is connected with definite, specific historical facts. This has two consequences for the concept of history in Israel: a) Because of the connection of the covenant with historical events, the history of the people, insofar as it occurred *prior* to these events, necessarily appears in a particular light. It is not simply empty time, but a time which leads up to the events of the covenant, a time of promise.[54] Occasionally the history of the patriarchs Abraham, Isaac, and Jacob is depicted so that it anticipates the later covenant events in a mysterious way. The establishment of a covenant with Abraham is related, a covenant of fire and smoke, and Yahweh appears before him with the formula, "I am Yahweh, who brought you out of Ur-Kasdim."[55] The essential content of the patriarchal narratives is the promise of the

---

[52] I have in mind the semantic structure of the Canaanite language to which I refer on p. 56 above.

[53] Cf. G. VON RAD, Das formgeschichtliche Problem des Hexateuchs (Beiträge zur Wissenschaft vom Alten und Neuen Testament, Stuttgart, IV, 26), 1938 (= Gesammelte Studien zum Alten Testament, Munich, 1958, pp. 9 ff.); M. NOTH, Überlieferungsgeschichte des Pentateuch, Stuttgart, 1948.

[54] Cf. W. ZIMMERLI, "Promise and Fulfillment," p. 90.

[55] Gen. 15:7; cf. ZIMMERLI, p. 91.

land into which the descendents will eventually be led as the people of
Yahweh. Here history is more than merely the consequence of human
action, actualized by the gods according to the order of correspondence
between action and suffering, or any other aspect of experience. Here
history has a goal toward which it runs. b) Over against the actualization
of the covenant in historical events stands the disobedience and apostasy
of the people, the breaking of the covenant. According to the ancient Near
Eastern conception of history as | the consequence of human actions, such
an evil deed would necessarily lead directly to an outbreak of doom. Also
for Israelite thought doom necessarily follows; however, it cannot be
merely doom, but is rather punishment and chastisement. God does not
simply wipe out his inheritance and annul the covenant which had already
become reality in his great historical deeds. God punishes Israel and defers
the fulfillment, but his promises are not shaken. Thus God does not simply
react to human evil-doing with doom, but requites Israel in an active,
judging deed. Thereby the ancient Near Eastern conception of history as
consequence changes to the concept of history as *judgment*.

(2) If the apostasy of the people leads to punishment by God and the
deferring of the fulfillment of the covenant, but not to its withdrawal,
since God's promises are not shaken, this means that the whole history of
Israel is seen within the schema "promise and fulfillment." Or, to put it
another way, the actualization of the covenant is not a once-and-for-all event,
but a historical process – *Geschichte*. Consequently, according to the Israelite
view, Israel's history is based upon a divine *plan of salvation*, and this plan
is made known to Israel from time to time in God's promises. In the actualization of his plan of salvation God avails himself of the large and small
historical powers, which he uses as his instruments.

Given the profundity which historical thinking reached in Israel, it is
of course to be expected that the Old Testament would not be lacking in
historiographic works. In this essay I can only touch on a few of these works.
The history of the succession to King David[56] is characterized by the
literary gifts of the author, and it could only have arisen in a people with
a considerable feeling for the narrative form. This writer of history understands how to show, in the events of everyday life, the underlying forces
which make for history, namely the divine plan, within which everything
has to fit together as in a puppet play, although each person acts freely and
with his own intentions.

The great historical work of the Yahwist takes over the outline of official
Sumerian world history, which had reached Israel through some channel
of oral tradition: the history of creation, the primeval period, the flood,

---

[56] Cf. L. ROST, Die Überlieferung von der Thronnachfolge Davids, (Beiträge zur
Wissenschaft vom Alten und Neuen Testament, Stuttgart, III, 6), 1926.

and the new beginning of world history. But what becomes of this outline of history in the hands | of the Yahwist? According to the Israelite view, the time of promise began with the patriarch Abraham. So the Yahwist tells of the fall after creation; Cain's fratricide of Abel falls into the primeval period, and in this same period the sons of God marry the daughters of men, who then bear the giants of the primeval period. Consequently Yahweh shortens man's life span. When the world is newly founded after the flood, Yahweh says that the thoughts of human hearts are evil from their youth up; thus he will no longer curse the whole earth because of man. Then the crime of Canaan and the destruction of the tower of Babel are related. The time of blessing commences only with the patriarch Abraham.

In its history of Israel the deuteronomistic historical work[57] follows the continuous correspondence between promise and fulfillment, apostasy and punishment, until finally, because of Israel's stubborn turning from Yahweh, the existence of the people as a nation has to come to an end by means of the catastrophic blows of the Mesopotamian empires. But this historical work ends with a reference to the pardon given to the only surviving Davidic king, Jehoiachin, and his sons, who are in exile in Babylon.[58] Among his later descendents was Shesh-bazzar,[59] who was to return to Judah with the stolen temple treasures and serve as Davidic nāśi' and Persian deputy governor; along with him the first group of Jews returned to the land.

Recent Old Testament study has shown how firmly the prophets of Israel are rooted in the religious traditions of their people. Today they no longer appear to us as the preachers of a basically new understanding of God, as they did toward the end of the nineteenth century, when they were celebrated as the founders of ethical monotheism. Thus even the prophetic conception of history may not radically differ from that which we have attempted to characterize as the Israelite idea of history. However, it seems to me that they indicate a further development of historical thought, and I conclude with a few remarks on this subject, without, however, going into the question of the possible origin of these new insights in the cult. |

The Israelite view of God as the one who actualizes his covenant in history and judges Israel receives its classic expression in the prophetic proclamation of Yahweh's word as the effective power in history. But this history is neither eternal, nor infinitely extendable; it pushes on to a conclusion, whether it be the complete destruction of the people because of

---

[57] Cf. G. VON RAD, "Theologische Geschichtsschreibung im Alten Testament," Theologische Zeitschrift, 4, 1948, pp. 161 ff.

[58] II Kgs. 25:27 ff.; cf. VON RAD, p. 173.

[59] Cf. H. GESE, Der Verfassungsentwurf des Ezechiel (Beiträge zur historischen Theologie, 25), Tübingen, 1957, p. 118.

its apostasy from Yahweh, or the final fulfillment of the divine promises. Amos takes up the popular conception of the day of Yahweh, which may well stem from the cult. This day will not be light, but darkness.[60] But perhaps a remnant will remain.[61] Then justice and righteousness will reign, then there will be no more sacrifice, just as there was no sacrifice at the beginning, during the sojourn in the wilderness.[62] In my opinion we have here for the first time the view of a correspondence between the primeval period (Urzeit) and the eschaton (Endzeit), whereby the salvation-acts of Yahweh constituting the covenant are understood as the Urzeit.[63] Hosea goes considerably further in this train of thought: Israel will again experience an urzeitliches event, will again be led into the wilderness; the covenant with Israel, indeed the whole creation, will be made new.[64] In Isaiah the idea of the remnant of Israel is developed in a decisive way.[65] He sets forth the promises of the Davidic covenant,[66] and to a considerable degree makes use of mythical elements in the characterization of Zion as an impregnable, divine establishment.[67] Finally, Deutero-Isaiah, in his proclamation of Yahweh's forthcoming acts in history, portrays them with the colors of the Urzeit. Just as Yahweh led Israel out of Egypt through the wilderness, so also he will lead her home out of Babylon;[68] just as Yahweh made a covenant with Noah when the world was reestablished after the flood, so also he will do it again with Israel.[69] And the exodus from Egypt is described by Deutero-Isaiah with the mythologoumena of the battle with the chaos dragon.[70] So for prophetic thought history pushes on to its goal. And the more this goal is identified with the salvation acts of Yahweh, which had once established the covenant, the more eschatological the | idea of history has to become: history finds its end. Apocalyptic has expanded this idea to the doctrine of two aeons: the aeon of world history, which is that of periodic cycles, will be replaced by the kingdom of God, the coming aeon.[71] The end of history has broken in when the kingdom of God appeared in history – a kingdom not of this world.

---

[60] Amos 5:20. [61] Amos 5:15. [62] Amos 5:21–25.

[63] The imperfect with wāw copulative וְיִגַּל, Amos 5:24, is to be translated as consecutive-final (cf. J. P. HYATT, "The Translation and Meaning of Amos 5:23–24," ZAW, 68, 1956, pp. 17ff.); מִשְׁפָּט and צְדָקָה, Amos 5:24, are to be taken as positive. The unit concludes with a rhetorical question which establishes the relationship of the final (endzeitliche) events to the primeval period (Urzeit).

[64] Hos. 2:16f. (EVV 2:14f.); cf. 11:10f.

[65] Isa. 6:13; 8:18; 10:19; 11:11, 16; 28:5.

[66] Isa. 9:5f. (EVV 9:6f.); 11:1ff.

[67] Isa. 8:18; 28:16; 29:7; 31:9.

[68] Isa. 43:16–21; 48:20f.

[69] Isa. 54:9.

[70] Isa. 51:9ff.

[71] E.g., Dan. 2; 7.

»We« in Acts and the Itinerary[*]

by

Ernst Haenchen

Translated by Jack Wilson

1. The Situation

For a long time the occurrence of "we" in Acts has given people occasion for thought.[1] It first appears in chapter 16. Previously, the stories of the earliest period in Jerusalem, the origin of the congregation at Antioch, the first mission to the gentiles, originating from Antioch, and the approval of this mission at a conference in Jerusalem were related. Then at 15: 36 the story of a second missionary journey begins. In this narrative "we" suddenly appears in 16: 10 but then disappears again in 16: 17. Only after several years in the narrative have elapsed does the word recur in 20: 5, and it continues in use until 21: 18 (to be sure with one omission, 20:16 to 38). Again after several years have passed, it reappears finally in 27: 1 and continues through 28: 16.

We are not told who it is that speaks in this "we." Ordinarily, it means "Paul and his companions," including the narrator. But it has been observed that before the last occurrence of "we" in chapters 16 and 21 it ceases to be linked with Paul.[2] In 16: 17 and 21: 18 it refers only to his traveling companions.[3] In sum, "we" occurs only in the description of Paul's | trips. Although it appears each time without preparation, its disappearance is prepared for by literary means.

How can one explain this special use of "we"?

---

[*] "Das 'Wir' in der Apostelgeschichte und das Itinerar," ZThK, 58, 1961, pp. 329–366.

[1] So far as we know, the church father Irenaeus was the first to note its importance; cf. Adv. haer. III 1; 10: 1; 14: 1f. He proved the Lukan authorship on the basis of Col. 4: 4 and II Tim. 4: 9ff. together with the "we" sections and the prologue to Luke's gospel.

[2] The Beginnings of Christianitye, d. by F.J. FOAKES-JACKSON and K. LAKE, IV, London, 1933, p. 193: "Both here and in xxi. 18 Paul is distinguished from the 'us'. Is this an indication by the writer that he proposes at this point to drop out of the story and leave the whole stage to Paul?" In fact, this change in meaning is found also in 20: 13f. and 21: 12–14.

[3] Also in 27: 20 only Paul's companions are meant. For, corresponding to Luke's

2. The Traditional Explanation of "We"

At first this occurrence of "we" was explained in a very simple way: The author, i. e. Luke the physician[4] mentioned in Col. 4: 14, II Tim. 4: 11, and Philem. 24, met Paul and his companions, Silas and Timothy, in Troas and immediately joined them. He came with them to Philippi and remained there (which is the reason, it was assumed, that this "we" section ends here), perhaps as leader of the new congregation (and as a physician). Years later when Paul again came through Philippi, Luke once more joined him and followed him to Jerusalem. It is not certain where Luke stayed while Paul was a prisoner in Caesarea ("we" is missing in this section). But because Paul's departure for Rome came quite suddenly and Luke went with him, according to "we" in chapters 20–21, Luke must have remained in or near Caesarea.

Thus the occurrence of "we" from chapters 16 to 28 seems to be well understood: The narrator who speaks in "we" and the author are identical, i. e. Luke the physician. Nevertheless, the problems still remain why "we" appears each time so abruptly, without any explanation to the reader, and why its disappearance is prepared for by literary means. It is also worthy of consideration that someone who knew only Acts would not arrive at the conclusion that Luke was its author. It is at these points that one can begin a criticism of the traditional explanation of "we."

3. Historical-critical Theology: Differentiation between Author and Source ("We")

Especially since the end of *Tendenzkritik*, the historical-critical consideration of Acts has sought to find the sources of this work. One obvious approach was to explain the "we" sections as a "we" source. Awkward, however, was the fragmentary character of this source: the first section contains only eight verses. How can one visualize the handing down of such a document? | As an example of the way in which historical-critical scholars attempted to avoid this difficulty, we cite E. Norden. He regarded it "as an assured result of source analysis of Acts" "that even in its original form the 'we' account contained not just 'we' sections in the strict sense of the word but also data concerning events about which the author could not report as

---

depiction of Paul, "we" to be sure, but not Paul himself, are in despair. In 27: 16 "we" includes Paul and the others on the ship this one time.

[4] Only Col. 4: 14 designates Luke as a physician. The idea that Luke was something like the first bishop of the Philippian congregation appeared first in the time when one reckoned with the monarchial episcopacy, an institution not found in the Pauline congregations. E. ZELLER, Die Apostelgeschichte kritisch untersucht, 1854, p. 454, thought: Luke "could also have come back from Philippi to Troas, or wherever else he was from, and could have met Paul intentionally again in Philippi."

an eyewitness; the relationship of 16: 6–9 to 20: 5f. admits of no other interpretation."[5] "This basic document was therefore the combination of an account of what he himself had experienced plus a report in the third person. Consequently, the redactor expanded from other sources a work which he already possessed and which showed the form of composition mentioned above, retaining the 'we' found in the basic document."[6] According to Norden, then, the author of Acts edited this basic document; the document itself was a ὑπόμνημα in which the "we" or "I" style was combined with a report in the third person. As examples of such works Norden named ancient accounts of expeditions and works of Hellenistic historiography.[7] The hypothetical basic document of Acts would have belonged to such a group.[8] Yet why did the redactor keep the "we" of the basic document, which went back to firsthand experience and thus was an eyewitness account, although the redactor himself was not an eyewitness? "This is the real problem."[9] Norden solved it by the reference to the books of Ezra and Nehemiah. The redactor of these books used original, firsthand accounts, even written in the first person, and in some instances left them unchanged.[10] Thus Norden thinks that the "we" in Acts goes back to the firsthand accounts of one of Paul's traveling companions. But these accounts also contained reports in the third person about those parts of Paul's journeys in which the narrator himself had not taken part. The redactor, to whom Norden attributes the composition of Acts, should have changed this "we" into the third person in order | to preserve the stylistic unity. But the example of the Biblical books Ezra and Nehemiah, moved him to take over the "we" unchanged.

Important in this solution is the distinction made between the eyewitness who speaks in the "we" section (though not only there!) and the redactor. It is also important, however, that here the hypothetical written source contains more than just those sections in which "we" appears. To be sure, all in Acts which contains a "we" is from the source for Norden, but

---

[5] EDUARD NORDEN, Agnostos Theos: Untersuchungen zur Formengeschichte religiöser Rede, Leipzig and Berlin, 1913, p. 314.

[6] NORDEN, p. 315.

[7] NORDEN mentions Velleius Paterculus, Cassius Dio, Ammianus Marcellinus, the Novel of Alexander, and apocryphal acts of the apostles.

[8] NORDEN, p. 326.

[9] NORDEN, p. 327.

[10] NORDEN, pp. 330f. He had read in EDUARD MEYER, Der Papyrusfund von Elephantine, Leipzig, 1912, p. 3: "The author [of the books of Ezra and Nehemiah] had absolutely no notion of the actual events and their inner relationships. But the source material which he used was excellent, especially the memoirs of the very personalities involved, Ezra and Nehemiah. He took them over in part in their original form but in part abbreviated and changed them from the first to the third person." NORDEN adds to this quotation: "It appears to me that here is where one should look for the answer to the riddle."

not everything in the source contains a "we." Thereby the connection between "we" and the source began, unnoticed, to be weakened.

4. Harnack's Proof of the Stylistic Unity of Acts:
Redactor = Narrator

Even before Norden's book, Harnack[11] had argued against the distinction between the "we" narrator and the author of Acts. He maintained that the two were identical. His method of proof was a simple as one could desire: He printed the above-mentioned "we" sections and emphasized by bold type all of the words and expressions which also occur in the third gospel and the rest of Acts. A look at these pages has been enough to convince most readers that the writer of the "we" sections was also the author of Acts.

But what had Harnack really demonstrated? At best the unity of style in the "we" sections and in the rest of Acts. This unity can, however, also have come about through the editing and stylistic revision by the writer of Acts of *all* the sources he used. It would be rash to maintain that on the basis of style one can draw definite conclusions about the source used. Rather, we must distinguish carefully at least three problems in Acts: those of the author, the style, and the sources. That this distinction was neglected is due to the theory that the sources were simply copied verbatim, a theory we have already encountered in Norden and which today appears to us as almost naive. Yet a glance at those passages in which the Third Gospel uses Mark as a source would suffice | to show that the writer of the Third Gospel certainly did not simply render his sources unchanged. But the article by F. C. Burkitt which proved this appeared first in 1922 in the second volume of the *Beginnings of Christianity* (pp. 106–120).

In his meritorious essay, "Stilkritisches zur Apostelgeschichte," which appeared in 1923 in the Festschrift for Gunkel, Martin Dibelius performed the service of beginning to separate clearly the problem of style from that of the sources.

---

[11] ADOLF HARNACK, Neue Untersuchungen zur Apostelgeschichte und zur Abfassungszeit der synoptischen Evangelien (Beiträge zur Einleitung in das Neue Testament, 4), Leipzig, 1911, pp. 3–9. Earlier EDUARD ZELLER (see n. 4) had written (457): "...the parts in which the narrator used the first person demonstrate absolutely no essential departures from the plan, tone, and style of the book as a whole. In particular, the language differs to such a minor degree from the other part of the writing that even an advocate of the Timothy hypothesis like DE WETTE (Einleitung in das Neue Testament § 115a) found it necessary to assume that the sources had been revised freely by the author." It is astonishing how many important insights can be found in older literature, which were later forgotten and have to be discovered anew.

5. The Beginning of the Clarification of the Problem of Style by Dibelius

Between 1923 and 1947 Dibelius worked out a new view of the whole question [12] which we will summarize in three theses:

1. Luke the physician wrote the third gospel and Acts.
2. He used an itinerary as a source for chapters 13–21.
3. He indicated his own presence on Paul's trips each time by means of "we."

The view on Lukan authorship, which we have included as thesis 1, is quite new in that Dibelius substantiated it in an entirely new way. He employed a method of logical conclusion, beginning with the observation that the Third Gospel and Acts are dedicated to Theophilus. This fact Dibelius interpreted in the following way: [13] A dedication proves that an ancient writing is a literary work intended for the book market. But it could not appear on the book market without the name of its author. (It is improbable that Acts originally bore the name of an author other than that which church tradition mentions.)

Thesis 2 gives the result which grew out of Dibelius' style criticism. Again and again, Acts contains "information about the stations on the journey, the hosts, the preaching and the results of preaching, the founding of communities, disputes and either voluntary or forced departures... We cannot imagine that these records, with their concise and impartial styles, | were written down with the purpose of edifying or of entertaining. Nor are they colourful enough to be regarded as the local traditions of individual communities." [14] Thus one has to think of "a list of stations [which] might well have been used on such journeys for the practical reason that, if the journey was made on another occasion, the route and the same hosts might be found again." [15] This is therefore the setting (Sitz im Leben) for this itinerary.

Thesis 3 depends basically upon two observations. In the first place, Dibelius saw what Harnack had already noticed: "We read the same sort

---

[12] MARTIN DIBELIUS, Aufsätze zur Apostelgeschichte, ed. by HEINRICH GREE-VEN, Göttingen, 1951. Translated by MARY LING and PAUL SCHUBERT as: Studies in the Acts of the Apostles, London, 1956. Cited as Studies with the page number of the English translation first followed by the page number of the German in parentheses.

[13] The development of this line of thought can still be followed clearly. While DIBELIUS in 1923 called the author "Luke" "without prejudice to the question of authorship," p. 2 (9), he considered as a possibility in 1927 (Geschichte der urchristlichen Literatur, vol. I [Sammlung Göschen No. 934], Berlin and Leipzig, p. 47) that the Third Gospel and Acts "even from the beginning on circulated under the name of their author." Since 1939 Dibelius has presented the view indicated in the text above again and again: Studies, p. 65, n. 7 (60, n. 6), 89 (80), 95 (85), 135f. (118f.), and 146–48 (127).

[14] Studies, p. 69 (64).   [15] Studies, p. 199 (169).

of account about Philippi (first person) as about Corinth: [third person]:
where Paul lived and where he preached, how long he worked and what
success he achieved."[16] There is a problem here which we must investigate
in more detail later. In this "same type of account," is the problem one of
content or of style? At any rate Dibelius maintains that the author of Acts
is the narrator who speaks in "we"; yet from this datum he comes to a
different conclusion than had Harnack. That is, he disagrees with the
theory that the "we" sections are accounts by an eyewitness. He sees the
proof for this disagreement in the depiction of the trip to Rome (chapters
27–28). And thus we come to the second observation on which the third
thesis then depends: The depiction of the journey to Rome contains marks
of a literary character in great abundance. From this Dibelius concludes
that this travel account is "one of those literary descriptions of a voyage,
which had already become the convention in Greek literature."[17] Although
the depiction of the journey to Rome employs the "we" style, it is the
most strongly literary section in all of Acts. Therefore, it cannot be a
firsthand account. The observation that the parts about Paul, vv. 9–11,
21–26, 31, 33–36, and 43, are secondary insertions makes the proof even
stronger.[18] Dibelius explains this "we" in chapters 27–28 by the assumption that Luke as historian wishes "to portray and illuminate what is
typical."[19] "This practice of aiming at what is typical and important
allows the author of Acts partly to omit, change, or generalize what really
occurred."[20] As a historian, Luke wrote of a typical sea voyage and passed
over his own travel experiences in favor of a purely secular account, for
which "a secular description of the voyage and shipwreck served as a pattern, basis or source."[21] From this two-fold conclusion (1. "We" and
"they" accounts agree stylistically; 2. "We" style in a literary section)
Dibelius concludes: | In every case Luke indicated with "we" his personal
participation in the respective parts of Paul's missionary activity: "The
'we' is not at all remarkable in such descriptions of travel, and so is not in
the least an indication that his is a non-literary account of a journey which
originated from among Paul's associates."[22] "We" is not "an original
element, but an addition."[23]

6. What Objection is there to Dibelius' Interpretation?

The solution which Dibelius suggests for the problem of "we" is at first
very impressive. But a more thoroughgoing consideration shows that there

---

[16] Studies, p. 70 (65).   [17] Studies, p. 213 (180).
[18] Studies, p. 205 (173); somewhat different, Studies, 213f. (180).
[19] Studies, p. 136 (119).   [20] Studies, pp. 136f. (119).
[21] Studies, p. 205 (174).   [22] Studies, pp. 205f. (174).
[23] Studies, p. 136 (119).

are serious difficulties (we think they are insuperable) with all three theses.

A. Let us begin with the reason which Dibelius gave for the first thesis, that method of logical conclusion which allowed Dibelius to believe that Luke the physician wrote Acts. The argumentation employed here has proved to be faulty. For A. D. Nock[24] has shown in his extremely instructive review of Dibelius' essays on Acts: Dibelius has misunderstood both what a dedication meant in antiquity and the nature of the ancient book market.[25] If Dibelius were right, i. e. if in ancient times the dedication and naming of the author would always have gone hand in hand, then there could have been no literary work in antiquity which was anonymous but contained a dedication. But there were such works. People referred to them simply by the name of the one for whom they were intended in each case. Dupont[26] in dealing with Nock's objections gives as examples the well-known "Epistle to Diognetus," the four books on rhetoric "ad Herennium" and finally also the epistle "to the Hebrews." Thus, it is illegitimate to conclude that because a book contains a dedication it must at one time have borne the name of its author. The dedication in antiquity means in the first place only that the author has concluded the work on his composition. When the one to whom he has dedicated it contributed to its circulation, so much the better. But at that time the circulation did not take place, as was earlier assumed, by means of some kind of a copying factory which would throw 500 or even 1000 copies on the market. Ordinarily the circulation of a writing took place in a way which can still be studied in the case of Augustine's "De Trinitate:" | From the autograph a few copies were made, and these then served as models for other copies.[27]

With this, the argument collapses which Dibelius again and again brought forth[28] to prove that Luke the physician wrote Acts, as church tradition had said. Dibelius never gave another reason. Thus when some one today[29] refers to Dibelius' affirmation of the church's tradition concerning Luke, he must not forget that the basis no longer exists on which Dibelius then relied.

B. The second thesis reads: Throughout Acts 13–21 Luke used an itiner-

---

[24] ARTHUR DARBY NOCK, Gnomon, 25, 1953, pp. 497–507.
[25] NOCK, p. 501: "In any event, the suggestion of Dibelius involves a misunderstanding of book-dedications and indeed of the nature of publication in antiquity."
[26] Dom JACQUES DUPONT, The Sources of Acts. The Present Position, London, 1964, p. 138, n. 3.
[27] Cf. H. I. MARROU, "La technique de l'edition a l'époque patristique," Vigiliae Christianae 3, 1949, pp. 208–224.
[28] See n. 13.
[29] DUPONT, pp. 135, 140.

ary as a source.[30] In discussing this question, Nock[31] already raised the
objection: This by no means says that there was only one document;
moreover, it would scarcely have survived the shipwreck at Malta. According to Nock, the numerous omissions point rather to the possibility that
there were different documents, of which each – as a private travel-diary –
covered a certain part, e. g. the collection trip to Jerusalem. Nock does not
appear to have seen what far-reaching results this assumption that there
were different "documents" has: different documents of this type no longer
necessitate that they go back to one and the same author.

Also, Nock thinks of this type of document not quite in the manner Dibelius conceived his "itinerary." For if "any companion keeping a travel-
diary might well have lost it in the shipwreck,"[32] then according to Nock,
chapters 27–28 reproduce only the recollections of a traveling companion
about the voyage, not however a travel-diary written during this voyage. It
is questionable if we have a basis for the assumption | that the author of
Acts possessed such exact information about each day for all of Paul's
journeys as seems to be the case in 20: 5ff.

Furthermore, we have an objection to consider which Alf Kragerud[33] has
raised against Dibelius' concept of the itinerary. He reproved Dibelius by
charging[34] that he has isolated the itinerary subjectively on the basis of

---

[30] Studies, p. 86 (77).

[31] NOCK, p. 500: "May there not rather have been several distinct travel-diaries
covering separate periods, e. g. that of the collection for the saints in Jerusalem
(cf. 20, 3–5)? ... The question whether this travel material comes from one or
from more documents is not very important, save for the fact that if there was only
one, it is perhaps harder to account for some of the many omissions in this part of
the story."

[32] NOCK, p. 499, n. 3: "Any companion keeping a travel-diary might well have
lost it in the shipwreck; to be sure, Julius Caesar preserved his papers while swim-
ming 200 paces (Suet. Iul. 64)."

[33] ALF KRAGERUD, "Itinerariet i Apostlenes gjerninger," Norsk teologisk tids-
skrift 56, 1955, pp. 249–72.

[34] KRAGERUD, p. 250. He thinks of an itinerary as sketches for a missionary
report which the missionary later had to make in his home congregation. He thinks
that "style-critical analysis and historical construction" allow the hypothesis of such
an itinerary. But what he calls "style-critical analysis" here is only a picking out of
those sentences which report about the trip and the results of the mission. Is it not,
in these circumstances, really the analyzer himself who on the basis of his leading
concept of the itinerary selects what he thinks must have been in such a document
and through this selection, so to speak, brings the itinerary into existence? Thus, has
he eliminated the subjectivity of which he reproaches DIBELIUS? (Of course,
DIBELIUS and KRAGERUD are not the only ones confronted by this difficulty!) His
"historical construction" makes it even clearer that KRAGERUD does not avoid
subjectivity. In the case of the so-called first missionary journey one can easily
imagine (from 14: 27, which KRAGERUD, however, assigns to Luke's redaction) the
giving of such a report following a successful return home. But later Paul carries
out his own missionary campaign and is no longer commissioned by the congregation

content and historical-critical considerations. This objection deserves our careful examination. Dibelius approached the text with a set conception of what an itinerary would have contained (stations on the journey, hosts, results of preaching, etc.). He assigns sentences which contain this information to the itinerary. One must ask if in this case the presupposition does not already determine all that is to follow, if it is not thus the analyzer himself who on the basis of his leading concept produces the itinerary through his choice. Dibelius thought he was establishing the itinerary on the basis of style-critical observations. Kragerud[35] objects that it is not the style but the content of the sentences which causes Dibelius to classify them as part of the itinerary. In fact, two thoughts enter side by side in Dibelius' mind when he speaks about the style of the itinerary. | In the first place he means by this particulars about stations on the journey, hosts, etc.; all these are actually characteristics of content. In addition, however, he mentions genuinely stylistic peculiarities: the brief and neutral depiction, the exactness of the information, which nevertheless does not serve an edifying purpose. Yet one must ask somewhat skeptically if this second point alone can prove that an itinerary was used. At this point we want only to indicate the difficulty present; in reality, the problem is even more complicated. Thus, we shall discuss the pertinent parts of Acts in a later section and in this connection deal with the question in its full dimension.

C. The third thesis may be divided into two parts: 1. "We" is a literary device by which the author indicates in every instance his participation in Paul's journeys. 2. Luke the physician is the one who employs this literary means in order to indicate his own participation. This second assertion, however, demands from the (conjectured) traveling companion of Paul that he passed over his own experiences on Paul's trip to Rome, thus that he was silent about actual events known to him as an eyewitness and replaced them with a fictitious narrative outline and fictitious content – only in order to elevate this voyage into a "typical" one because he was a "historian."[36] This appears to us to be extremely improbable. Here Dibe-

---

at Antioch. How then would the itinerary fit in as an account to the home congregation? KRAGERUD is aware of the difficulty: according to his letters, Paul does not consider himself as an official pledged to give a report (KRAGERUD concedes this, p. 268). But KRAGERUD tries to help his theory with the expedient that "theory and transcendental perspective" on the one hand and "practice and immanent level" on the other are two different things even for Paul. This means, however: KRAGERUD decides against Paul's own testimony (as only a "theoretical" speculation) in favor of a source hypothesis which he needs for Acts.

[35] *Ibid.*, p. 250.

[36] In 1923 DIBELIUS saw two possibilities for chapters 27–28 (Studies, p. 7f., n. 15 [14, n. 2]): "He [the author] may possibly have accompanied the apostle (and there is a hint of this in the 'we'); in that case he has invested his own memories with a literary veil and suppressed what was individual in favour of the conventional,

lius has evaluated quite highly the author's ambition to prove that he was
a historian; but he has not proved that the exhibition of such a "typical"
case played such a role anywhere in the program of the historian. It is
certain that a "we" can be used as a literary means in order to indicate an
eyewitness account. | But one must ask if the author himself has to be this
eyewitness, or if it would be sufficient that his authorities were.

7. A New Examination of the Account of Paul's Journeys

In view of the questions raised in connection with Dibelius' theses, it
would be profitable once more to examine chapters 13–21 and 27 and 28
anew and independently. Do these chapters in reality show us a consistent
pattern of how a journey is depicted, and do they give indications of what
the author actually wished to express with "we"?

A. We begin with chapters 13 and 14. They depict for the reader the
so-called *first missionary journey*.[37] To be sure, much about this journey
remains problematic, above all the first half, the missionary journey to
Cyprus. We learn very little about it. Not one host who accommodated the
travelers is named, and yet Barnabas as a $K\acute{v}\pi\varrho\iota o\varsigma\ \tau\tilde{\omega}\ \gamma\acute{e}\nu\varepsilon\iota$[38] probably had
relatives and acquaintances on Cyprus. But not only the names of the hosts
are omitted, but also the information about the result of the preaching.
Apart from the confused story of Elymas/Bar-Jesus, what we do hear is
astonishingly little and allows no conclusion concerning an itinerary behind

but it is also conceivable that he gained possession of a short account of the events
from somewhere else, secured credibility for the section provided by the witness by
the use of the word 'we,' and then extended the account to a literary composition."
It is precisely this second possibility which DIBELIUS offers as a choice that we
favor (without agreeing that the "information" was so sparse as DIBELIUS thought),
while DIBELIUS finally decides in favor of the first because of his erroneous concept about dedication and the book market in antiquity. See esp. Studies, p. 134
(118): "He [Luke] does ... emphasize the significance of the story of the voyage by
adding nautical details and so giving prominence to the story as such ... So we see
Luke once more as a historian who expounds the meaning of an event by striking
description." We think that such a procedure whereby Luke suppresses his own
memory and replaces what was individual in favor of the typical would have demonstrated not so much that he was a historian but rather that he was a novelist
who took account of the average taste of the public.

[37] HANS CONZELMANN, Die Apostelgeschichte (Handbuch zum Neuen Testament,
volume 7) Tübingen, 1963, has recently expressed doubts (but he was by no means
the first) that this first journey ever took place at all. But in II Timothy, which
in 1 : 5 reveals the use of an extra-canonical source, there is a tradition visible in 3 :
11 which knows of Paul's persecutions and suffering "in Antioch, in Iconium, in
Lystra." That seems to us to speak for the historicity of the journey reported by
Luke. – HANS CONZELMANN has given me access to his manuscript before its publication; I would like once again to express to him my hearty thanks for this.

[38] Acts 4: 36.

it, concerning a travel-diary, or even a recollection of the journey by an
eyewitness. Obviously, one could not have traveled directly from Syrian
Antioch to Cyprus but only from the harbor city Seleucia, and then one
would have arrived at the Cyprian harbor Salamis, which lay opposite it.
Philo and Josephus report that there were many Jews in Cyprus.[39] Thus,
it is quite believable that there were numerous "synagogues" in Salamis.
But there is no mention of the establishing of a congregation. The three
missionaries appear forthwith to travel on, crossing the entire island.
That would have taken more than a week, even if they did not have to
support themselves by working, as Paul and Barnabas later did. Probably
the congregation at Antioch supported the journey not only with their
faith and prayer | but also financially. For friendly Jews did not dwell
everywhere (especially not in the inner sections of Asia Minor), and even
the most frugal missionary had to eat. Unfortunately, the narrator (whom
for the sake of brevity we shall call "Luke") does not inform us if they
preached anywhere as they traveled on the island; perhaps he inferred
this traveling only from the fact that the episode delivered to him concerning the governor of the province, Sergius Paulus, took place on the
west coast of the island in (New-) Paphos, the official residence of the pro-
consul. If one trusts the Lukan account of this journey, then one would
have to conclude from Luke's silence that either the entire mission to
Cyprus was one unmatched, huge fiasco, which the scene (not to be expected in an itinerary) about the governor with its ambiguous ἐπίστευσεν[40]
conceals with difficulty. Had a gentile Christian (!) house church been
formed in Paphos with the chief Roman official on Cyprus as its leader,
this would have been depicted in an edifying way. The other possibility,
which we think more probable, is, however: Luke knew nothing about the
journey to Cyprus except the episode before Sergius Paulus. This was
important, however, since Luke could push Paul into a place of primary
importance at this point. One cannot use in chapter 13 the expedient
which Dibelius employed to explain the brevity of 16: 6ff., that the
historian omits everything in order to make clear the "directional sense of
the event,"[41] and Dibelius did not use it either. Precisely at the juncture
where divine instruction (similarly as in 16: 6–10) could have shown that
God was guiding the missionaries in a quite definite direction, that is,
when they were turning away from the Pamphylian harbor town Perga
into the interior of Asia Minor,[42] nothing along this line is indicated. It

---

[39] Philo, *Legat. ad Gaium*, 282; Josephus, *Ant.* XIII, 287, with a reference to
Strabo.

[40] According to other occurrences in Acts ἐπίστευσεν would mean: "He became
a Christian."

[41] Cf. the quotation from DIBELIUS, Studies, p. 134 (118), above n. 36.

[42] Luke does not indicate why the missionaries carried on their tasks in these out

appears rather as if the two missionaries went through the wild territory between Perga and Pisidian Antioch (which did not yet enjoy the blessing of the *Pax Romana*) in a non-stop march and when they arrived at their goal went immediately into the synagogue. Luke sets forth only Paul's speech [43] in detail. It is not mentioned where Paul and Barnabas | lived during their week's stay (13: 42ff. would have given an opportunity for this). Instead Luke makes one of his typical statements (v. 52) speaking of "disciples": This means that the missionaries have succeeded in establishing a congregation! But the formula-like depiction of the turning away from the Jews [44] does not change the colorlessness of the description. Dibelius thought that he detected the itinerary in 14: 1–6.[45] But what we read here is certainly not the text of an itinerary, whether we think of it as a travel-diary or an account of a mission. Rather, they are edificatory phrases which Luke himself prefers to employ.[46] All concrete statements, such as we find in the description of the so-called second and third missionary journeys, are missing here. Once again, as in 13: 14 the missionaries apparently go into the "synagogue of the Jews" immediately after their trip there and are extremely successful among Jews and Greeks. But again Luke speaks of this only in quite general terms. Even the reaction of the unbelieving Jews to these numerous conversions is described (principally with phrases from the Septuagint) without concrete particulars. According to v. 3 a tense situation exists for quite some time: [47] the missionaries preach on fearlessly and even perform signs and miracles, without even faintly attaining the effect of the miracle depicted in 14: 10. They escape from a planned perse-cution in the nick of time and flee "to the cities of Lycaonia, Lystra and Derbe, and to the surrounding country, and there they preached."

The following passage, 14: 8–20, once again concerns Lystra. Accor-

---

of the way places, which could be reached only by difficult and dangerous routes. There is no indication here of divine direction, unless one takes 13: 2 as such.

[43] Cf. ULRICH WILCKENS, Die Missionsreden der Apostelgeschichte. Form- und traditionsgeschichtliche Untersuchungen (Wissenschaftliche Monographien zum Alten Testament und Neuen Testament, ed. by GÜNTHER BORNKAMM and GERHARD VON RAD, vol. V), Neukirchen, 1961, pp. 50–55 and 70f.

[44] Acts 13: 46; cf. to this turning away from the Jews of Asia Minor the corre-sponding turning away from the Jews of Greece in Corinth 18: 6 and from the Jews of Rome in 28: 28.

[45] Studies, p. 86 (77f.).

[46] DIBELIUS himself refers to this, Studies, p. 187, n. 83 (160, n. 1).

[47] It has been thought that 14: 3 is the trouble maker which confuses this pre-sentation. But according to 14: 2 the gentiles become unfriendly because of the Jews' influence; yet according to 14: 4 some of the people side with the "apostles," others with the Jews. Each of these features has parallels in Acts: the first is like 13: 50; the other, that two groups who think differently about Christianity oppose each other, is a continuing motif throughout Acts up to 28: 24f. This does not mean that this is a realistic depiction of the situation.

dingly, their moving on to Derbe must be related again in v. 20. Dibelius
has claimed several times [48] that this is an indication that here Luke has
broken an itinerary open by the insertion of the story about the lame man.
We will soon turn to a detailed discussion of this objection, but there is
actually another objection still nearer at hand: On the basis of the words
just quoted from vv. 6 f., the reader receives the impression that the mission
in Lystra and Derbe proceeded without interruption. But that would be an
incorrect | conclusion drawn from Luke's phrasing. In actuality, Luke is
concerned that at this point nothing be said about persecution; instead, he
intends expressly to play up admiration of the gentiles for the missionaries
as much as possible. In addition, mentioning Lycaonia here (even apart
from the question of language) [49] has a particular meaning: again a new
territory is opened to the Christian message, after 13: 13 had mentioned
Pamphylia and 13: 14 Pisidia.

We have already said that Dibelius finds the reverting to Lystra objec-
tionable. Apparently at this point he has not observed exactly enough that
Luke includes not only the story of the healing of the lame man but also
the story of Paul's stoning in Lystra. First Luke gives a general survey and
then transmits the entire tradition about Lystra which he possesses. One
misunderstands this process if he assumes that Luke has mechanically
transcribed an itinerary. Rather, here is a major composition by Luke
which with very little material aims at a major effect. Paul himself confirms the second story, although he does not say where he was stoned. [50] Yet,
upon reflection, the first story, the worshiping of the "apostles" [51] as gods,

---

[48] Studies, p. 6 (13), 72 (66), and 198 (168).

[49] Acts 14: 11.

[50] II Cor. 11: 25: ἅπαξ ἐλιθάσθην.

[51] GÜNTER KLEIN, Die zwölf Apostel. Ursprung und Gehalt einer Idee, Göttingen,
1961, p. 212, finds the explanation for the fact that in these verses Barnabas and
Paul are called "apostles" in the assumption: "that this terminology is an ingredient
of the mimicry which he [the author] uses as a protection as he brings about the
momentous modification of the traditional concept of the apostle." Thus, KLEIN
thinks that the author does not want his readers to note that he is taking the honor
of being an apostle away from Paul. After the readers have already learned that
only the twelve are "apostles," he designates Barnabas and Paul as apostles here in
order to camouflage what he is doing. One would really be forced to say in this case
that Luke went to work with "extreme craftiness" (KLEIN). But perhaps even KLEIN
would prefer another explanation. In any case, he points to the D-Text in Acts 14: 14,
citing L. CERFAUX: ἀκούσας δὲ Βαρναβᾶς κτλ. This according to him is without
question the more difficult reading. "If the idea of apostle were missing in v. 14,
G. SASS has already seen (Die Apostel in der Didache, 235) that v. 4 'would no
longer clearly refer to Paul and Barnabas.'" (213) We think the theory that a reader
could have connected the apostles mentioned in v. 4 not with Paul and Barnabas
but with the twelve apostles who stand behind them puts one on what is clearly the
wrong track. The concept, "more difficult reading" means basically that one must
search for that reading from which the other(s) developed; in special cases it is

sounds like a literary piece. | Dibelius himself had sensed this; he became
convinced that v. 18 was not the original conclusion of the story and conjectured:[52] "Originally the crowd was probably not persuaded, but became
angry and attacked the apostles." Unfortunately, it is not clear if he connected Paul's stoning with this attack. We prefer not to take up Dibelius'
venturesome conjecture. It is more probable that Luke has dressed up a
Lystran healing story from tradition by using some learned data, which
he arranged into the imposing scene in which the "apostles" are worshiped
as gods. But he did not combine the second tradition, about Paul's stoning,
with this scene. Consequently, he did not employ any changing of mind by
the disappointed crowd as the motive which incited the mob to riot;
rather he used the machinations of Paul's old enemies, the Jews, who had
arrived from Antioch (!) and Iconium.

Yet one does justice to Luke as author only when one realizes that he
had to overcome a serious difficulty in composition here. The author likes it
best of all when the high point of the action comes immediately before the
conclusion. But that was not at all the case here. For Luke's readers probably felt that the high point was the worshipping of Paul and Barnabas as
gods; the overwhelming impression which they made could not have
appeared more clearly. But Luke could nevertheless not leave the matter
here, as in the parallel account in 28: 6. | There the Maltese say that Paul is
a god. Because this produces no consequences, Luke does not need to add
the correction which Zahn supplied on his own: the Christian reader
already knew that Paul was only the messenger of a higher power, who
protected him. But in our passage, according to Luke's description, there

---

the difficult reading which has been changed into a simpler one. In order to establish
the original reading in our passage, however, one must look at the context in D and
the Old Latin manuscripts. The reading of D in 14: 14 "διαρρήξαντες ... καὶ ἐξ-
επήδησαν" arose when, during the making of the bilingual manuscript, someone for-
got the Greek counterpart to the "et" of the Latin (consciverunt vestimenta sua et
exilierunt) and, unconcerned about grammar, inserted a καὶ between the participle
and finite verb. D is thus here a mixed text from the "neutral" text (διαρρήξαντες)
and the Old Latin d (which is by no means, as some have occasionally assumed, a
"slavish translation" of D). Examples of such a process are numerous in D; see my
commentary on Acts, p. 51 f. Now there is a similar situation with respect to the
beginning of v. 14. The Old Latin translation which serves as a basis had replaced
"Paul" in v. 9 with "the apostles." (The text of h shows this.) Consequently, it
omitted the word "the apostles" in v. 14. It translates the ἀκούσαντες of the Greek
text with "cum audissent." This text is in d in the distorted form "cum audisset."
D contains a mixed text from ἀκούσαντες ("neutral" text) and "cum audisset":
ἀκούσας. This text is anything but original. WILCKENS (p. 208, n. 1) comments on
14: 4, 14: "...one finds here usage of the language common in early Christianity
(ἀπόστολοι = missionaries), not specifically Lukan usage." That is quite right, but
it does not enter into the D text in v. 14. When WILCKENS adds: "material from a
source?" he is posing the question about the origin of the tradition of 14: 9 ff.,
which we cannot pursue any further here.   [52] Studies, p. 21 (25).

was danger that the people would offer a regular sacrifice to these men whom they took to be gods. Such an apotheosizing of men had to be prevented. In expressions from the Septuagint but also thoughts which he would use in the Areopagus speech, Luke therefore has the men "rush out" – but where from, really?[53] – and preach a short, explanatory sermon about the true God. Only a few readers note that Paul, who had preached before (14: 9), must in actuality already have said this. If the scene described here had really taken place in this way, then these words would have come too late. Bauernfeind[54] has perceived correctly in this matter that in such a situation, although a few horrified and indignant cries were possible, an address so well organized was not. We have mentioned Dibelius' conjecture above that the scene at one time concluded in a different way. But such a criticism easily overlooks what Luke wants to say with the phrase $\mu \acute{o} \lambda \iota \varsigma$ $\check{\varepsilon}\pi a v \sigma a v$: the impression that the apostles are divine persists to such a degree that even this informative and persuasive address can scarcely keep the people from sacrificing. Thereby Luke maintained the theme of the worshipping of Paul and Barnabas as gods up to v. 18 and prevented the high point of the story being reached and passed over back at v. 13.

To be sure, this meant that adding the second story, which told of Paul's stoning, would be even more difficult. Nevertheless, Luke did his best to make the event understandable. He had the Jews from Antioch and Iconium provoke it. The entire drama is depicted in two parts. The decisive point is that this messenger of God is not discouraged but resumes his task. The fact that we hear nothing more about activity in Derbe is not viewed by the reader as a deficiency. By reporting about Derbe with the same words used in v. 7, Luke gives the reader the feeling that he is already well informed and needs no more information. How precisely balanced Luke's presentation is and how evident his ability in composition is can be seen in v. 22. Here Luke has the apostle speaking in direct discourse to the Christians and thus also to the reader: | "Through many tribulations we must enter the kingdom of God." Each Christian must be prepared for suffering such as Paul has borne.

That we have before us a composition by Luke and not an itinerary is proved, however, not only by the expressions from Luke's edifying vocabulary and speeches inserted by Luke, but also by his assertion that Paul and Barnabas appointed elders in the congregations. Thus, a later situation, of which we get no hint in the letters of Paul, is ascribed naively to the time of Paul.

---

[53] In the Old Testament parallel Judith 14: 16f., the steward Bagoas: $\delta\iota\acute{\varepsilon}\varrho\varrho\eta\xi\varepsilon\nu$ $\tau\grave{a}$ $\grave{\iota}\mu\acute{a}\tau\iota a$ $\acute{\varepsilon}av\tauo\widetilde{v}$ ... $\grave{\varepsilon}\xi\varepsilon\pi\acute{\eta}\delta\eta\sigma\varepsilon\nu$ $\varepsilon\grave{\iota}\varsigma$ $\tau\grave{o}\nu$ $\lambda a\grave{o}\nu$ ... $\varkappa\varrho\acute{a}\zeta\omega\nu$. Here, the situation is clear: Bagoas rushes out of Holofernes' tent.

[54] O. BAUERNFEIND, Die Apostelgeschichte (Theologischer Handkommentar, vol. 5), Leipzig, 1939, p. 183.

Once more in v. 24 there is mention of the new territories reached by
the mission, in reverse order from that of 13: 13ff. In v. 25 [55] there is a brief
notation about a sermon in Perga; perhaps the establishment of a congregation is thereby indicated. Then the missionaries sail from the harbor city
Attalia "to Antioch," as if this city were located directly on the sea. Yet it
is sufficient for Luke that he had already indicated to the readers in 13: 4
that Seleucia was Antioch's harbor. Verses 26–28 are especially rich in
Lukan expressions. In fact, they are a model of how one speaks in edifying
language about a missionary journey.

What has been the result of this examination of chapters 13 and 14?
This "first missionary journey" does not show a single trace of an itinerary.
The material from which the author constructed these two chapters
consisted, so it appears, only of a few independent stories (encounter with
Bar-Jesus, worshipping of the missionaries as gods, stoning of Paul) and of
a tradition about Paul's suffering and persecutions "in Antioch, in Iconium,
in Lystra." Because no dramatic event took place during the mission to
Derbe, it left no concrete image in the memory of the Christians; they
remembered the unusual and striking. Chapters 13 and 14 are a Lukan
composition from the first to the last verse, quite different from the style in
which Luke narrates the second and third missionary journeys. We will
pass on now to these.

B. The so-called *second missionary journey* is reported in 15: 36 to 19:
30. It has long been noted that Luke betrays nothing of the bitter conflict
between Paul and Peter in Antioch, depicted in Gal. 2: 11ff. Instead, we
learn of a personal dispute between Paul and Barnabas over John Mark.[56]
In view of this observation, it is only too easy to forget something else:
Luke, who must have at least formulated 15: 36–41, does not introduce
the second missionary journey, the most important of all, with the plan for
a | new missionary journey into an untouched territory: Paul proposes
only to visit congregations already established on the first journey. And at
first this remains the plan even when the alienation between Paul and
Barnabas is brought in. They only divide the mission territory (already won)
among themselves: Barnabas goes with John Mark to Cyprus, but Paul and
Silas go through Syria and Cilicia to Derbe and Lystra. Iconium is mentioned in 16: 3, but there is nothing more said about Pisidian Antioch. The
fact that Luke speaks only in passing of the departure of Barnabas and
Mark, while according to 16: 4 Paul and Silas are ceremonially and officially
"commended by the brethren to the grace of the Lord," corresponds to
Luke's intention from this point on to deal almost exclusively with what
Paul does. One may suppose that in reality Barnabas enjoyed no less sym-

---

[55] These words were added by the translator.
[56] Acts 15: 36–38.

pathy in Antioch; probably he even embarked on the journey as the representative of this congregation. We see already from the way things begin: we do not have before us a copy of an itinerary but a Lukan composition, according to which Paul and Silas carry out the so-called apostolic decree everywhere.

Without the reader noticing or being supposed to notice, in this entire presentation Luke escapes a major difficulty. Obviously the congregation at Antioch neither decided upon nor supported this new missionary journey by Paul. One can recognize this from the fact that Paul was forced to earn his living by working at the trade[57] in which he was trained (when voluntary donations from one of the newly established congregations did not make this unnecessary for him).[58] Because, as Luke depicts it, Paul's inspection journey automatically becomes a new, major missionary offensive, Luke did not need to speak concerning how the congregation at Antioch felt about Paul's new missionary undertaking.

But neither 15: 36–41 nor 16: 1–5 recapitulates an itinerary. Dibelius did not discuss this passage. Kragerud[59] assigned the ἰδού in v. 2 and vv. 4f. to Luke and the remainder to the itinerary. But the possibility that this circumcision story comes from an itinerary and thus corresponds to what really happened is out of the question.[60] To be sure, Bauernfeind[61] has indicated that Timothy as the son of a Jewess was a Jew according to Jewish law[62] and thus should have been circumcised. | But Timothy was already a Christian (cf. I Cor. 4: 17), converted by Paul himself, and probably, in addition, baptized. But then, as Paul understood the situation, he was "neither Jew nor Greek," and this belated circumcision would have been a falling away from Christ, a falling back into a life under the law.[63] Thus at this point Luke has obviously become the victim of a corrupt tradition. It had begun to circulate in Paul's lifetime; in Gal. 5: 11 Paul defended himself against the rumor that he was still preaching circumcision. If he had actually circumcised Timothy as reported in Acts, then he would have done everything possible to play into the hands of his opponents. In 16: 3 one reads a tradition contrary to the facts, not an itinerary.[64]

---

[57] Acts 18: 3 (σκηνοποιός probably means "leather worker" not "weaver").

[58] II Cor. 11: 8; Phil. 4: 10, 15.

[59] KRAGERUD, p. 253.

[60] Here is one of those rare instances in which the content excludes the possibility of the passage belonging to an itinerary (regardless of whether one thinks of it as travel-diary or missionary report or recollections of the journey).

[61] BAUERNFEIND, p. 205.

[62] Yebamoth 45b.

[63] Neither BAUERNFEIND nor DUPONT (p. 141, n. 10) has considered the case from this point of view.

[64] OLOF LINTON, "The Third Aspect," Studia Theologica 3, 1950, pp. 79–95.

At 16: 6–8 we arrive at the peculiar passage in which Dibelius[65] conjectured that there had been an abbreviation of the itinerary: Luke wished
to show the "directional sense" of the event and thus stressed heavily the
leading of the Spirit. Therefore, all exact geographical references were
omitted. To be sure, this explanation is possible. But this is not to say that
Luke possessed more data for this trip through Asia Minor than in 18: 23
(or 19: 1), where Dibelius himself reckoned with the possibility that no
itinerary was kept. Yet, however this may be, in this respect Dibelius is
right in any case: that Luke wished to show in 16: 6–8 that God himself
led Paul's journey to the right goal. There is a quite exact parallel to this in
Acts: the Cornelius episode, in 10: 1 to 11: 18. There Luke wished to make
it clear to the reader that it was God who caused Peter to baptize the gentile Cornelius. This divine direction becomes evident in the angel who
visits Cornelius, in the vision of Peter at Lydda, in the orders given to
Peter by the Spirit, and finally, in the fact that the Holy Spirit falls on those
gathered to hear the apostle. Here in 16: 6–8 we encounter phenomena
which correspond exactly: the Holy Spirit does not allow the missionaries
to preach in Asia Minor; the Spirit of Jesus stops their journey to Bithynia.
Thus, only the road to Troas remains open. But ships sail from there in
many directions. Which one did God decide upon for Paul? Paul's vision in
the night gives the answer; in it a man from Macedonia asks him to come
and help them.

If, however, God's intervention is depicted in the same denseness as in
the Cornelius scene, then it follows: here also the | reader is shown that a
particularly important decision in the story of the mission is decided not by
men but by God himself. The missionary epoch which begins here is the
Pauline mission in the real sense. Luke is not concerned simply about
Macedonia.[66] This province is only the point of departure for the larger
mission of Paul, which includes Greece and wins in Corinth the decisive
base for his operations. The man who asks for help "for us" represents

---

[65] Studies, p. 148f. (128f.), etc.

[66] To be sure, DUPONT, (p. 129, n. 63) thinks: "The journey from Troas to Philippi and the foundation of the church in Philippi do not appear as particularly
striking events in the plan of the book. To speak in this connection of the starting
point of the evangelization of Europe or of the Greek world is to place ourselves
at the point of view of a modern reader; Acts only speaks of the evangelization of
Macedonia." DUPONT errs when he holds that distinguishing between the continents
of Europe and Asia is a modern opinion. Philo not only emphatically juxtaposes the
two in *In Flacc.* 46: ἐν Εὐρώπῃ καὶ Ἀσίᾳ, but also distinguishes in *Legat. ad Gaium* 283,
τὸ Εὐρωπαῖον, τὸ Ἀσιανόν, τὸ Λιβυκόν. In vv. 7–9 of his didactic poem, Dionysius
Perihegetes confirms that three continents are meant. Here he says about the earth
(I am quoting from the Latin translation): "Una autem quamvis sit, homines in tres
eam continentes partiti sunt, primum in Libyam (Africa) deinde in Europam Asiam-
que" (Geographi Graeci Minores, ed. C.MULLERUS, vol. II, Paris, 1851, p. 105.
MÜLLER dates Dionysius in the first century A.D.).

basically all of the gentile world, to whom Paul now brings the gospel. Luke thus makes it clear to the reader in 16: 6–8 that the beginning Pauline mission, exactly as formerly the baptism of the gentiles by Peter, goes back to unmistakable directions of God. Luke demonstrates this at the beginning of the mission; only 18: 9 comes as a later confirmation.

Luke reports the crucial part of this demonstration, Paul's vision, in 16: 10 in "we" style: "And when he had seen the vision, immediately we sought to go into Macedonia, concluding that God had called us to preach the gospel to them." Thus, it is not left to the reader to draw the conclusion for himself; rather, the vision is interpreted by the "we" in this sense.

Herewith we have arrived at the first passage[67] in which Acts reports in "we" style about the Pauline journeys. The "we" is not restricted, however, only to 16: 10, but it also depicts the beginning of the mission in Macedonia, or, to be more precise, in Philippi. At first glance, to be sure, one might think that we were reading *verbatim* the notes of one who had taken part in the journey, | and people have preferred to hold on to this impression unchanged. Yet if one looks at the text more closely, it becomes clear: in spite of "we," it is not a case here of an itinerary simply being transcribed.

The information about Philippi (i. e. that it belonged to the first of four parts of Macedonia set up by Aemilius Paulus and was a [scil. Roman] colony) is not paralleled exactly in later statements in Acts about the localities where the mission took place. Here we get an exact datum (even if it is obliterated in the present text), but it takes on meaning first through what is related in vv. 20 ff. That is, we have before us a statement by the author, not the notes of a traveling missionary. By this we do not wish to assert that Luke worked here without a written source which came from an eyewitness; on the contrary, we presuppose such a source. Our concern is, however, that it is not related in a *verbatim* form but in Luke's redaction. This will become even clearer in what follows: "We remained in this city some days." It is to be understood that the missionaries were not idle but at least made inquiries which could be useful in carrying out their assignment. If there was really a travel-diary which told of the days' activities in a few phrases (as one could imagine on the basis of 20: 7 ff.), then we would not have this colorless expression about "some days" placed before us. Obviously, here Luke has abbreviated his source to what was important for him. If Luke did not have the travel-diary of one of the participants at hand but, what appears more probable to us, what such a participant remembered and related, then certainly we cannot state with

---

[67] When it appears that Irenaeus has "we" beginning earlier in Acts 16, 18 (*Adv. haer.* III 14, 1), he is quoting inaccurately from memory. On the other hand, his silence on Acts 11: 28 shows that in his "western" text there was not yet this "we."

certainty what the latter told about the activities in Philippi during this time. In any case, Luke repeats only the first prominent scene: going to the προσευχή on the sabbath and the conversation with the women. Luke's style in v. 14 (one of those clauses apparently relative, which in reality are main clauses) is unmistakable, but not only that: "We" talk with the women, but by "what was said by *Paul*" the Lord opened Lydia's heart. The words ὑπὸ Παύλου, moreover, are emphasized by their position at the end of the sentence. Here again it should certainly be clear that we have before us not a note about the result of the preaching but the quite deliberate stylization of the author, Luke. That he has edited the passage is demonstrated clearly in what follows, "and when she was baptized, with her household." He skips over the time between the first meeting of the missionaries with Lydia and her baptism. We get no information of how the other Christians, of whom v. 40 speaks, were won. Luke concentrates all of his | interest on a very few but impressive episodes, in the depiction of which his own hand can clearly be detected.

Despite the initial "we," the next narrative about the possessed, soothsaying slave girl came to Luke from another tradition.[68] Luke does not stop using "we" so abruptly as he began, but at first uses it in the sense, "Paul and those who travel with him" (through v. 16), then switches to the meaning "those who travel with Paul" (in v. 17). After this, he speaks only of Paul. This deserves some reflection. First we have seen: it would be judging too hastily to find here personal notes repeated verbatim. And yet what we have found by no means eliminates the possibility that Luke got such details about the trip from what a traveling companion of Paul remembered, details available to him in oral or written form, which he then edited in literary fashion by excerpting and reshaping them. The section is thus not a Lukan composition if one means thereby that Luke made up these details of the journey, but it is when thought of in this way: that he put in his own words the particulars which came to him from an eyewitness, concentrating on a few very impressive scenes.

The fact that at the beginning of the narrative about the slave girl Luke drops the "we" raises the question why Luke precisely at this point no longer wishes to emphasize the authority of the eyewitnessing. The expedient that here he alludes to his being an eyewitness (Dibelius), or uses the notes of an eyewitness or the reports of what such a one remembered, does not explain the dropping out of the "we" in the middle of the narra-

---

[68] DIBELIUS opined (Studies, p. 198, n. 14 [168, n. 3]): "It would be difficult to decide what relationship there is between the preceding story of the healing of the girl, and this story of release on the one hand, and the source on the other." We think: It is clear that there was originally an independent exorcism story which Luke used here to demonstrate Paul's miraculous power and to trace the enmity against him back to the personal egoism of his opponents.

tive.[69] To phrase the question in more general terms: why is the "we" missing in other parts of the depiction of the journey which show Luke to be just as well informed as in this section? We have already found a partial answer: The beginning of Paul's own mission is just as critical a moment as the beginning of the gentile mission by Peter. The fact that this decision is brought about by a vision given by God to Paul receives, so to speak, its documentation by means of "we." | But, and only now do we come to the complete answer to the question, the "we" form can be used only sporadically and only in those places where no special action or speech by Paul is recorded. Of course, "we" gives the reader the certainty that he is learning firsthand about these things, even that he is participating in the experiences with the eyewitness who is narrating. But it may well conflict with Luke's real intention which is to focus all attention on Paul alone.[70] Thus, "we" disappears before Paul drives out the demon. We will see later that the following instances in which "we" appears and then disappears also follow this rule exactly: as soon as the spotlight of interest is directed on Paul, "we" is omitted.[71]

Admittedly, Kragerud[72] believes that the narrative about the slave girl likewise comes from the itinerary, for the tumult of the people in 16: 22 must have a basis, and only this narrative offers it. But this is wrong. We find the real basis of the "tumult of the people" in 16: 21. The citizens of the Roman colony of Philippi defend themselves against the "Jewish" propaganda – outlawed among Romans – which Paul is putting forth. According to Luke's depiction, this is, of course, only a pretense. But in reality Paul must have had here in this Roman colony where the Christians were of course still regarded as Jews, the painful experience of the limits which Rome imposed on Jewish propaganda. Originally, the story of the exorcism of the soothsaying demon was intended to show the miraculous power of Paul – and of his heavenly Lord. But Luke used it to blunt the sharpness in the serious political conflict and to represent disappointed greed as the real basis for the enmity against Paul.

The next episode which Luke reports is Paul's preaching in Thessalonica, which at the end[73] changes into direct discourse. But we | hear only the

[69] Acts 16: 17.

[70] This is especially beautifully illustrated in chapter 27; see section D below.

[71] Luke brought "we" and an incident involving Paul together in 21: 6 and 21: 12–14.

[72] KRAGERUD, p. 225.

[73] Acts 17: 3. ZELLER (see n. 4) back in 1854 had pointed out that the calumny "These men who have turned the world upside down have come here also" comes too early at this passage: "Because at that time, when they first appeared in Europe, such a calumny could not have been made against those who proclaimed Christianity, for it had scarcely spread beyond the borders of Syria." (p. 259) According to ZELLER this depiction can surely "more accurately be ascribed to someone

major themes: scriptural proof that the messiah must suffer and rise from
the dead and that Jesus is this messiah. First with the scene of the persecution, which concerns Jason as Paul's host, does the depiction become
really graphic. Here, and only here, Luke intimates that the proclamation
of "Jesus the king" can be misinterpreted politically as opposition to the
emperor. In what follows, only Paul and Silas are spoken of; Timothy
meets Paul again no earlier than in 18: 5. After another general and brief
account of the mission in Beroea, the famous chapter 17 contains the
magnificent description of Athens. Concerning this, Nock says in his
excellent review, which we have already quoted several times: "...bril-
liant as is the picture of Athens, it makes on me the impression of being
based on literature, which was easy to find, rather than on personal observation."[74] The speech on the Areopagus is not an address by Paul. Nock
reminds us that the Areopagus council met in the *Stoa Basileios* and at its
sessions had the precincts roped off so that its deliberations could remain
secret.[75] Acts 17: 22 f. together with the introduction describes an imagin-
ary scene. It can be proved that Acts 17: 16 ff., the introduction, does not
repeat an itinerary verbatim. According to Acts 17: 15 and 18: 5 Paul was
alone in Athens; Timothy rejoined him in Corinth. But on the basis of
I Thess. 3: 2 it follows that Timothy was with Paul in Athens and that Paul
sent him from there to Thessalonica. In our particular context it does not
matter if one explains this difference by saying that Luke was not accurately informed or that he wanted to simplify the presentation. In any case it is
shown here: His account is neither a verbatim nor a factually true repetition of an itinerary. Dibelius conjectured[76] that the itinerary contained the
names Damaris and Dionysius, found in 17: 34; this datum, he says,
because of the mention of Dionysius the Areopagite had prompted Luke
to sketch the Areopagus scene. But there is no certain proof for the itinerary at this point; the situation can be explained otherwise, e. g. by the
conjecture that the Athenian congregation (which was established later,
after Paul's time) held the names of Dionysius and Damaris in honor as the
first converts. This in no way forces us to assume that Paul himself had
already won some few followers. For Paul's own testimony in I Cor. 2: 3
speaks against this view. Here he writes that he came to Corinth in much
fear and trembling. This would not be understandable if he had just
succeeded in establishing a congregation in the famous city of Athens. |
On the other hand, it is quite understandable if his missionary preaching
in Athens ended in failure.

living at a later time who saw the οἰκουμένη really put into an uproar by Christianity" "than to the time in which this movement, with its meaning for world
history, just began."

[74] Nock, (see n. 24), p. 506.
[75] Nock, p. 506, n. 5.   [76] Studies, p. 75 (68).

Luke had a few accurate particulars about *Corinth*. But one may ask if the information that Aquila and Priscilla had gone from Rome to Corinth because of Claudius' edict would have been in an itinerary. Yet also here this much is certain: Luke is not repeating a hypothetical source verbatim. For, corresponding to his concept of Paul, once again he has the apostle performing all of the missionary task alone. But against this view is the statement from II Cor. 1: 19 that Silvanus and Timothy participated in the missionary preaching. Once more, in his depiction of the Corinthian period Luke offers the reader only a few, graphic scenes: Paul's working at his trade, the turning away from the Jews and moving to Titius Justus' house, his vision in a dream one night, and the hearing before Gallio. That is certainly not much for an effort that lasted one and a half years. Yet Luke did not find any more material which was usable for his purposes.

For the presentation of the *second missionary journey*, the result is: That which is included in the supposed itinerary because of the "we" is best understood if Luke in 16: 10ff. is testifying to the historical certainty of a critical moment in Paul's mission by referring to the fact that his authority was an eyewitness. There is no support for the theory of a *verbatim* repetition of a continuous report; the fact that Luke revises, e.g. in Acts 17: 6, has been proved. Despite what one would like to have for apologetic purposes, this should be obvious: The report of the freeing of Paul and Silas from prison was not written by a man who lived in Philippi at that time as a Christian and who must have spoken with Paul before he left (16: 40). On the other hand, 18: 18–21 shows that Luke has revised a written source. Luke had access, directly or indirectly, to the recollections of someone who had accompanied Paul at the time, but not to an itinerary. These recollections furnished the concrete statements which we have for this journey. It would be quite possible to consider Timothy as the authority. Contrary to the opinions of Conzelmann now and Zeller earlier, this is not disproved when Luke speaks of him in 16: 3 and elsewhere in the third person; we will discuss Zeller's reference to Acts 20: 4f. on pp. 88f.

C. And so we come to the so-called *third missionary journey*. I have shown in my commentary[77] that the statements in Acts 18: 18–22 have been revised by the author of Acts: he has given Paul the honor of delivering the first Christian sermon in Ephesus. As for the journey through Asia Minor, | which is depicted in terse style in Acts 18: 23, even Dibelius[78] leaves it open whether the itinerary is to be found here. For there is nothing about "spiritual influence" mentioned here: the Spirit of God does not intervene miraculously in the action. Also, the information about Apollos and about the Baptist's disciples cannot originate from an itiner-

---

[77] pp. 483 f.
[78] Studies, p. 5 (12).

ary. [79] What Luke reports about the σχολὴ Τυράννου [80] can very well be a local tradition of the Ephesian congregation.

When one takes into consideration all that Luke reports about the period of Paul's work in Ephesus (the handkerchiefs with miraculous powers, the adventure of Sceva's sons, the burning of the magicians' books) and then considers the fact that Paul according to 20: 31 spent a τριετία in Ephesus, it then becomes evident how little in the way of concrete data we really learn about Paul's activity there. This, of course, may in part be due to Luke's desire to relate only graphic events which put the result of Paul's work in the best light. The type of dry data about the progress of the mission which the modern investigator would like to know did not at all interest him. Yet one may not forget that the narrative about the riot of Demetrius and Paul's speech at Miletus communicate indirectly several things about Paul's missionary work in Ephesus. Finally, one may not expect an itinerary from a period in which Paul made no long missionary journeys. It is very doubtful if Luke knew anything at all of the tensions between Paul and the Corinthian congregation, which came in this period. But even had he known about them and the trips which they required of Paul, he would hardly have gone into them. This would have upset far too much the harmonious image of the situation among the Christians which Luke presupposed.

It was all the more necessary from the literary point of view to have the conflict of Paul in Ephesus itself – which became his lot – end with still another triumph of the great missionary, not with a narrow escape of one who already despaired about his life being saved (II Cor. 1: 8). What there is of historical reminiscences in the Demetrius story is difficult to decide. Zeller [81] pointed to the mention of Gaius and Aristarchus | on the one hand and of Alexander on the other. But Paul's own life must have hung in the balance, and the Demetrius story is so full of internal contradiction that one cannot make use of it as a historical account. [82]

In chapter 20, finally, the "we" reappears, but under very odd circumstances. Luke's account of Paul's journey from Ephesus to Macedonia, Hellas, then back to Macedonia, and on to Troas is, first of all, characterized by a puzzling vagueness. We learn no more about what congregations Paul visited on the journey there in Macedonia than about the name of the Greek city where he stayed three months. Only from the epistle to the Romans [83] does one learn that it was Corinth. The riddle of the indefinite-

---

[79] Acts 18: 24–19: 7. What is told about Apollos took place while Paul was away. The disciples of the Baptist, however, are only very loosely connected with Paul's activity in Ephesus, the account of which, moreover, has been revised to a great degree, unless one imagines that Luke has simply put together isolated material.

[80] Acts 19: 9.   [81] ZELLER, p. 266.

[82] Cf. my commentary on Acts, pp. 511–14.   [83] Rom 15: 22–29.

ness of the whole presentation is answered by the recognition of the fact that Luke did not know how to deal with the collection[84] and therefore did not mention it.[85] Accordingly, the representatives of the congregations which took part in the collection had to become a sort of honorary escort. The text just allows us to conjecture that they gathered in Corinth: Originally, Paul wanted to go from Corinth to Palestine. Thus, all the delegates of the congregations, obviously including those of Philippi, had to come to Corinth. At the last minute it seems that Paul found out that the Jews wanted to attack him on the ship; he therefore decided to go by land through Macedonia and by sea from Troas, or rather from Neapolis, the harbor of Philippi. The representatives of the congregations who would have carried their respective share of the collection (presumably changed into gold) "followed him." Luke lists the names of only seven of them and mentions in the list neither the Corinthians (otherwise he would have indicated to the readers that hidden behind this vague "Hellas" was simply Corinth) nor the Philippians, for then it would not have become difficult to understand why they joined Paul in their city. Furthermore, Luke leaves unclear | exactly whence the seven followed Paul. They are mentioned as late as possible, so that the reader is not at all astonished that they appear immediately before Troas is named. One can scarcely assume that Paul had the delegates of the congregations travel on before him (including the one or ones from Philippi) while he alone made an extended excursion to Philippi. Rather, all would have traveled the *Via Egnatia* from Thessalonica to Philippi. Only for the two from Asia Minor, Tychicus and Trophimus, could one consider the possibility that they were sent ahead. They had to arrange for a ship in Troas which did not dock at the dangerous city of Ephesus; but such ships were probably not numerous. Certainly, Luke could not detail all of this for the reader. It thus appears as if v. 5 would prove that some unnamed person from Philippi is speaking in "we," which begins again here.[86]

---

[84] Luke wrote in Acts 11: 29 f. of a collection brought by Barnabas and Saul to Jerusalem. He must also have learned that many years later Paul went to Jerusalem with a large collection. But he did not interpret and depict it gladly as a sign of the unity of the gentile Christians with the Jewish Christians; rather, he mentions only the demand of the Jerusalem elders that Paul assume the expenses for the four Nazarites. But this certainly shows that the problem of the collection and how the Jerusalem church received it was something which could not be inserted without creating a great deal of tension in Luke's depiction of Paul's mission.

[85] To the reader who knows Paul's letters, Acts 24: 17 appears as an allusion to the collection. But this verse speaks of Paul's action on behalf of his people, not the Christian congregation.

[86] The travel account, which appears in a more revised form (e. g. 20:16 – 21:1a is an insertion by Luke) can certainly go back to recollections of one of Paul's traveling companions; in any case, I know of nothing which speaks decisively against this theory.

In v. 7, similarly as in 16: 16ff., "we" appears in the introduction to a
miracle story. But once again, Paul is the center of attention; thus "we"
disappears until after v. 12. An indication of how unsuccessful the inter-
weaving of "we" has been from a literary standpoint is the statement that
"they" (the Christians of the congregation at Troas), not "we," rejoiced at
the fortunate outcome of the accident which befell Eutychus. Then there is a
passage composed of just a travel account, with a small, everyday episode:
For some reason Paul wants to go from Troas to Assos by land, not by sailing. Just because the detail is so unimportant, it shows the reader that
the narrator who speaks in "we" is informed even of the most trivial
details. The reason given for Paul sailing past Ephesus is that it supposedly
saves time, as if bringing the elders from Ephesus had not demanded quite
some time! Since Paul's address to them is in reality only the literary form
of a testament to the readers, to the church, one need not worry about
"we," which stops again. From the standpoint of content, the account
proceeds from ἀπὸ δὲ τῆς Μιλήτου in 20: 17 directly to εὐθυνδρομήσαντες
(21: 1). In the preceding words, "and when it came to pass that we parted
from them," Luke tried for the first time to connect "we" with an insertion of his own in the account of the trip; in 21: 12, 14 he has been more
successful.

Farther on in the account of the trip, the author intersperses warnings to
Paul about Jerusalem. Luke appears not to have noticed the difficulty into
which this gets him: the congregations warn | Paul against a visit to
Jerusalem "through the Spirit," and yet Luke does not want to say that
Paul goes there contrary to the direction of the Spirit. Basically Luke only
wanted to announce the coming trouble first vaguely, then clearly; the
second way is the meaning of the Agabus episode. The prophet does not
tell Paul what he should do but what will happen.

In the instant in which Paul again stands alone as the center of the
action, "we" stops. Since Luke was silent about the collection (in 24: 17
the reader can see only the expenditure for the four men who had taken an
oath and the releasing of whom involved the presentation of the offering of
which 24: 17 speaks)[87] he does not need to say anything about the Jerusalem-
ites accepting or rejecting it.

What do we learn from the account of the so-called third missionary
journey? We have seen that Luke by no means repeated an itinerary
verbatim but that he revised the account of a source. The fact that the first
"we" ends in Philippi and the second begins there speaks quite strongly
and convincingly for the theory that this account comes from the same

---

[87] To be sure, Paul could not foresee this. But if such a thought had occured to a
reader in antiquity, then he would have concluded: Paul could have used the money
which he gave out for the Nazarites instead for charitable purposes on behalf of his
people.

narrator as the "we" passage in chapter 16. If one has recognized that Luke really needs the obscurity in 20: 1–4 and that this obscurity would be out of keeping with "we," then the argument above loses some of its weight. Conzelmann has pointed out that "we" occurs exclusively on sea voyages. This is not entirely accurate, for the journey by land from Caesarea to Jerusalem also contains "we," yet the statement applies in most cases. We have attempted to understand this from the circumstance that such sea voyages contain no special adventures by Paul. Yet where Paul comes to the fore, "we" stops immediately. First in 21: 6, and then in 21: 12–14 Luke tried to connect it with the account about Paul. Moreover, the connection of "we" in 20: 6 with Philippi is not at all without its problems; one could not sail from Philippi, only from Neapolis. In favor of the theory that Luke is writing here is the acknowledged fact that in other places too he simplifies as much as possible: a further argument is that he has included "we" in the beginning of the story about Eutychus, although it really has nothing to do with "we" (otherwise the conclusion should have read: "and we were all greatly comforted"). Thanks to "we," however, Luke can allow the reader to take part personally, as it were, in Paul's destiny laden trip to Jerusalem. | When stopping points where nothing at all "pious and edifying" is to be related are named along the way, this does not mean that Luke has simply transcribed his data mechanically. He who imagines Luke as a copier of others' (or even his own) notes sees him with the eyes of the nineteenth century as simply a "collector and transmitter" and forgets that he was an author, even an author of rank. It is such traits not intended for edification which give to the narrative a realistic lifelikeness: One may think for example of 20: 13: Paul prefers to go from Troas to Assos by land and then is again taken on board. This information probably appeared in similar form in the source which Luke used here. But this is not to say that Luke took everything he found or that he arbitrarily picked out this or that. It is especially true with regard to the third missionary journey: One sees a narrator at work, one who with a few strokes lets the reader see more than is on paper. Sketching is the art of leaving things out. But the few things which remain must be those things which are important (for the author).

D. The journey to Rome was no longer a missionary trip by Paul but the transporting of a prisoner. Nevertheless, Luke employed "we" in the same way as previously in order to indicate the eyewitness character of his authority. This has led to difficulties in 27: 1 and 27: 6 which have frustrated all attempts by well-meaning scholars to solve them.[88] In v. 3 once

---

[88] Recently, J. Rougé, "Actes 27, 1–10," Vigiliae Christianae 14, 1960, pp. 193 to 203, has taken as his point of departure the "western" text in 27: 1 as allegedly the *lectio difficilior* and has deduced from it: Actually the centurion was supposed to have brought his prisoners by land through Asia Minor and Thessalonica to the

again only Paul is spoken of; again in this presentation "we" disappears
when Paul acts. Throughout vv. 4–8 "we" appears uninterruptedly. In
insertions which Dibelius, following Wellhausen's example, called Lukan,
vv. 9–11, 21–26, 31, 33–36, and 43[89] "we" is missing. That is especially
notable at the end of chapter 27. If an | account by an eyewitness had been
repeated unchanged here, then the last sentence obviously should have
read: "And so it was that *we* all escaped to land." But this ἡμᾶς is missing,
and v. 43 speaks only of the centurion wanting to save Paul. This led
Dibelius to the conclusion: "that a secular description of the voyage and
shipwreck served as a pattern, basis or source for the account of the journey, and that the writer inserted into this description a few short references
to Paul (because he had some special knowledge?)." "It is a secular
composition with insertions concerning Paul. The 'we' ... is simply the
normal usage in a literary description and indicates that the author was
present on the journey."[90]

But this hypothesis runs into difficulties. If a "secular" depiction served
as "pattern, basis or source," then there must have been mention in it of
the soldiers who by cutting the rope let the skiff drift (27: 32). For on the
following morning if the skiff had still been there, they would not have
been forced to have beached the ship and could have avoided the shipwreck.
Thus the soldiers belong to what Dibelius regarded as a narrative frame
and not to the Lukan additions. Yet such a feature does not appear in the
travel novels of that time, although the skiff does play a certain role in
them. Thus in my commentary[91] I have assumed that Luke did not use a
literary source but rather that he revised the accounts recalled by one of
Paul's companions and enlarged them by scenes which exalted Paul.

Against this view, Conzelmann now asserts: the conjecture that this is a
firsthand account "too easily passes over the fact that in any case Paul does
not appear in it, thus that one cannot speak of a firsthand account." There
appears to me to be a misunderstanding of the phrase, "firsthand account"
here: for what could a friend of Paul who sailed with him on the ship to
Italy report about Paul at all? One must assume that Paul did not sail as a
sort of chief guest, as one of the authoritative men on the ship, but as one

Adriatic (197). Since, however, there was a ship in Caesarea's harbor ready to sail,
which would reach the land route again in Adramyttium, Paul or someone else
suggested to the centurion (198) that they take the ship at their own expense; this
considerably shortened the exhausting march on foot. The centurion agreed and
later, when they by chance stopped in Myra and a ship bound for Italy lay at anchor
there, he suggested to Paul and his friends that they board it. ROUGÉ finds all of
this indicated in v. 6. In reality, the "western" text of 27: 1 is an attempt to eliminate the difficulty caused by "we" in this verse, a difficulty which ROUGÉ himself
has recognized. ROUGÉ's attempt to correct L. CASSON's version of the routes in the
Mediterranean appears to us to be unsuccessful.

[89] Studies, p. 205 (173).   [90] Studies, pp. 205 f. (174).   [91] pp. 634–636.

among other prisoners. Accordingly, one could report nothing special about Paul himself. A true "firsthand account" could only describe how the voyage proceeded: naming the stations and depicting above all the storm and beaching. For just this reason Luke was forced to insert scenes which contained particular acts of Paul. Obviously Luke revised the entire passage stylistically; from this procedure is derived the literary character of this chapter which Dibelius, with his very | sensitive feeling for style, detected. If one assumed some such firsthand account, he would trace the technical details back to one who made the journey; one could ask at most if Luke repeated all of them accurately. Very striking in chapter 27 are the imperfect tenses where one would expect an aorist. I have corresponded with A. Debrunner about this. They were also enigmatic for him; yet he would hear nothing of my suggestion to recognize them as tenses of narration. And yet in these tenses an older account which Luke used may be shining through.

Conzelmann himself emphasizes: V. 12 can be understood properly only when one eliminates vv. 9–11. But this would mean that Luke did use a written report. It surely goes without saying that he revised it. Cadbury[92] noted: "Like the rest of us, he has the habit of soon repeating a word when he has once used it." This is shown by $\delta\iota\alpha\sigma\dot{\omega}\zeta\epsilon\iota\nu$ which reappears in 27: 43, 44 and 28: 1, 4. It might well be possible that in this manner Luke wanted to underscore the motif "escape" as the theme. But there are enough other repetitions of a similar nature in Acts where this explanation does not fit. Conzelmann thinks that "we" changes its character from Malta on. With regard to this, it is correct that Luke henceforth no longer mentions the soldiers and the centurion. Only in 28: 16 is a $\varphi\upsilon\lambda\dot{\alpha}\sigma\sigma\omega\nu$ $\sigma\tau\rho\alpha\tau\iota\dot{\omega}\tau\eta\varsigma$ named. But the fact that Paul's being a prisoner is spoken of as little as possible after the arrival on Malta has at first nothing to do with "we." To be sure, one can ask: Who really is meant by "we" in 28: 2, Paul's group or all of the passengers? Verses 3–6 suggest that Luke here as in most instances previously thought about Paul and those around him.[93] Luke's style is evident throughout. The kind barbarians (cf. Cadbury)[94] of v. 2 show that God continues to protect his own in a special way. According to the clichés circulating at that time, barbarians were ordinarily brutal and cruel and murdered anyone who shipwrecked, in order to take his possessions. Luke had used the phrase $o\dot{\upsilon}$ $\tau\dot{\eta}\nu$ $\tau\upsilon\chi o\tilde{\upsilon}\sigma\alpha\nu$ in 19: 11; the counterpart to $\varphi\iota\lambda\alpha\nu\vartheta\rho\omega\pi\dot{\iota}\alpha$ is offered in 27: 3. The passage about the avenging $\delta\dot{\iota}\kappa\eta$ in v. 4 was, as Cadbury has shown,[95] an essay theme in the

---

[92] The Making of Luke-Acts, London, r.p. 1958, p. 218.

[93] It is difficult to imagine that all 276 passengers from the ship gathered around the stick fire; once again Luke thinks only of Paul (and his companions). Only they could be meant by the "us" in 28: 10.

[94] The Book of Acts in History, London, 1955, pp. 25 f.   [95] Ibid., p. 27.

school instruction of antiquity. Dibelius has emphasized several times[96]
that the Maltese call Paul a god without | being corrected: "Here, the
sentence 'they said that he was a god' serves as praise of him and with it
the narrative triumphantly ends. This represents not a Christian but a
pagan point of view." (214 [180]) This was a special trump card, especially
welcome to Luke at just this point, shortly before the end of the book, as a
counter-weight to the depressing fact that Paul remained a prisoner. Luke's
hand is visible not only in evidences of composition but again and again
in stylistic traits also. From 25 : 2 we recognize ἄτοπον; instead of the simple
εἶναι Luke likes to write as here in v. 7 the more sophisticated ὑπάρχειν.[97]
In οἱ καί in v. 10 we again come across a phrase which Luke especially
likes: a καί after the relative pronoun which cannot be translated into
German. But Luke shows himself even more strongly than in such stylistic
peculiarities through the way in which he lets Paul move around like a
free man, who if he wishes can take a week's vacation on his trip (v. 14!).
When Luke depicts Paul as a traveler who has complete control of his
time, this is an indication of poetic freedom. At the same time, the news
that Paul is close by can reach the Roman Christians in the intervening
period and bring them to the *Forum Appii* and *Tres Tabernae:* two names
which give a bit of local color to the account.

"We" occurs for the last time in 28 : 16. This is not because Luke had no
further information: the two years in 28 : 30 were probably no more made
up out of thin air than Paul's appearance before Nero's tribunal in 27 : 24.
No, the "we" must step back because now Paul – for the last time – stands
alone on the stage. Once more Paul is the missionary who proclaims the
"salvation of God" (28 : 28) and must undergo the rejection by the Jews.
This feature shows the reader that now, in Luke's day, the church has
only one way open to it: to the gentiles.

This last travel narrative in Acts does not by any means repeat *verbatim*
a travel-diary; in this respect Dibelius is quite right. What information
Luke had about this trip (we think it was a great deal more than Dibelius
presupposed) he edited with complete freedom: he changed, abbreviated,
and enlarged. Dibelius made a basic distinction between the depiction of
this trip and the former ones: only here did Luke replace his own recollections with a typical depiction, into which he inserted individual episodes.
We are skeptical about this difference in the travel reports.[98] We do not see
how one could expect from a traveling companion of Paul's | that he, to

---

[96] Studies, p. 8, n. 16 (15, n. 1), 20 (25), 204, n. 27 (173, n. 1).

[97] How poorly a later period understood this fine point is shown in the way d
renders the expansion by D, quite Lukan in style, in 14: 9 ὑπάρχοντα ἐν φόβῳ:
possidens in timore!

[98] Actually, Luke works in basically the same way as in chapters 27–28 when he
inserts episodes in chapters 20–21.

Paul's honor, suppressed his own recollections and instead of them offered a fictitious narrative framework enriched by fictitious insertions. Yet we do not overlook Dibelius' statement: [99] "The story of the centurion's apt decision... has nothing to do with Paul... but by the introduction of four words, has been made into an account concerning Paul." Here Dibelius clearly presupposes a written source, according to which the prisoners were guarded by soldiers on the transport ship. We believe we are aiding this contribution by Dibelius when we presuppose a firsthand account of one of Paul's companions, an account which Luke, as others had already done, edited and, by inserting "we," characterized as going back to an eyewitness.

E. There still remains the assignment of discussing the prologue to the Third Gospel.[100] The problem of this prologue is connected with "we" insofar as many scholars, among them an authority like Cadbury, hope to find in the Lukan prologue the proof that Paul's traveling companion Luke wrote Acts and that it is he who speaks in "we."

We will go briefly and in order through the statements of the prologue. V. 1 begins with $\dot{\varepsilon}\pi\varepsilon\iota\delta\dot{\eta}\pi\varepsilon\varrho$. In this prologue Luke likes to use words and phrases distinguished by their important sound, even though they run the risk of being somewhat out of place. This is the case with $\dot{\varepsilon}\pi\varepsilon\iota\delta\dot{\eta}\pi\varepsilon\varrho$; correctly, it should *follow* a main clause and should not, as here, *precede* it.[101] Eduard Schwartz has shown[102] and Cadbury has confirmed that $\pi o\lambda\lambda oi$ was popular at the beginning of a speech. From Acts, 24: 2 and 24: 6 serve as examples; especially pronounced is the $\pi o\lambda\dot{v}\varsigma$ in Heb. 1: 1. In such rhetorical usage the word no longer has its full, old meaning; if Luke knew of two or three "gospels" (understood in the modern sense), this would justify the use of $\pi o\lambda\lambda oi$. The word $\dot{\varepsilon}\pi\iota\chi\varepsilon\iota\varrho\varepsilon\tilde{\iota}\nu$ can, to be sure, mean "bad attempts," but it does not intrinsically have such a pejorative connotation; e. g. in Acts 9: 29 such a connotation comes in only from the $\dot{\alpha}\nu\varepsilon\lambda\varepsilon\tilde{\iota}\nu$ which follows; in Josephus, *Vita* 9, from the participle $\vartheta\alpha\varrho\varrho\tilde{\omega}\nu$ which precedes. As Cadbury has already seen, in reality $\dot{\varepsilon}\pi\varepsilon\chi\varepsilon i\varrho\eta\sigma\alpha\nu$ $\dot{\alpha}\nu\alpha\tau\dot{\alpha}\xi\alpha\sigma\vartheta\alpha\iota$ replaces the simple $\dot{\alpha}\nu\varepsilon\tau\dot{\alpha}\xi\alpha\nu\tauo$; it is due "to the desire for rhetorical fulness." (404) The word $\sigma\nu\nu\tau\dot{\alpha}\xi\alpha\sigma\vartheta\alpha\iota$ would have been more customary. | All of the preceding could have been expressed much more simply with "Since many have told." Concerning $\pi\varepsilon\pi\lambda\eta\varrho o\varphi o\varrho\eta\mu\dot{\varepsilon}\nu\omega\nu$, Cadbury writes (496): "Perhaps for a second time in this preface Luke has chosen a longer and more sonorous word when a simple $\pi\lambda\eta\varrho\dot{o}\omega$ would have served his purpose as it has done

---

[99] Studies, p. 205 (173).

[100] Thus, we shall give the reasons, which DUPONT (110, n. 51) noted were missing, for our assertion: "This proëm applies only to the Third Gospel" (Commentary on Acts, p. 105, n. 3).

[101] CADBURY, Beginnings of Christianity, II, p. 492.

[102] Nachrichten von der Gesellschaft der Wissenschaften zu Göttingen, Phil.-hist. Klasse, 1907, p. 294.

elsewhere, e. g. Acts xix. 21 ὡς δὲ ἐπληρώθη ταῦτα." "The suggestion that
the fulfillment of Scripture is what Luke means need hardly be taken
seriously... The simpler meaning of the word is 'complete.'" The phrase
πεπληροφορημένων ἐν ἡμῖν πραγμάτων refers to the events which have
happened "among us," i.e. us Christians. All of the content of this first
verse may be summarized in the words: "Since some have already reported
the events which have happened among us," scil. in writings. This makes
clear even at this point that the prologue is intended only for the gospel:
there were several gospels, in the sense in which we use the word today,
but not acts of the apostles.

Now v. 2 gives the presupposition for this composition of gospel writings:
"As they" – that is, the events – "were delivered to us by those who from
the beginning were eyewitnesses and ministers of the word." The eyewitnesses (Luke would be thinking primarily of the twelve) did not leave behind anything which they had written; but they preached missionary
sermons (this is the preferred meaning for λόγος in Luke) which transmitted the tradition about Jesus. Thus, Luke knows of no gospel which claims
to have been written by an apostle. It is likewise clear that Luke distinguishes the authors of gospel writings and himself from the eyewitnesses, to
whom one ultimately owes the tradition. They delivered to us, the Christians, the gospel of Jesus.

At v. 3 Luke turns to his own work: "(Since some have written gospels),
I decided also... to write." Thus Luke gives the reason for his undertaking
quite simply. He does not assert that the writings of his predecessors were
bad; this has been read incorrectly into the word ἐπεχείρησαν. The most
that one can infer is that when he wrote his own gospel, despite the fact
that others had already appeared, he saw a need to supplement them.
Characteristic for what people later felt was lacking here is the addition by
b, q, and the Gothic tradition: "(mihi) et spiritui sancto."

But now we come to the crucial part of the sentence: Connected with κἀμοί
one reads: παρηκολουθηκότι ἄνωθεν πᾶσιν ἀκριβῶς. Dupont[103] would like
to detach ἄνωθεν from ἀπ᾿ ἀρχῆς and insure the meaning | "depuis long-
temps" [for a long time]. That would be necessary if παρακολουθέω meant
personal participation in the events, as Dupont finds is expressed here for
a part of the action depicted in Acts.[104] But when he cites Acts 26: 4f.,
where ἄνωθεν appears beside ἀπ᾿ ἀρχῆς, we cannot agree with him. According to Luke's depiction Paul came to Jerusalem when he was a small child.
Therefore, he can have Paul say here: "My manner of life from my youth,
spent from the beginning (ἀπ᾿ ἀρχῆς) among my own nation and at Jerusa-

---

[103] DUPONT, p. 106f.; cf. H. CADBURY, "'We' and 'I' Passages in Luke-Acts," NTS
3, 1956/57, p. 130, to which we will often refer below.
[104] CADBURY, p. 131.

lem is known by all the Jews. They have known me from the beginning
(ἄνωϑεν), if they are willing to testify, that according to the strictest party
of our religion I have lived as a Pharisee." Obviously it is a question here,
in the total context, of the Jews of Jerusalem. Paul assumes here that they
are all informed about the life he has led from youth on and that they could
testify to his experience as a Pharisee if they only wished to do so. The
clause ὅτι ... ἔζησα clarifies the phrase he has used at the beginning τὴν ...
βίωσίν μου. There is therefore no basis here for the distinction between
ἄνωϑεν and ἀπ᾿ ἀρχῆς at this point which Cadbury, followed by Dupont,[105]
hoped to establish.

But now Cadbury has injected another argument in the debate: that the
verb παρακολουϑεῖν [106] in such contexts always refers to "firsthand knowledge," not, however, to secondhand knowledge gained by asking someone
else. Unquestionably, the verb has such a meaning in many passages. But
it appears to me to be equally clear that it does not have such a meaning
here. For this meaning cannot be connected with ἀκριβῶς. I can be informed
"accurately," | but I cannot participate in a war "accurately." But that is
not all: the word πᾶσιν also stands in the way of the meaning given by
Cadbury and Dupont. This is evident by the effort with which Cadbury
opposes this counter-argument: "From πᾶσιν one would expect the
author's first-hand knowledge to apply to the whole section, whereas the
'we' sections are intermittent."[107] But, according to Cadbury, there are
reasons for the belief that this part of Acts is more uniform than the pronouns
indicate. Or πᾶσιν is an exaggeration. But with all this, nothing is accomplished. For it is not at all simply a question if Luke personally followed
Paul where "we" occurs. (He who denies this or rejects my explanation

---

[105] DUPONT, pp. 106 ff.

[106] CADBURY, p. 130. When DUPONT, p. 102, n. 3, asserts: "W. BAUER remains
hesitant (Wörterbuch⁵, 1227; English translation, 624)," this is not correct.
BAUER clearly decides in favor of the meanings: "follow a thing, trace or investigate
a thing," and cites as documentation the passages discussed by CADBURY: Demosthenes 18, 172 and 19, 257. In fact, contrary to DUPONT's thesis, neither means
firsthand information. For in *De corona* Demosthenes means by the words παρηκο-
λουϑηκότα τοῖς πράγμασι ἐξ ἀρχῆς καὶ συλλογισμένον an investigation of the events
in which (as the continuation of the passage demonstrates) ἐξετάζειν plays a role.
Demosthenes had made inquiries. The fact that he was one of the statesmen on the
side of Athens, acting against Philip, certainly does not eliminate this possibility! The
second passage, from *De legatione*, reads: ἀκριβέστατ᾿ εἰδὼς ἐγὼ καὶ παρηκολουϑη-
κὼς ἅπασι κατηγορῶ. The perfect is used in all these and similar passages (as also
by Luke, who here uses a common idiom) not because the information took place
long ago but because it began long ago or concerns a development which began a
long time ago. Therefore, the word παρακολουϑέω does not at all necessarily mean
for Luke, as DUPONT seems to assume, 'follow things as an eyewitness," although
it can have this meaning in other cases.

[107] CADBURY, p. 131.

certainly will have difficulty in explaining the transition to "we" in these parts. To be more exact: he can then give no reason for this transition.) The word ἄνωθεν used with the meaning "for a long time" really gets the exegete who defends this meaning into a predicament. If one were to assume that Cadbury and Dupont were right and that the clause means: "(to me) since I have followed all things closely for a long time" and applies this to the second half of Acts, then the whole thing would be senseless: Luke in his foreword to the Third Gospel would only be indicating his qualification as a writer of history in the second half of Acts but would be saying nothing about his qualification as writer of the *historia Jesu*.

If one puts together all of the arguments presented here, then it becomes evident: Luke is making clear at this point to what extent he is qualified as one who depicts the story of Jesus, as the author of the Gospel of Luke. He indicates this by referring to the fact that he has followed everything accurately from the beginning – from the infancy stories of Jesus on! Only by this explanation can one take the word πᾶσιν seriously and treat the word "accurately" according to its real meaning. Only in this way – and with this we come to the conclusion – do we remain in the direction mapped out by research.

For research really has proceeded at a very equal and consistent pace; this will become clear now in retrospect. The "we" in Acts has stimulated and driven it forward again and again. Scholars agreed among themselves that it referred to eyewitnessing. But this eyewitness "account" could be a "source" which the author wove in or his own notes. The unity of style in the "we" parts and the remainder of Acts appeared to speak for the second possibility. But this could also be interpreted to mean that the author had revised his source stylistically, and the way Luke used Mark's text pointed in this latter direction. But if "we" belonged to the revision (this thought is the decisive advance which Dibelius made), then there is the question why the author | begins "we" so suddenly precisely at these places and, in part, stops using it so abruptly. From his concept of dedication and the book market (current at his time), Dibelius came to the conclusion that Luke the physician wanted to indicate with "we" that he had participated in these parts of Paul's journeys. Since, however, these presuppositions about the meaning of dedication and the requirements of the book market have proved to be erroneous, we must look for another reason which will make "we" understandable. The new solution was already prepared for. On the one hand, by Nock's conjecture that for the different sections of Paul's trip several "documents" existed, not just (as Dibelius with his theory about one long itinerary had assumed) a single one. On the other hand, Dibelius himself had already seen the possibility (at first only for the trip to Rome) that the author revealed with "we" the fact that his authority was an eyewitness. We have carried through these two thoughts with the result:[108] even sections which appear to be taken over *verbatim* from an itinerary have in reality been revised and throughly reshaped by the author of Acts. At the same time we have attempted to explain why Luke uses the "we" so sparingly (his sources probably would have allowed him to have used it more often and in longer passages). At one place (chapter 16) it serves to insure historically a crucial moment in Paul's mission; in other places it makes the reader feel himself directly connected with Paul's life (chapters 20–21, 27–28). Since, however, Luke (apart from a few tentative attempts) does not connect "we" with the depiction of Paul's acting and speaking and since Paul is the real center of attention in the second half of Acts, "we" according to the second meaning could be used only in sections which did not report any special deeds of Paul. If Luke had connected "we" by literary means with the story of Paul, then this would not have been a story of Paul but a novel about Paul. But Luke, despite his considerable ability as a narrator,[109] is not a novelist but a historian.[110]

---

[108] In my commentary on Acts, pp. 77 f., I listed three possibilities of how Luke could have obtained data: a) traveling himself, b) obtaining information from others who had traveled, c) asking for information by letters. I have not asserted that Luke in actuality went over the routes Paul took, either all or part of them.

[109] Perhaps this sounds like an exaggeration when one thinks of the primitive means with which Luke worked. However, it is not the means that matter, but rather the effect he was able to attain with their help.

[110] This does not exclude the possibility that at times he invented an entire scene, as the conversation between Festus and Agrippa, 25: 13–22, and the accompanying trial.

God's Righteousness in Paul *

by

Ernst Käsemann

Translated by Wilfred F. Bunge

The letter to the Romans places the entire proclamation and theology of Paul under the one theme of the self-revealing righteousness of God. Undoubtedly the distinctively Pauline message thereby acquires a focus and appellation which very clearly set off its individuality from the rest of the New Testament. On the other hand, the problems arising with the Pauline theology are also centered in this theme, as I shall briefly recall at the outset. For only when these problems are clearly seen one can achieve the precise interpretation which is here required, a task which, in my opinion, in spite of many attempts, has not yet been satisfactorily accomplished.

The difficulties begin immediately with the question whether the genitive construction, δικαιοσύνη θεοῦ, is to be analyzed as a subjective or objective genitive, that is, whether it means the righteousness which belongs to God and issues from him or that which is valid before God and is given us by him. There can be no question but that the general trend of the Pauline statements, as well as the reformation tradition which has shaped us, speaks for the objective genitive. Phil. 3: 9 emphatically and, as has been said, in authentic interpretation sets the δικαιοσύνη ἐκ θεοῦ over against one's own righteousness. The status παρὰ τῷ θεῷ is characterized, according to Rom. 2: 13, by δικαιοῦσθαι. The basic alternative between righteousness from (or through) faith or from works is comprehensible only from this perspective, and thus Rom. 5: 17 speaks expressly of the δωρεὰ τῆς δικαιοσύνης. Nevertheless, one should not be too quickly satisfied with these | highly impressive arguments. Is there really no basis for Paul's speaking emphatically about God's righteousness, instead of the divine righteousness which is bestowed on us, is declared ours, and justifies us? Is it permissible to overlook the fact

---

* "Gottesgerechtigkeit bei Paulus," ZThK, 58, 1961, pp. 367–378. – A short paper read at the Oxford Congress on "The New Testament Today," September 14, 1961. Other interpretations were of course considered in the preparation of the paper, but the exegetical and systematic discussion with them could not be explicitly included in this framework. Furthermore, the consequences of my own understanding are more alluded to than developed.

that the δικαιοσύνη θεοῦ in Rom. 1: 17; 10: 3ff. appears personified as a
power, and therefore in the hymnic citation I Cor. 1: 30 can be identified
with Christ, that it describes the reality of the redeemed community in
II Cor. 5: 21, and that at least in Rom. 3: 5, 25f., in an incontestable
subjective genitive, it characterizes God's own activity and nature? Is this
only an inconsistency on the part of the apostle, the reasons for which
require clarification? Or does the tension here reveal a profound problem
of content, whose proper understanding will provide a basis for judging
every further interpretation?

For the time being the question may remain open. As is well known,
there are significant exegetical difficulties connected with the aspect of
the righteousness of God as a gift. These must be taken into consideration
from the start. Again I begin from an unquestioned fact: This gift is
almost always received as something which is already present. It is described
as effective in and through us, and II Cor. 9: 9f.; Phil. 1: 11 even name its
fruit. This makes it the more striking that Gal. 5: 5 views it as an object
of hope and leaves its final realization still open. Our theme thus leads us to
encounter that phenomenon which has somewhat unsatisfactorily been
designated the double eschatology of Paul. Even God's righteousness has
the double aspect, that salvation and the benefits of salvation appear at one
time as present with faith and baptism and at another time as fully realized
only through the parousia. More than this, the dialectic of having and not
fully having is here projected into the present of the Christian life. For the
formula λογίζεσθαι εἰς δικαιοσύνην, which is used technically in Rom. 4
and Gal. 3: 6, signifies that in this world we have the righteousness only as
a gift which is declared ours, which is constantly assailed and must be
confirmed. That is, we have it under the sign of promise and expectation.
Paul uses himself as an example of this in Phil. 3: 12: "Not that I have
already obtained this or am already perfect; but I press on to make it my
own, because Christ Jesus has made me his own." Even the gift of divine
righteousness places us not at the goal but on the way. It is given us in such
a way that it at the same time always lies ahead of us and must be grasped
anew. On the basis of Rom. 5: 6–10, the following formulation may be
given: It has us before we grasp it, and we keep it only as long as it holds
us. Accordingly, the gift itself has the character of power. It is completely
clear what this signifies concretely. Paul | knows no gift of God which does
not obligate us to service and make this service possible. A gift which is not
put to the test and passed on loses its specific content. In this connection,
the departure into the ever new future of receiving and grasping and the
resulting transformation of the gift into service is apparently to be understood, on the basis of Gal. 5: 5, as a reflection of the fact that God's final
righteousness is still to come.

To be sure, it is not yet clarified to what degree these conclusions necessarily follow from the character of the divine gift. It is by no means permissible to answer in the line of idealistic tradition that the gift is in the final analysis the essential principle of our vocation, which we in our actions are to realize ever anew and concretely. For then it would be mis-understood as law, and righteousness by works would inevitably take the place of righteousness by faith. Furthermore, the texts do not support the distinction which has sometimes been made between initial and final right-eousness, or between righteousness of faith and righteousness of life. On the contrary, this distinction reveals merely the impasse into which the apostle plunges his modern readers here, in precisely the same way as does the dif-ferentiation between ethical-juridical and sacramental-mystical viewpoints, which earlier generations favored. Paul, who in Rom. 4 clearly describes God's δικαιοῦν as a forensic act of declaring righteous, says in Rom. 5: 19 just as categorically that the status in righteousness has been established. He has characterized this status with especial clarity in the hymnic or liturgical passages, Rom. 8: 30 and I Cor. 6: 11, as the reality of the existence which has been transformed through baptism, and he bases the new obedience of the Christian on this status. This corresponds to the structure of the letter to the Romans as a whole. Not even justification and sanctification can be materially or chronologically separated. Christian worship in everyday life, parenetically depicted in Rom. 6: 11ff. and Rom. 12–14, which replaces the Jewish and Gentile cult, is the manifestation of God's righteousness on earth. This is the δουλεία τῆς δικαιοσύνης which can be effected only by the grantee who has been placed in the freedom of the child of God. It may be sufficient, for purposes of introduction, to leave the analysis at this point. My initial concern was only to recall the tensions connected with the Pauline doctrine of justification and the theological dialectic which is manifested in this doctrine. Such dialectic can rightfully be explained by the fact that the apostle stands against the double-front of nomism and pneumaticism and defends himself alternately against the one opponent with the terminology and motivation of the other. Our problem, however, is to determine from what unified center he could combine present and future eschatology, "declare righteous" and "make righteous," | gift and service, freedom and obedience, forensic, sacramental and ethical outlook. Only when this is answered with complete clarity will it be possible to say whether we still can and must carry out this dialectic. One should not be satisfied with partial solutions, even if they are correct. And if the individual aspects are absolutized, as often happens, the Pauline dialectic is destroyed.

I shall introduce my own attempt at interpretation by stating that the expression δικαιοσύνη θεοῦ was not created by Paul. The way in which it appears independently in Mt. 6: 33 and James 1: 20 can be traced in the Old Testament as far back as Deut. 33: 21. Two citations will verify that it

370/371 God's Righteousness in Paul 103

continued to be used in Judaism. In the original text of the Testament of Dan. 6: 10 we read:[1] ἀπόστητε οὖν ἀπὸ πάσης ἀδικίας καὶ κολλήθητε τῇ δικαιοσύνῃ τοῦ θεοῦ, and again in the Qumran Manual of Discipline: "If I stumble by the iniquity of my flesh, my vindication is in the righteousness of God" (1 QS XI 12). The significance of this fact is usually not seen and considered. Methodologically, the fact that Paul takes over a fixed formula certainly means that his phrase "God's righteousness" may not automatically be subsumed under the general concept δικαιοσύνη and thereby robbed of its individuality. Naturally it is of unusual significance that God's redemptive activity is designated by the apostle as righteousness, and we shall have to deal with this thematically in our conclusion. From the beginning it should also be noted that in the sphere of the Old Testament and Judaism righteousness means primarily not a personal, ethical quality, but a relationship. Originally it meant loyalty to the community, and in a trial referred to the restored "status" of the member of the community who has been declared innocent.[2] However, every interpretation which starts from the general concept and its distinctly juridical usage will necessarily be oriented toward the character of righteousness as a gift and in fact toward anthropology. The formula taken over by Paul, on the other hand, speaks first of all about the redemptive activity of God, which manifests itself in the gift without being absorbed in it. Naturally the entire emphasis will fall on the gift when righteousness by faith and righteousness by works must be sharply contrasted. Only it should not be overlooked that the phrase "righteousness of God" parallels the other phrases, the power, the love, the peace, and the wrath of God, which can likewise be personified | and designate divine power. Thus Rom. 1: 16 and 3: 21 speak of its revelation as its earthly epiphany; it is depicted in Rom. 10: 6 as speaking and acting; and it appears in I Cor. 1: 30 as nothing less than the manifestation of Christ, in II Cor. 5: 21 as the manifestation of the community. It is not without basis that Rom. 5: 21 is concerned with the βασιλεύειν of grace through righteousness, Rom. 6: 13 and II Cor. 6: 7 with the warfare, Rom. 6: 19 f. with the δουλεία, II Cor. 3: 9 with the διακονία of righteousness, and that all of this is summed up in the characteristic phrase of Rom. 10: 3: "submit to righteousness." This shows that Paul retained the aspect of righteousness as power which was a part of the formula as such and is corroborated by the parallels. The power becomes a gift when it takes possession of us and thereby, as it were, enters into us, so that, as in Gal. 2: 20: "It is no longer I who live, but Christ who lives in me." From this is to be understood the double signification of the genitive

---

[1] Cf. A. OEPKE, "'Δικαιοσύνη θεοῦ' bei Paulus in neuer Beleuchtung," ThLZ 78, 1953, cols. 260 ff.

[2] See R. BULTMANN, Theology of the New Testament, New York, II, 1955, pp. 271 ff.

construction: The gift which is here given is not and never will be severed from its giver. It participates in the character of power, in that in it God himself enters the scene and with it remains on the scene. Thus demand, obligation, and service are also inseparably connected with it. When God enters the scene, we experience his dominion even in his gifts. It is precisely his gifts which place us under his dominion and thereby in a position of responsibility. The widespread view of God's righteousness as a divine attribute can now be rejected as misleading. It derives from Greek theology which speculates about the attributes of God; it contradicts the basic Old Testament, Jewish understanding of righteousness as loyalty to the community; and it breaks down on the point that the conferral of a divine attribute on men cannot be convincingly made intelligible. Δικαιοσύνη θεοῦ is for Paul as well as for the Old Testament and Judaism a noun of action, which does not describe God as he is in himself but God as he reveals himself.

The decisive step toward understanding Paul properly is made only when one grasps the inseparable connection between power and gift in our concept. It is amazing that this has not long since been accepted as self-evident. For it is a basic phenomenon in the entire Pauline theology. A few examples will demonstrate its variational breadth. According to II Cor. 12: 9 and 13: 3f., God's *power* operates at the same time as a *gift* within us. Likewise the Spirit who awakens the dead is at the same time the πνεῦμα ἐν ἡμῖν which has been given us, and Christ, whom Paul extols as the Lord of the world, not only gives himself for us, but also dwells and lives in us. | Though χάρις means primarily the power of grace, it means concretely the individuation of χάρις in the χάρισμα conferred on us. In Rom. 8: 39 the love of God is the power from which nothing can separate us, while in Rom. 5: 5 it is the gift which is poured into our hearts. The gospel appears in I Cor. 9: 16 as ἀνάγκη upon the apostle and in II Cor. 2: 14ff. as a power unto life or unto death, so that Rom. 1: 16 expressly designates it as δύναμις θεοῦ. Nonetheless in the kerygma we participate in it and Paul can speak of "his" gospel. The σῶμα Χριστοῦ of the Lord's Supper joins us, according to I Cor. 10: 16, to the body of Christ, the Church.

The key to the Pauline view lies in the observation that power always seeks to and must become operative. This occurs most effectively when it does not remain outside of us but enters into us and thereby makes us its members, as the apostle says. The conception of Christ or the Spirit dwelling in us, which has so frequently been called "mystical," may in fact, as far as its manner of expression is concerned, be explained from the analogy with concepts and forms of hellenistic mysticism. However, essentially it is not in the least in contradiction with the conception of the Christ *extra nos*. Rather it radicalizes this conception: The dominion over us is precisely then totally effected when it masters even our heart and takes us into its service. Conversely, every gift which is no longer interpreted as the presence of its giver and therefore loses the character of a claim is an abused and detrimental grace. Justification and sanctification must coincide, if indeed justification means that Christ assumes power over our life. At the same time this understanding excludes the possibility of righteousness by works and of boasting on the basis of one's own accomplishment. The same Lord who calls us to his service makes possible this service which he demands in such a way that his gift is passed on. If one is the instrument used by grace, one cannot meaningfully speak of one's own accomplishment. Here applies always: "Let him who boasts, boast of the Lord." Thus there is no real tension anymore between sacrament and ethics. The Lord who is received by us in and with baptism in the gift of his Spirit, i. e., the power which establishes dominion, drives us, precisely as our Lord, to constantly new service and into the ever new future. We do not exist anymore for ourselves alone and therefore we cannot even stop with what we have received. Only as we continue on the way and are daily summoned anew into the dominion of Christ do we remain in the gift which we have received. And only thus does the gift remain alive and effective in us.

The relationship between the Pauline indicative and imperative is often described with the formula: "Become what you are." | This, to be sure, is not false, but in view of the origin of this formula in idealism it is not without danger. For Paul it was primarily not a matter of the Christian in isolation, which is only conceivable in the abstract, much less of the Christian personality. The fact that one believes only as an individual means that in this as in service he cannot avoid responsibility. However, I cannot possibly agree that Paul's theology and view of history are oriented to the individual.[3] It is the unfortunate consequence of understanding God's righteousness exclusively as a gift that in this case Pauline anthropology falls necessarily into the rut of an individualizing way of thinking. The meaning of the hortatory imperative as the consequence and confirmation of the indicative is much better described with the formula: Abide with the Lord who has been given you and in his dominion, just as the Johannine farewell discourses center around the theme of "abiding." In precisely this way the Christian becomes what he is. For in Paul existence is at all times determined by the Lord to whom we belong. When a transformation of existence occurs in baptism and the word of God effects a new creation, this means nothing other than a change of Lordship. The new Lord separates us from what we were, and he never allows us to remain what we are at any time, for otherwise he would be the first cause but not really our Lord. According to this theological context man is never free in the manner of autonomy. Eschatologically, however, he is given the

---

[3] Against BULTMANN, The Presence of Eternity, New York, 1957, pp. 40 ff.

possibility of choosing between the kingdom of Christ and the kingdom of Satan. And temptation as well as the call of the sermon place the Christian ever anew before this choice, so that Christian life may aptly be viewed as a constant return to baptism.

From this standpoint the tension in the relation between "declare righteous" and "make righteous" can also be resolved. If one sees in God's righteousness only an isolable gift, it must appear as though God imparts to us in principle something which we have to realize ourselves, or as though he transforms our existence in a natural, automatic way. In either case the Pauline dialectic is not understood. The situation is different, on the other hand, if the power character of the gift is respected and Christ's Lordship is recognized as the actual content of the gift. According to I Cor. 12: 2 the power of God, in contrast to that of the idols, is not dumb but bound to the word. It speaks to us in love and judgment, so that we experience its will, and it places us through the gospel in a position "in the presence of Christ" which is determined by it. The righteousness which is given us consists of this status, which is only to be attained through the gospel. | This is the possibility of access to God, in which, according to Rom. 5: 1f., we have peace and, according to II Cor. 5: 19ff., we are reconciled with God. However, a Lord is not a guaranteed possession and is not subject to our self-willed disposal. That he is there for us is experienced only in the form of promise, is confirmed only to the faith which trusts the promise, the faith to which the παρ᾽ ἐλπίδα ἐπ᾽ ἐλπίδι of Rom. 4: 18 applies. On the other hand, the status under such Lordship is no phantom or ideological program. According to Rom. 10: 6ff. the righteousness of faith, in contrast to the law, proclaims the nearness and presence of grace. And the new obedience demonstrates that the promise is heard and received, that faith is right hearing. The divine promise therefore produces reality. It remains bound to the actuality of the promise, however, that such reality stays alive and that in obedience the status before God – Paul can say "in the presence of Christ" as well as "in Christ" – is maintained.

Up to this point I have passed over the question why Paul designates the eschatological redemptive activity of God as δικαιοσύνη and not consistently as ἀγάπη θεοῦ, as he occasionally does. That he thereby stands in the Old Testament, Jewish tradition cannot be disputed, but this gives only a start toward an explanation. Frequently the problem is not even raised, so that God's righteousness is defined simply as redemptive activity and salvation. However, the Pauline theology gives evidence of careful reflection and naiveté is the last thing that characterizes it. One comes further with the insight that in Rom. 3: 25f. the apostle, citing a Jewish-Christian creedal fragment,[4] can speak of the δικαιοσύνη θεοῦ as divine loyalty to

---

[4] Cf. my essay: "Zum Verständnis von Römer 3:24–26," (in: Exegetische Versuche und Besinnungen, Göttingen, I, 1960, pp. 96–100).

the covenant. If one asks why that does not happen more often and why the citation is even corrected and in any case commented upon in verse 26, the answer must be given: Paul does not think, as the immediate post-Easter community did, in terms of the renewed covenant and of the holy remnant, or he does it only rarely and in an auxiliary fashion. For him Christ is not the second Moses, as he is for example in the infancy narratives of Matthew, but the second Adam, who for that reason introduces the new covenant and the new creation. For this reason God's righteousness can no longer be for him primarily the divine loyalty to the covenant with Israel. Conversely, however, he has nevertheless been able to take up the Jewish-Christian citation in Rom. 3: 25 and to parallel the motifs of καινὴ κτίσις and καινὴ διαθήκη. Even for him God's righteousness remains – and indeed precisely in a juridical sense[5] – ἔνδειξις of the divine loyalty to the | community, to be sure not only with regard to Israel, but with regard to the entire creation.

Usually the Pauline doctrine of justification is distinguished from the Jewish doctrine by connecting the antithesis between present justification and justification still unrealized or even uncertain with the antithesis of faith and works. There cannot be the slightest doubt that Paul lays the strongest emphasis on the presence of salvation. Rom. 1: 16 and 3: 21 alone would prove the point. Nevertheless it is not sufficient merely to assert this. For just as the apostle in Gal. 5: 5 can speak of the righteousness which is still *unrealized,* so the Thanksgiving Psalms of Qumran offer evidence that already in apocalyptic Judaism the *present* manifestation of God's righteousness could be extolled with as much emphasis as in Paul. Realized eschatology, if one wishes to use this catchword at all, is certainly not the exclusive mark of the early Christian proclamation. And Paul, so far as it can characterize him, stands in the first instance entirely within the sphere of possibilities and realities of at least one definite stream of Jewish apocalypticism. Naturally, the christological orientation separates his theology from the latter. However, everything depends on making clear what that means as far as the content is concerned. It seems to me, in the light of the Thanksgiving Psalms, that one can no longer do this satisfactorily on the basis of an understanding of self and history which is governed alone or primarily by present eschatology. The presence of the Spirit was experienced not only by Christian pneumaticists, but also by Jewish apocalypticists. What distinguishes the Pauline theology from both of them is rather the unprecedented radicalization and universalization of the promise in the doctrine of the justification of the sinner. The Jewish point of view is expressed in the Damascus Document 20:20: "Salvation and righteousness are revealed to those who fear God." Even the Thanksgiving Psalms, of

---

[5] Cf. W. G. Kümmel, "Πάρεσις und ἔνδειξις," ZThK, 49, 1952, pp. 154–167.

course, remain faithful to the thinking in the covenant pattern. The additions in which Paul speaks interpretatively of God's righteousness and its
revelation χωρὶς νόμου are the distinguishing mark of his theology. It is not
by chance that, according to the context of Rom. 3: 22 and 8: 29, the δόξα
θεοῦ which was lost to all men through the fall is given again with the
righteousness of God and, according to II Cor. 3: 18 and 4: 6, now shines
into the world in the διακονία τῆς δικαιοσύνης. It is further not accidental
that in Rom. 1: 18–3: 20 Paul views the world before and outside of Christ
not under the goodness and forbearance of God, but under the judgment
of wrath. This jugdment is manifested in the accumulation of guilt, in
impenitence and condemnation. It affects Jews and Gentiles alike and is
revealed together with the gospel.

| Only in such a framework can Paul in Rom. 9–11 speak also of God's
righteousness in relation to Israel. Doubtlessly Israel presents a special case,
insofar as it is the people of the promise and of the experiences of grace and
is thereby the very prototype of the *homo religiosus*. It is to be asked
whether God acts differently toward this people, and therefore toward
pious man, than he does toward the rest of the world,[6] and whether his
faithfulness is maintained here in immanent continuity. Rom. 9–11 shows
that this is not the case. In these chapters the course of the entire letter is
being rehearsed, with the demonstration of the freedom of God, the indict-
ment of the guilty, the establishment of their condemnation, and finally
the apocalyptic promise. Rom. 11: 32 summarizes almost triumphantly:
"God has consigned all men to disobedience, that he may have mercy upon
all." In any event, Israel is not a special case in the sense that God's
righteousness is shown differently toward her than otherwise. On the
contrary, it is demonstrated here most clearly and incisively that the way
of salvation always leads over the way of the justification of the sinner. The
attempt to achieve status before God and to establish one's own righteousness by means of pious works and an appeal to the fathers characterizes,
even more than does heathen idolatry, the will of the flesh to achieve inde-
pendence from the Lord who claims us totally and constantly. Therefore it
falls under the wrath of God. For it means that God is no longer God and
man is no longer man in the sense of being subject to the power of God
and fully dependent on the mercy of God. The attempt to preserve independ-
ence over against God is the basic sin, no matter how it is manifested
concretely, and it is always answered as in Rom. 1: 24ff.: διὸ παρέδωκεν
αὐτούς. The eschatological salvation thus begins with the revelation of the
godhood of God and the necessity of man becoming man. In the new creation there is reference back to the *creatio ex nihilo* and preparation for the

---

[6] See my essay: "Paulus und Israel," in: Juden, Christen, Deutsche, ed. by H. G.
Schultz, 3rd ed., Stuttgart, 1961, pp. 307–311.

resurrection of the dead. The καινὴ διαθήκη is not simply the renewed and broadened covenant of Sinai, and its sign is πίστις, not νόμος.

Nevertheless, God keeps that faithfulness, called צדקה in the Old Testament, which is bound to the covenant both in the Old Testament and in Judaism and is prominently recalled in Rom. 9: 4f. In spite of everything, Paul clung to the conviction that God displays his righteousness, not in a renewed, but in a new covenant. Therefore he could transfer the motif of the people of God to the Christians as the eschatological Israel. In this he | has in mind that faithfulness which the creator maintains toward his work of creation in spite of the revolt of his creatures, the faithfulness with which he guards and grounds anew his dominion over his creation. Thus δικαιοσύνη θεοῦ and πίστις θεοῦ are joined in Rom. 3: 3–5 in the sense of such faithfulness. At the same time it becomes clear that God's righteousness is what it has to be as the power of the sinner's justification, namely God's victory amidst the contradiction of the world. With it, all human righteousness and insubordination come to naught, while, according to Rom. 4: 17, that which does not exist is called into existence and the dead are made alive. Christ is the new Adam, because as the bearer of destiny he introduces the world of obedience. Everything which has been said can be summarized in the statement that δικαιοσύνη θεοῦ for Paul is God's dominion over the world, which is being revealed eschatologically in Christ. If one thinks etymologically, he may also say: that right with which God carries out his claim over the world which is fallen from him and yet, as creation, belongs inviolably to him.

If this is true, Paul does not relate God's righteousness primarily to the individual. And it is not to be understood exclusively from the context of anthropology, as must be the case if its character as a gift is the first and only concern. To be sure, Paul, in sharp polemic against the Jewish scheme of the covenant people, presented the believer and him alone as the recipient of salvation. Nevertheless, the category of the individual man which thereby appears does correspond to the intention of salvation for all, which is directed toward the entire world and no longer restricted by the Law. At the same time, Pauline theology is unique in the New Testament in presenting a developed anthropology. It is impossible to comprehend its distinctiveness, if this is not taken into consideration systematically from the very beginning. On the other side, however, this anthropology is only a part of Pauline theology, and as such it has a specific function in it. It shows in the trials of life the present reality of the activity of God directed toward the new creation. The believers are the world restored to God's dominion, the host under the eschatological right of God, in which, therefore, God's righteousness is manifested on earth, according to II Cor. 5: 21. However, the theological perspective is shortened and even Pauline anthropology misinterpreted, if one stops with such a conclusion. It is precisely Paul's doctrine of justification which shows that God's action in Christ as well as in the creation has to do with the world, and that the dialectic of present and future eschatology overarches the Christian existence. Anthropology is not the real concern of this doctrine. Paul saw his task in the world mission, consciously and under apocalyptic | urgency. An interpretation which loses sight of this fails to give historical research its due and reduces as well the theological problematic with which Paul confronts us. The present eschatology of the apostle cannot be separated from the context of future eschatology, just as the gift of justification is not to be isolated from the context which speaks of God's righteousness as a power which establishes salvation. Even as a Christian Paul remains an apocalypticist. [7] His doctrine of the δικαιοσύνη θεοῦ proves this: God's power grasps at the world, and it is the world's salvation that it is brought back under God's dominion. Precisely for this reason, it is God's gift and the salvation also of the individual, that we become obedient to God's righteousness.

---

[7] With this I extend the lines laid down in my essay: "Die Anfänge christlicher Theologie," ZThK, 57, 1960, pp. 162–185, and meet the criticism of my friends E. FUCHS ("Über die Aufgabe einer christlichen Theologie," ZThK, 58, 1961, pp. 245–67) and G. EBELING ("Der Grund christlicher Theologie," ZThK, 58, 1961, pp. 227–44) for the time being by taking the offensive. The defense will still have to wait. Time is not only something we have to be granted. We have to be able to take our time, too. In any case the problem is just as important as the problem of the historical Jesus, and perhaps it should even be dealt with first. It would only be of advantage for our theological situation if the fire which has been kindled were not too quickly extinguished. Whether it is burning on a stake will become clear. There are also Easter fires!

History and Cult in the Gospel of John and in Ignatius of Antioch[*]

by

Helmut Koester

Translated by Arthur Bellinzoni

I. The Problem

Few men of the first hundred years of Christianity have as much in common as do the author of the Gospel of John and Ignatius of Antioch. They use nearly the same language; they employ closely related terminologies; and in their theological thought, both are apparently influenced by Gnosticism. Moreover, both stand in close proximity in time – the Gospel of John was written shortly before, the epistles of Ignatius one or two decades after the turn of the century –, and both probably come from the same geographical vicinity, i. e. from Syria.[1]

There is less certainty with regard to the question of literary relationship. Did Ignatius know the Gospel of John? Is it possible to prove the presence of quotations? Until the beginning of the 20th century the answer to this question was almost always affirmative; e. g. D. Völter: "The acquaintance of the author (of the epistles of Ignatius) . . . with the Fourth Gospel can be taken as absolutely certain."[2] However, since the investigation of von der Goltz[3] the opposite opinion has prevailed. "Even though the fourth Gospel already existed, which cannot be doubted, the bishop of Antioch did not know it, in any case did not know it in such a way that his mode of thinking could be traced back to the fact that he had read it." This is the way von der Goltz formulates his solution, and most of the recent scholars have followed suit, while emphasizing at the same time the common history-of-religions background more strongly.[4]

---

[*] "Geschichte und Kultus im Johannesevangelium und bei Ignatius von Antiochien," ZThK, 54, 1957, pp. 56–69. – Inaugural lecture delivered on July 3, 1956, before the theological faculty of the University of Heidelberg.

[1] For John see W. BAUER, Das Johannesevangelium (HNT 6) 1933³, pp. 243f.

[2] D. VÖLTER, Die Apostolischen Väter neu untersucht, Leiden, II, 1910, p. 112; similar conclusions are reached by F. C. BAUR, A. HILGENFELD, G. VOLKMAR, H. J. HOLTZMANN, B. WEISS, TH. ZAHN, J. B. LIGHTFOOT.

[3] E. VON DER GOLTZ, Ignatius von Antiochien als Christ und Theologe (Texte und Untersuchungen, XII, 3), Leipzig, 1894.

[4] E. g. W. BAUER, G. KRÜGER (in: HENNECKE, Neutestamentliche Apokryphen, 1904), H. SCHLIER, H. W. BARTSCH and R. BULTMANN.

The most recent major investigation of this subject comes from Christian Maurer.[5] Maurer tries to make the hypothesis of a literary dependence again respectable. He argues that Ignatius is combining various passages from the Synoptic Gospels, from John, and from Paul, and it is for this reason that it is so difficult to recognize that real | quotations are involved here. Ignatius' literary dependence upon the Gospel of John is, however, beyond question, once his method of conflating quotations has been clarified. On the other hand, Maurer now puts the emphasis upon the essential difference between the two writers, also with respect to their history-of-religions background. The dividing line between Gospel and Gnosticism separates John and Ignatius. Whereas John is still completely filled with the "Old Testament spirit of the Bible," Ignatius is proclaiming a Christian Gnosis and a Christian Mysterion.

Inasmuch as Maurer's hypothesis regarding Ignatius' method of conflating quotations is contestable, the question of the literary relationship of John and Ignatius remains uncertain even after his investigation. This problem will not be pursued here.[6] It appears to me, however, that in principle Maurer is quite right in his emphasis upon the fundamental and essential difference between John and Ignatius.[7] Yet, Maurer's formula for this difference is much too simple. As much as John does not simply think in "Old Testament" terms, Ignatius is not just a representative of Gnosticism. It is necessary to add, moreover, that such a classification does not automatically imply a theological judgment of the subject matter. One certainly has to recognize the shades of difference in their history-of-religions background. But this does not mean that it is possible to explain the terminological relations as literary dependence and to deny flatly the proximity in terms of history-of-religions background. After all, an essential difference does not have to result exclusively from a difference in history-of-religions motives and thought forms. Such essential differences might also result from a difference in decision with respect to theological questions in each case.

In my opinion, E. Fuchs has correctly grasped the basic intention which is consistently carried through in the Gospel of John: "He (the evangelist)

---

[5] CHR. MAURER, Ignatius von Antiochien und das Johannesevangelium, Zürich, 1949.

[6] Cf. the critical review of E. KÄSEMANN, Verkündigung und Forschung, 1950, pp. 221 f., and the favorable evaluation of E. SCHWEIZER, Theologische Zeitschrift, 5, 1949, pp. 463 ff.

[7] One should not overemphasize the fact that literary knowledge and essential misunderstanding always go hand in hand in Ignatius. For it is certainly true that with respect to the relation of Ignatius to Paul, Ignatius knew and made full use of the Pauline Epistles. At the same time, however, he understood and interpreted Paul much better than many others, as BULTMANN has most recently shown: "Ignatius und Paulus" (in: Studia Paulina in honorem Ioannis de Zwaan, Haarlem, 1953), pp. 37–51 (Eng. tr. in: Existence and Faith, ed. SCHUBERT M. OGDEN, New York: Meridian, pp. 267–277).

has seen that theology is not permitted to put the problem of the historical pastness of Jesus into parenthesis . . ., but that theology must be developed on the basis of the distance of faith from the historical Jesus."[8]

That is a "theological" question which enables us, as I believe, to lay open an important difference between John and Ignatius, precisely in view of their strong relationship in terminology and history-of-religions background. How did the author of the Gospel of John solve this problem of the distance from the historical Jesus? Did Ignatius see this problem at all? How did he solve it? In the same way in which the author of the Gospel of John solved it? Or do fundamental differences appear here?

Taking this formulation of the question as the starting point, I will try to examine two topics in John and Ignatius: a) the work of Jesus and its appropriation; b) the unity of the church and Christian existence. The concern here is primarily to contribute to the understanding of the Gospel of John rather than focusing upon Ignatius. The latter will be referred to only as an example of a theological point of view which is quite similar in appearance, but in reality rather different.[9]

II. The Redeemer in Ignatius and John

Ignatius is capable of describing the work of the Redeemer in the colors and terms of the Gnostic myth, as he does most noticeably in Eph. 19.[10] The virginity and parturition of Mary as well as the death of the Lord are secret facts of which the ruler of this aeon does not receive any knowledge. It is only with the ascension of the Redeemer that the accomplished work of salvation is made known. From then on all works of the old dominion are in the state of dissolution: μαγεία, δεσμὸς κακίας, ἄγνοια and θάνατος.[11]

This Gnostic cosmological aspect of salvation shows similarities throughout with the statements of the Gospel of John, although the latter lacks a coherent myth of descent and ascension. But single features of this myth are also present in John: The Son of Man descended from heaven and he will ascend into heaven again (Jn. 3:13; 6:33, 50, 62; 20:17). Faith in the Redeemer is characterized as γινώσκειν (the corresponding negative term ἄγνοια does not appear in John). The believer has gone from death

---

[8] E. Fuchs, Hermeneutik, Bad Cannstatt, 1954, p. 242.

[9] I make no claim that the details of the following discussion are new. My intention is solely to re-examine the comparison between John and Ignatius under a fresh formulation of the question with the result that much already said elsewhere will have to be repeated.

[10] See H. Schlier, Religionsgeschichtliche Untersuchungen zu den Ignatiusbriefen, Gießen, 1929, pp. 5 ff.

[11] As in Paul in I Cor. 15:26 "death" is here emphasized by its position at the end.

into life | (Jn. 5:24; I Jn. 3:14), – this corresponds to the dissolution of death in Ign. Eph. 19:3.

In the Gospel of John, however, these concepts do not have a cosmological but an existential meaning. Consequently, there is nothing in John that corresponds to μαγεία and δεσμὸς κακίας, and nothing is said about the appearance of the star of the ascending Redeemer. The exaltation, the δοξασθῆναι, refers to the cross (Jn. 7:39; 12:16 *et passim*). Whoever sees him who became flesh sees the δόξα (Jn. 1:14). This is plainly the fundamental statement of the Gospel.

But such a comparison between Ignatius and John still falls too short, because for Ignatius also the emphasis is not on the myth of secret descent and spectacular ascension, but similarly on the coming of the Redeemer into the flesh. To be sure, in Eph. 19:3, Ignatius speaks only in colorless terms about the θεὸς ἀνθρωπίνως φανερουμένος, yet in other places he says ἐν σαρκὶ γενόμενος θεός (Eph. 7:2, cf. Smyrn. 3) or Χριστὸς σαρκικός (Eph. 7:2), in kerygmatic formulations also Χριστὸς ὁ κατὰ σάρκα ἐκ γένους Δαυίδ (Eph. 20:2). Ignatius even far exceeds the Gospel of John in the frequency of emphasis upon the fleshly appearance of Jesus, even if the σὰρξ ἐγένετο of John 1:14 is lacking in Ignatius. Yet this unanimity is only an apparent one. Σάρξ does not mean the same to John and Ignatius.

For Ignatius σάρξ is a sphere which corresponds to the other sphere πνεῦμα. Therefore the statement of the fleshly appearance of Jesus always appears together with the other statement of his pneumatic existence:

Eph. 7:2:   εἷς ἰατρός ἐστιν,
                σαρκικός τε καὶ πνευματικός,
                γεννητὸς καὶ ἀγέννητος,
                ἐν σαρκὶ γενόμενος θεός, ἐν θανάτῳ ζωὴ ἀληθινή,
                καὶ ἐκ Μαρίας καὶ ἐκ θεοῦ,
                πρῶτον παθητὸς καὶ τότε ἀπαθής,
                        Ἰησοῦς Χριστὸς ὁ κύριος ἡμῶν.
Smyrn. 3:3: ... συνέφαγεν αὐτοῖς καὶ συνέπιεν ὡς σαρκικός,
                καίπερ πνευματικῶς ἡνωμένος τῷ πατρί.

Even if this terminology is dualistic in origin, the examples presented here (they can easily be multiplied) | show that Ignatius' thought is not essentially dualistic, but rather a soteriological "monism." Two spheres, flesh and spirit, things procreated and things unbegotten, man and God, are made a unity in Christ. There is no irreconcilable antagonism like that which is characteristic of genuine dualism where the battle is to the end and the battlecry is irreversible separation. In Ignatius the theme is synthesis and unity which is present in perfection with the person of the Redeemer who is both flesh and spirit at once. The presupposition for this description of the Redeemer and his work is the Hellenistic concept of substances, which makes possible the thought of a unification of two spheres, if they are conceived of as substances. According to Ignatius, this unification has been accomplished in Christ who, being spirit, took on flesh also.

In the Gospel of John, especially in the prologue, a truly dualistic concept seems to appear: The light shines in the darkness, and the darkness did not comprehend it (Jn. 1:5). The statement "light *and* darkness" is impossible for the Gospel of John. The opposites are irreconcilable. Yet the statement about the Logos becoming flesh neither belongs in the categories of such an antithetical dualism nor does it intend to describe the accomplishment of a synthesis as it does in Ignatius.

The term σάρξ, rare in the Gospel of John anyway, as a rule is neutral and simply designates the world in terms of the things which are in existence, in terms of that which belongs to man and to history, – but never the world as hostile to God (Jn. 1:14; also 8:15; 17:2!).[12] Σάρξ is used in contrast to πνεῦμα only twice: Jn. 3:6 and 6:63. Both times, however, we are not dealing with a dualistic statement, but with a general maxim about the impossibility of taking possession of the divine by means of natural criteria: It is the Spirit that gives life, the flesh is useless.

If σάρξ, therefore, is the neutral sphere of that which belongs to man and history, the fundamental assertion Jn. 1:14: ὁ λόγος σὰρξ ἐγένετο, says that the divine Logos comes into the historical realm of human existence, not in order to bring about a uniting of metaphysical substances, but in order to work as the historical word of a historical man.

III. The Work of the Redeemer in Ignatius

As far as the work of the Redeemer is in question, the differences between John and Ignatius lie in the same direction. In Ignatius' epistles the Redeemer appears to be speechless. | Not only is the completion of the three secrets of Eph. 19 (virginity and parturition of Mary, the death of the Lord) brought about in the "silence of God," but also "what he (Christ) has done silently, is worthy of the Father" (Eph. 15:1). That indicates that according to Ignatius the work of Christ is not word, is not address, neither as a whole nor in what he happens to have said;[13] it is rather the accomplishment of a unification of substances, a work that is concerned with metaphysical principles and elements. Consequently he says about Christ: "He was born and baptized in order to purify the water through suffering" (Eph. 18:2). Thus the meaning of Jesus' baptism is the consecration of the baptismal water for the Christians.

---

[12] R. BULTMANN, Das Evangelium des Johannes, Göttingen, 1941, pp. 39f.

[13] The designation of Jesus as the διδάσκαλος, however, is strikingly rare in Ignatius (only Eph. 15:1; Magn. 9:1f.); what its meaning is has to be discussed in another context.

Above all, his coming in the flesh had the purpose of mediating the sacred food to his people. The eucharist is the flesh of the Redeemer (Smyrn. 7:1). His flesh is the medicine of immortality (Eph. 20:2), which is effective because in Christ the unity of flesh and spirit is present. Therefore, whoever eats his flesh partakes of this unity and consequently also of the πνεῦμα. Stated paradoxically: "You are made alive through the blood of God" (Eph. 1:1); "What I desire is the bread of God, which is the flesh of Jesus Christ, who is of the seed of David; and for drink I desire his blood which is an imperishable meal of love" (Rom. 7:3).

The appropriation of salvation is possible through sacramental means and possible only in this way. At the same time one understands why it was a must for Ignatius to argue in terms of a strict antidocetism. The absolute denial of the fleshliness of Jesus would have implied the impossibility of obtaining salvation, because the sacrament then would also be only a semblance. The ultimate purpose of the mysterious coming of the Redeemer into the flesh, therefore, is not understood in terms of Gnosticism as the deception of the rulers (one is tempted to interpret Eph. 19 in this way at the first reading); it is rather to bring about the unification of flesh and spirit in order to give to those who are flesh the possibility of partaking of the spirit through the sacrament.

IV. Historical or Sacramental Redemption in John?

Returning to the Gospel of John, in chapter 6 we find a number of sentences which seem to fit rather well into Ignatius' understanding of the sacrament and of salvation, i. e. the controversial passage Jn. 6:51b–59. In agreement with Ignatius these verses designate the eucharistic bread as the flesh of Jesus: "The bread which | I shall give for the life of the world is my flesh" (vs. 51b); "He who eats my flesh and drinks my blood has eternal life" (vs. 54). The Ignatian term "medicine of immortality" lies within close proximity of this passage. Exegetes have observed and noticed this fact again and again. Indeed, the eucharistic character of these verses is beyond any doubt.

What is to be doubted, however, is whether these words are an original part of the text of the Gospel of John – these doubts must be raised in spite of some recent attempts to retain them as genuine.[14] I am grateful to be permitted to make use of an essay by Günther Bornkamm which is as yet (i. e. 1956) unpublished.[15] G. Bornkamm takes as his starting point the observation that the offence caused by Jesus' words, which is discussed

---

[14] Recently E. SCHWEIZER has spoken for the genuineness: "Das johanneische Zeugnis vom Herrenmahl," Evangelische Theologie, 12, 1952–53, pp. 358–361.

[15] This article has since appeared under the title, "Die eucharistische Rede im Johannesevangelium," ZNW, 47, 1956, pp. 161–169.

in Jn. 6:60ff., cannot refer to the questionable passage Jn. 6:51b–59, as many exegetes maintain.[16] Actually, vs. 63 is only a maxim which does not say anything with respect to σάρξ as a (sacramental) element, nor anything about Jesus as being "in the flesh." As Jesus' words in vs. 62 indicate, the subject matter in question is rather Jesus' claim to be the bread from heaven; vs. 62: "What if you now see the Son of Man ascend where he was before?" refers back to vs. 50: "This is the bread which has descended from heaven." The verses in which the *flesh* of Jesus is spoken of as the food that gives life are not in view at all. Therefore, in addition to other, older arguments against the authenticity of Jn. 6:51b–59,[17] there is further reason for eliminating these verses. This is how far G. Bornkamm's argumentation brings us.[18]

Thus, it seems to be necessary to admit that this sacramental passage Jn. 6:51b–59 rather characterizes the view of Ignatius and should not be employed for the interpretation of Johannine thought. It should not be overlooked, however, that even after the elimination of this passage, there remain certain elements in the words about the ἄρτος τῆς ζωῆς in Jn. 6 which are possibly determined by cultic language. To be sure, the background may be a metaphor originating in Gnosticism; yet a Christian of the second generation could hardly speak about the "bread of life" without thinking of the eucharist. Firstly, ἄρτος in Early Christianity is the technical term for the eucharistic food (documentation is not necessary); secondly, the comparison | of the bread which Jesus gives (or *is* himself) with the manna of the fathers always occurs in the context of the eucharist (with Jn. 6:31, 49, cf. I Cor. 10:3f. and Rev. 2:14, 17).

The reference to the eucharist, however, is not the case in point in the argumentation of Jn. 6. Rather the discourse only starts from the above-mentioned term (bread of life) in order to point in another direction, i. e. to the words which Jesus speaks. To the sentence 6:51a: "He who eats of this bread (which has come down from heaven – which is I) will live in eternity," corresponds vs. 63b: "The words which I have spoken to you are spirit and life." The case in point are the words of the Revealer who has come into history, the words to which Peter confesses: ῥήματα ζωῆς αἰωνίου ἔχεις (6:68).

---

[16] So again E. SCHWEIZER, "Das johanneische Zeugnis," p. 358.

[17] Cf. most recently R. BULTMANN, Das Evangelium des Johannes, pp. 161f., and Ergänzungsheft, 1953, p. 25.

[18] At the same time G. BORNKAMM's interpretation shows convincingly that one cannot separate Jn. 6:60ff. from 6:1–51 as BULTMANN has done (Das Evangelium des Johannes, pp. 214ff.).

V. The Transposition of Cultic Categories into Historical Categories
in John

In Jn. 6 we have thus observed the tendency to appropriate cultic terminology and by means of it to refer back to the revelation which has the
character of historical event. This same tendency can be noticed also in
other passages of the Gospel of John.

Jn. 3:5: "Whoever is not born again of water and the spirit cannot
enter the Kingdom of God." *Water* and spirit can only refer to baptism.
Bultmann also recognizes this. [19] In his opinion, however, ἐξ ὕδατος is a
later addition that belongs to the redaction of the church, which subsequently wanted to introduce a connection to baptism into this passage. [20]
But is this connection to baptism not present even without this controversial word?

I think the connection with baptism is already quite certain through the
phrase ἄνωθεν γεννηθῆναι (vs. 3), because this expression is obviously
formulated with reference to the terms ἀναγέννησις (I Pet. 1:23) and
παλιγγεννησία (Tit. 3:6), terms which are always designations of baptism
(λουτρον Tit. 3:6 and Justin in Apol. 61, 3f.). Furthermore, the saying
quoted in Jn. 3:3 as the theme for the following discourse also occurs in
Justin Apol. 61, 3f. in a reading that cannot be derived from the Gospel
of John (Ἄν μὴ ἀναγεννηθῆτε, οὐ μὴ εἰσέλθητε εἰς τὴν βασιλείαν τῶν
οὐρανῶν), but which apparently depends on older oral tradition. [21] Justin
uses the saying as a proof for baptism. |

Wherever there is mention of "rebirth" in early Christianity, the idea
of baptism is always present. [22] This connection would have suggested itself
quite naturally and is traditional. It would be present in Jn. 3:3ff. even if
ἐξ ὕδατος were not to appear in 3:5. The saying quoted in Jn. 3:3 apparently
already contains a reference to baptism in any case. Accordingly there is
no reason to assume that the Evangelist could not possibly have also written
ἐξ ὕδατος in 3:5. However, the quest of the Gospel of John is not about
the meaning and significance of the element of the sacrament, but about
the "Mystery of the Son of Man." This title which Bultmann gives to the

---

[19] Das Evangelium des Johannes, p. 98.

[20] *Ibid.*

[21] I refer to the proof offered by W. BOUSSET, a proof which in my opinion is
still valid: Die Evangelienzitate Justins, 1891, pp. 116ff. It is very doubtful anyway
whether Justin knew the Gospel of John. Justin's use of this gospel can in no case be
proved with certainty.

[22] We should also refer to Ps. Clem., Hom. IX 26,2 (ed. REHM, p. 167; cf.
BOUSSET, loc. cit.) where the same saying is quoted in connection with baptism. As
in the case of Justin, here too εἰς τὴν βασιλείαν τῶν οὐρανῶν (Jn.: τοῦ θεοῦ) and
ἀναγεννηθῆναι (Jn. ἄνωθεν γεννᾶσθαι) speak against dependence on John and for
dependence on the free tradition.

section 3:9–21 is very much to the point.[23] It is the Son of Man to whom the community bears witness (3:11: "We bear witness to what we have seen"), i. e. the one who has come down from heaven (3:13). Here, too, the witnessing community only takes its starting point from the sacrament of baptism in order to point back to the Word that has become flesh – to the Jesus of history!

On the basis of the understanding of baptism and eucharist given by Jn. 3 and 6, it is also necessary to interpret the equally controversial passage Jn. 19:34b–35.

Bultmann also tries to solve the difficulty in this passage by a deletion.[24] v. 34b *καὶ ἐξῆλθεν εὐθὺς αἷμα καὶ ὕδωρ* and v. 35 as a whole ("and he who has seen it gave witness, and his testimony is true"), he considers as additions of the church's redactor, who at a later time wanted to tie baptism and eucharist to the cross by means of an eye-witness. Also, vss. 34b–35 interrupt the connection between the piercing of his side (v. 34a) and the quotation of Zech. 12:10 (vs. 36f.) that reflects upon it.

The latter observation is certainly correct. This connection, however, is not typically Johannine. It belongs rather to the narrator whose passion narrative John has used.[25] The Gospel shows that elsewhere also the author of the Gospel of John is accustomed to disrupting a traditional connection, | and what has been brought into this passage appears to me to be typically Johannine. It is questionable, however, whether it is really the purpose of this insertion to authenticate the sacrament through the suffering of Jesus.

With the phrase *αἷμα καὶ ὕδωρ* we have to compare I Jn. 5:7f. *ὕδωρ*, *αἷμα* and *πνεῦμα* as the three witnesses; with *ὁ ἑωρακὼς μεμαρτύρηκεν*:

Jn. 3:11: *ὃ ἑωράκαμεν μαρτυροῦμεν*;

I Jn. 1:2: *καὶ ἑωράκαμεν καὶ μαρτυροῦμεν*;

I Jn. 5:7f.: *τρεῖς εἰσιν οἱ μαρτυροῦντες*.

What is being witnessed here is not the sacrament, but the reality of the historical existence of the Revealer. This is shown by the use of the verb "to witness" in the Gospel and the Epistles of John. For John the concern is not with the sacrament which can be conceived of also apart from the historical reality of salvation. Jesus is not merely the bringer of the water of life (*οὐκ ἐν ὕδατι μόνον*), but he who has come through water *and* blood,

---

[23] Das Evangelium des Johannes, p. 102.

[24] Das Evangelium des Johannes, pp. 525 ff.

[25] M. DIBELIUS has demonstrated this point conclusively: "Die alttestamentlichen Motive in der Leidensgeschichte des Petrus- und Johannesevangeliums" (in: Botschaft und Geschichte, I, pp. 235 f.). Zech. 12:10 must already have been applied to the passion before John and independent of him; cf. Rev. 1:7; Barn. 7:9; etc.

i. e. he who really was and who really suffered. In this way the Evangelist points from the sacramental term back to the reality of history.

The Evangelist is not aiming at sacramental participation anyway, but rather at the recognition that the historical Jesus is the Revealer who brings life. This recognition is given by the πνεῦμα. Therefore the πνεῦμα in I Jn. 5 is the third witness. For this reason, even if Jn. 3:5 first formulates ἐξ ὕδατος καὶ πνεύματος, Jn. 3:8 can say simply ὁ γεγεννημένος ἐκ τοῦ πνεύματος.

Our considerations fully confirm what G. Bornkamm notes with respect to Jn. 19:34f., viz. that John remains quite within the framework of sacramental concepts.[26] John indeed uses such sacramental concepts and terms, but he employs them in such a way as to point back to the history of Jesus. What corresponds to the sentence ὁ λόγος σὰρξ ἐγένετο in the beginning of the Gospel is the remark καὶ ἐξῆλθεν εὐθὺς αἷμα καὶ ὕδωρ in the conclusion of the Johannine passion narrative.

VI. The Church as a Historical Actuality in John

The πνεῦμα bears witness that the Jesus of history is the Revealer; the same πνεῦμα, as the Paraclete, recalls this revelation in the flesh. In | keeping with this "remembering" of the Paraclete, the narrative of the footwashing, Jn. 13:1–17, indicates that the Evangelist wants the church to depart from the understanding that the past presence of Jesus can be simply extended into the present as it is possible in the cult. He refers the church back to the historical "once for all" of Jesus' coming.

The context of the last supper of Jesus is no doubt presupposed in Jn. 13. Any reader of the Gospel in that time had to expect that the institution of the sacramental meal would follow after the entry into Jerusalem. Already in the tradition that Paul uses, the institution of the eucharist by the Lord is placed in the context of the last supper (I Cor. 11:23). Thus, the author of John must have known what it meant that the institution of the sacrament was *not* reported at this point.

Obviously the Evangelist consciously avoids making the last meal of Jesus a legend that institutes a cult. In the Fourth Gospel the service of the historical Jesus takes the place of the institution of the sacrament. This is emphasized in two respects:

Firstly, through the singularity of the service. He who is washed is pure and needs no further washing (Jn. 13:10). This feature probably was already part of the source which John uses here and which polemicized against repeated washings as were practiced, e.g., among the Essenes.

---

[26] G. BORNKAMM, "Das Anathema in der urchristlichen Abendmahlsliturgie" (in: Das Ende des Gesetzes. Paulusstudien, Munich, 1952), pp. 128f.

According to the intention of the Evangelist, however, the concern is not to justify the unrepeatable act of baptism, but to emphasize the "once and for all" of the historical ministry of Jesus. For what takes place in the footwashing is, to be sure, not the institution of the sacrament of baptism, but is the symbolization of the service which Jesus does to those who belong to him.

Secondly, at the same time this service establishes, in a non-sacramental fashion, the new existence of the church and the unity thereby effected. That is what the second interpretation which the Evangelist adds to the footwashing, vss. 12–17, says: "I have given you an example in order that you do to each other as I have done to you." Divorced from the symbolization through the footwashing, the same thing is said in Jn. 13:34: "That you love one another as I have loved you, in order that you also love one another." It is this love in which the unity of the church as the disciples of Jesus is founded: "By this all men will know that you are my disciples, if you have love for one another."

The scene of the designation of the traitor which follows the footwashing (Jn. 13:18ff.) is also intended to avert a sacramental interpretation. Closely associated with the disavowal of the sacramental communion is the repudiation of misconceived effects of the sacrament. | The service of Jesus is valid even for the traitor. The notion that this service might have results which come about by way of magic necessity is thereby explicitly excluded. The remark at the conclusion of the discourse on the bread from heaven has to be interpreted accordingly: "My words are life and are spirit; but there are some who do not believe; for Jesus knew from the beginning who would betray him" (Jn. 6:64f., 70f.).

Thus, according to the Evangelist, there is no guarantee for the unity and for the purity of the church. Even the sacrament cannot give this guarantee. There are only words and commands of Jesus with which the church is confronted time and again, which are "remembered" to the church, and which call the church to the service of love.

These statements of Jn. 13 are further developed in Jn. 15.[27] The myth of the tree of life probably provides the background for the discourse of the true vine in Jn. 15.[28] The fact, however, that this tree of life is not conceived of as an olive tree, or as an ash or pine or any other plant,[29] but precisely as a vine, perhaps points again to a cultic background.

One of the reasons for this assumption is the occurrence of the vine in the eucharistic prayers in Did. 9:2: "We praise you for the holy vine of David which you have made known to us through Jesus, your servant."

---

[27] I am inclined to agree here with R. BULTMANN who places chapter 15 immediately after 13:31–34 (Das Evangelium des Johannes, pp. 249f. and 401ff.).

[28] E. SCHWEITZER, EGO EIMI, Göttingen, 1939, pp. 39ff.

[29] R. BULTMANN, Das Evangelium des Johannes, p. 407 n. 6.

Secondly, the image of the vine elucidates the unity of the disciples among themselves and with Jesus. Elsewhere, however, this concept belongs to the eucharist (I Cor. 10, also 11; cf. Did. 9:4; furthermore Ignatius, see below). Thirdly, the χαρά (Jn. 15:11 *et passim*) also belongs to the context of the concepts associated with the Eucharist.

Through his use of this image, however, the Evangelist does not elucidate the sacramental unity, but rather the unity in the word and in love which has its basis in the love of this man Jesus and in his word. Jn. 15:7: "If you remain in me, my words also will remain among you." 15:10: "If you keep my commandments, you will remain in my love, because I have kept my Father's commandments and remain in his love." It is on account of this historical work in which the Son is united with the Father that the church lives in love, which is the historical unity of the church's work with Jesus, with his word and his service. Thus, obedience to the word and acting in this love, these two constitute the unity of the church. |

VII. The Cultic Unity of the Church in Ignatius

If in conclusion we look back once more at Ignatius, there emerges a quite different picture.

Here the unity is already arranged beforehand in the one and only Christ, who as the one and only bread, both bodily and spiritually, is always present as the foundation of the church. His existence is focused upon, not in terms of history but in terms of metaphysics. This by no means excludes the fact that the church is addressed in the imperative mode, just as it also includes the aspiration of the martyr to imitate in his own fate the fate of the Redeemer in order to achieve the final perfection of this unity. The road of the martyr, however, remains an "exceptional case." What is true for the martyr is not at the same time a demand directed to all Christians. These, nevertheless, have all reached perfection in the unity of the church, when they gather together with one mind in obedience to the bishop, in one faith, one prayer, one hope, and at one altar, to break one bread which is the medicine of immortality (Eph. 20:2; Magn. 7:1–2; Philad. 4 *et passim*).

This unity of the church is the presupposition for everything else. It is guaranteed solely through community with the bishop. He who does anything without the bishop is serving the devil (Smyrn. 9:1). Only he who is within the boundaries of the realm of the altar is "pure," i. e. in unity with the bishop and the board of presbyters (Trall. 7:2). How differently purity is defined in John! According to Ignatius, it is on the basis of this unity that love comes into existence (Magn. 6:2), and not the other way around.

With this sacramental unity all attacks of Satan are in vain. If gatherings of the congregation are held frequently, all attacks of Satan fail because of this unity of faith (Eph. 13:1). Heretics are those who stay away from the eucharist and from prayer (Smyrn. 7:1).

For Ignatius this argument is quite consistent and authentic; for it concerns people who do not confess that Christ has come in the flesh, that is to say, who therefore would have no interest in the cultic documentation of the flesh of Christ. Thus, for Ignatius also, what continues to be the criterion for heresy is christology, and by no means a self-appointed concept of unity with the bishop.

This, however, should not be allowed to mislead us. Actually, if Ignatius holds onto the concept that Jesus was in the flesh, he is holding onto something quite different from what the author of the Gospel of John expounds as the content of the statement that Jesus came in the flesh. To be sure, the terminology and | history-of-religions motifs of John and Ignatius are closely related; antidocetism is also common to both authors. But in John it is the once and for all historical event which is placed against docetism; in Ignatius, however, it is the supra-historical Henosis of flesh and spirit, understood in terms of metaphysics, extended into the sacrament, as Christ is truly in the flesh even after his resurrection and is not a "bodiless demon" (Smyrn. 3).[30] John also maintains, to be sure, that Christ is in the flesh after the resurrection, but he places such an emphasis side by side with the sentence: "Blessed are those who do not see and yet believe!" (Jn. 20:29). He is thus taking seriously the historical distance of the believing church from the Jesus of history, and he solely trusts the word which alone is capable of making past history present. Of this historical distance Ignatius is quite unaware, because to begin with, he understands the event of salvation in terms of metaphysics rather than in terms of history.

If the sacrament is thus understood in metaphysical terms as a *Christus prolongatus*, the cult as such gains ultimate significance, and with it also the bishop who demands obedience. As a consequence, the only possibility that remains is the service of the altar and submission. Faith and love are only a subsequent effect. Ignatius has thereby sacrificed everything that constitutes the essence of a historical revelation, i. e. the knowledge that there is a claim of Jesus on my history and that there is a ministry of the history of Jesus for my sake which constitutes my own existence in history. Only in the way in which John understands it is Christian existence able to remain an existence of obedience to the word and of the service of love. Only if understood as the appeal to the historical service of the Jesus of history can the cult represent the demand of a historical act of salvation.

---

[30] With respect to the difference in terms of history-of-religions perspectives it is necessary to point out that John's dualistic concept of realms has been replaced in Ignatius by a metaphysical concept that thinks in terms of substances.

Comments on the History of the Symbol of the Cross [*]

by

Erich Dinkler [1]

Translated by Gerhard Krodel

"Christianity grew up under the protection of the Jewish religion." This casual remark by Tertullian has been confirmed by historical criticism, even if the problem of how far this late Jewish religion had already been infiltrated by hellenistic syncretism is not hereby touched upon. Primitive Christianity, including its | earliest literature, stands at first not so much in opposition to Judaism, but rather shows itself to be a strongly competing confession, a sect, within the late Jewish tradition. Jesus' own work still took place within these bounds and even when he directs his sharp criticism against the degeneration of ritualism into mere customary formalism, he still remains within the frame of the radicalism possible within the Jewish prophetic tradition. [2] Even though in Jesus' own proclamation there is already an unmistakable universalistic tendency which rends all nationalistic bounds and which later became the factor that triggered the world-wide apostolic mission, nevertheless, on account of this we may not overlook the continuity of structures, of expressions, concepts and images, or even deny them on dogmatic grounds. It is indeed difficult to keep the proper balance and neither to minimize that which is new in Christianity by emphasizing the continuity with Judaism, nor, for apologetic reasons, to project the break with Judaism which later became plain back into the time of Jesus. This difficulty imposes itself upon every scholar in every period and its reasons lie not only in the pre-understanding, the pre-judgment, which each scholar always already has, but also in the fragmentary character of our sources. Therefore it is not surprising that all new discoveries, such as the Dead Sea Scrolls, produce difficulties because they do not fit so easily into the accustomed picture of that time. [3]

[*] "Zur Geschichte des Kreuzsymbols," ZThK, 48, 1951, pp. 148–172.
[1] The following article, written in honor of FRIEDRICH MATZ, archaeologist in Marburg, for the occasion of his sixtieth birthday, was presented to him in an unpublished "Festschrift" by friends and pupils.
[2] Cf. R. BULTMANN, *Primitive Christianity in its Contemporary Setting*, New York, 1956, pp. 71 ff.
[3] Cf. K. G. KUHN, ZThK, 47, 1950, pp. 192 ff.; M. BURROWS, *The Dead Sea Scrolls of St. Mark's Monastery*, New Haven, 1951, vol. II, fasc. 2.

Tertullian's above-quoted thesis, no matter how much it must be restricted or qualified, does not only have general historical validity. It also applies more and more to the area of primitive Christian art, a field which thus far has been investigated with respect to its relationship to the period of late non-Jewish antiquity. Now, however, the inner connection of primitive Christian art to Jewish art has become a real problem since the discovery of the synagogue in Dura-Europos.[4] The "dogma" of the Jewish indifference and hostility to art has finally been shattered, especially since it may be regarded as proven that the frescos of the Dura synagogue from the middle of the third century A. D. were not original creations, but incorporate a Jewish iconographic tradition which probably had its beginnings in Alexandria.[5] These conclusions can still be easily accepted | since the whole matter merely concerns Bible illustrations on the walls of a sanctuary, pictures which in themselves have kerygmatic character by proclaiming the holy history of the Jewish people. Much more revolutionary, however, is the evidence that in spite of the law and in spite of rabbinic tradition, Judaism employed pagan pictures and pagan symbols, the influence of which we have reluctantly become accustomed to acknowledging in early Christian art, but which had been regarded as being impossible in Jewish art.[6] Now the possibility has arisen that the syncretistic features of pagan symbols and mythology in early Christian art should be explained not merely on the basis of a direct transfer from hellenistic art, but rather on the basis of a hellenized Jewish art – or at least both sources should be taken into account. Indeed, it appears that we are only becoming fully conscious of the world-wide historical role which Jewish art, until recently unknown, has played, not least of all through its influence upon early Christian and thus medieval art.[7] It is inevitable that in such a revision of accepted notions, some monuments will receive a different interpretation.

At the center of this essay we want to place a Jewish ossuary find published by E. L. Sukenik in 1947.[8] Under the title "The Earliest Records

[4] Cf. Du Mesnil Du Buisson, *Les Peintures de la Synagogue de Doura Europos,* Rome, 1939; R. Wischnitzer, *The Messianic Theme in the Paintings of the Dura Synagogue,* Chicago, 1948.

[5] K. Weitzmann, *American Journal of Archeology,* 51, 1947, pp. 394f.

[6] E. R. Goodenough, "The Crown of Victory in Judaism," *The Art Bulletin,* 28, 1946, pp. 139 ff.

[7] Of special importance is the work of the scholars in Princeton on the LXX illustrations. Cf. K. Weitzmann, *Illustration in Roll and Codex,* Princeton, 1947. Idem, *The Joshua Roll,* Princeton, 1948. A good selection of old Jewish art is now offered by: A. Reifenberg, *Ancient Hebrew Arts,* New York, 1950.

[8] E. L. Sukenik, "The Earliest Records of Christianity," *American Journal of Archeology* (= AJA), 51, 1947, pp. 351 ff. A first critical appraisal of the find was given by C. H. Kraeling in: *Biblical Archaeologist,* 9, 1946, pp. 16 ff. – Unfortunately an article quoted in AJA, 53, 1949, was inaccessible to me. It was published by Bo Reicke in: *Svenska Jerusalems Föreningens Tidskrift,* 43, 1949, pp. 2–14. In it

of Christianity," he described an excavation about one mile and a quarter south of Jerusalem on the road to Bethlehem, near the suburb of Talpioth, where, during construction work, a Jewish burial chamber with some interesting ossuaries was discovered. Among these ossuaries are two with Jesus inscriptions, and one of them even bears a large cross on each of its four sides. It is Sukenik's opinion that the two Jesus inscriptions are acclamations to Jesus and that the crosses are to be understood as Christian signs. The family | chamber tomb in Talpioth therefore might reflect the transition of a Jewish family to Christianity. In the following pages I hope to show that this "earliest monument of Christianity" is a *Jewish* and not a Christian monument, and that *the sign of the cross has its home in Judaism* and can be found repeatedly, especially on ossuaries and tomb inscriptions. We begin first of all with the report of the find.

I. The Ossuaries at Talpioth near Jerusalem

During construction work in the autumn of 1945 a burial chamber was discovered which, measuring 3.36 meters by 3.42 meters, is almost square. Its average height is 1.14 meters. In this chamber, hewn into limestone, there runs from the entrance a trench, 0.70 meters to 0.80 meters in depth, 1.14 meters in width and 2.15 meters in length, so that one can stand upright in it. Along the three sides of the trench are benches on which the dead could be placed during the process of burial. Into the walls of the main chamber five loculi, vaults, are hewn. They are between 2.40 meters and 2.60 meters deep, average a width of 0.50 meters and a height of 0.73 meters.[9] This type of grave has many parallels in the

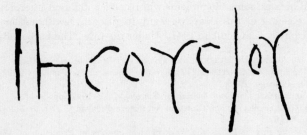

Illustration 1: Talpioth near Jerusalem –
Ossuary inscription *IHCOYC IOY*

Reicke states that he regards ιου and αλωθ as "proper names." – [The first century Jewish ossuaries around Jerusalem are small chests which received the bones of the dead one year after the original burial. Their approximate measurements are 0.50 meters long, 0.25 meters wide, 0.30 meters high. Translator's note].

  [9] Further differentiations are intentionally foregone.

necropolis of Jerusalem.[10] In the chamber tomb of Talpioth a total of fourteen ossuaries were found. They stood partially still *in situ* when Sukenik entered the excavation site, even though the chamber had been broken into earlier and partially searched. Among these ossuaries, also made of limestone, several bear inscriptions in Aramaic and Greek script. The following inscriptions are recorded:[11]

1) שמעין בר סבא Simeon Barsaba
2) מרים ברת שמעון Miriam daughter of Simeon
3) $I\eta\sigma o\nu\varsigma$ $\iota o\nu$ (Cf. Illustration 1)
4) $I\eta\sigma o\nu\varsigma$ $\alpha\lambda\omega\vartheta$ (Cf. Illustration 2)
5) מתי abbreviation for מתתיה = Mattathias

The fourth inscription is on the narrow side of the ossuary. This ossuary

Illustration 2: Talpioth near Jerusalem –
Ossuary inscription $IH\Sigma OY\Sigma$ $A\Lambda\Omega\Theta$

bears on all of its four sides a cross with four equal arms (See illustration 3) drawn in charcoal and still clearly recognizable. In this case a later addition of the cross is well-nigh impossible because the loculus containing the ossuaries with inscriptions 3 and 4 had not been disturbed in earlier times. The finding of a coin in the burial chamber gives us the year 42–43 A. D. as *terminus post quem* of the latest burial. Stylistic comparisons of the remaining ossuaries which bear the well-known and often found rosette ornament, | as well as the pottery finds (jars and lamps), make the period from 50 B. C. to 50 A. D. probable for all the remains found here.[12] Under no circumstances is Sukenik willing to go beyond the first half of the first century A. D. Interpreting the Jesus inscriptions as acclamations to Jesus and the sign of the cross as the oldest Christian sign Sukenik reaches the conclusion, "All our evidence indicates that we have in this tomb the

---

[10] Cf. K. GALLING, *Palästina–Jahrbuch*, 32, 1936. *Idem*, article "Grab" in: *Biblisches Reallexikon*, Tübingen, 1937, cols. 237 ff.

[11] The reading of inscriptions Nos. 1 and 5 is uncertain. Cf. SUKENIK, (note 8), pp. 357 f.

[12] Cf. E. L. SUKENIK, *Archäologischer Anzeiger*, (Berlin), 46, 1931, pp. 309 ff.

earliest records of Christianity in existence. It may also have a bearing on
the historicity of Jesus and the crucifixion" (op. cit. [above, n. 8] p. 365).

Illustration 3: Talpioth near Jerusalem –
Ossuary front view with sign of a cross

Before we enter into detail and examine the basis of Sukenik's thesis, it
should be recalled that as early as 1873 a similar discovery was made in
Jerusalem on the Mount of Olives.[13] At that time the French scholar Clermont-Ganneau wrote in a letter, "Some inscriptions, not only Greek, but
also Hebrew are accompanied by crosses which leave no doubt as to the
religion of those people whose bones rested here." Indeed, it was a coincidence that the ossuary inscriptions of that grave situated on the road to
Bethany bore the names of Lazarus, Simon, and Martha, among others,
names which in the Gospel story are connected with Bethany.[14] With
respect to the Jesus inscriptions one recalls the ossuary inscription, "Jesus,
son of Joseph,"[15] which was brought to light in 1931 in Berlin by Sukenik
and which at that time was taken up by newspaper bureaus, rather than by
theologians, and misinterpreted.

Since the interpretation of the finds at Talpioth is based essentially upon
the understanding of the Jesus inscriptions, we will begin with them.

---

[13] We follow the suggestion of C. H. KRAELING, (n. 8), pp. 16ff.

[14] Published in: *Palestine Exploration Fund, Quarterly Statement*, IV, 1873, pp. 7–10.
A facsimile of all finds is given by C. CLERMONT-GANNEAU, *Archaeological Researches
in Palestine*, London, I, 1899, pp. 381ff.

[15] A good reproduction is found in: REIFENBERG, (n. 7), p. 65. The most detailed
investigation of the inscription is given by: L. H. VINCENT, *Rendiconti, Atti della
Pontificia Accademia Romana di Archeologia*, VII, 1932, pp. 215ff.

II. The Jesus Inscriptions

Some of the inscriptions which are preserved on the ossuaries of Talpioth have been scratched into the limestone with a sharp object, others are merely drawn with charcoal. Aramaic and Greek inscriptions in undoubtedly Jewish graves occur quite frequently and even | bi-lingual inscriptions are often preserved.[16] Among those inscriptions which interest us most, the one reading $I\eta\sigma\sigma\nu\varsigma$ $\iota\sigma\nu$ is apparently drawn with charcoal, while the one reading $I\eta\sigma\sigma\nu\varsigma$ $\alpha\lambda\omega\vartheta$ is incised into the ossuary. What is the significance of these two graffiti?

The personal name $I\eta\sigma\sigma\nu\varsigma$ is the Greek form of יֵשׁוּעַ = Jeshua,[17] which is the shortened form, customarily used after the exile, of יְהוֹשֻׁעַ = Jehoshuah or Joshua. The number of persons known to have borne this name during the period of the first century B. C. and the first century A. D. is quite large. Josephus alone mentions approximately twenty of them, of which no less than ten belong to the time of Jesus of Nazareth.[18] So far we can say with certainty that six ossuary inscriptions have the name Jesus.[19] The widespread usage of this name in the diaspora is shown by the papyri.[20] These references are sufficient to conclude that Jesus was a name frequently used. Of course, one can see that through the veneration of Jesus of Nazareth as Christ this personal name became more and more a sacral name and was therefore avoided as a given name in Judaism and Christianity alike. Because of Judaism's reaction against the Church, the name Jesus here became unacceptable, while Christianity's reverence for the holiness of Jesus Christ caused his name to become a *nomen sacrum*.[21]

The name Jesus, as such, occurs so frequently that its mere occurrence cannot be regarded as a reference to one special person in history. Thus everything depends on the interpretation of the two words $\alpha\lambda\omega\vartheta$ and $\iota\sigma\nu$ which are connected with $I\eta\sigma\sigma\nu\varsigma$ in the ossuary inscriptions. The reading of $\alpha\lambda\omega\vartheta$ and $\iota\sigma\nu$ is absolutely certain. If we look first at the other inscriptions

---

[16] Cf. S. KLEIN, *Jüdisch-Palaestinisches Corpus Inscriptionum*, Berlin, 1920, pp. 8 ff.

[17] Cf. A. DEISSMANN in: *Mysterium Christi*, ed. by G. K. A. BELL and A. DEISSMANN, London, 1930, pp. 13 ff. Also, W. FOERSTER, article 'Ἰησοῦς in: *Theologisches Wörterbuch zum Neuen Testament*, Stuttgart: Kohlhammer, vol. III, 1938, pp. 284 ff. Also, F. VIGOUREUX, *Dictionnaire de la Bible*, vol. III, cols. 1422 ff., and its supplement in vol. IV, cols. 966 ff.

[18] Cf. DEISSMANN, (n. 17), p. 19.

[19] Cf. the information of VINCENT, (n. 15), pp. 221 f., and FOERSTER, (n. 17), pp. 285 f. – Furthermore see the list of note 29.

[20] Cf. F. PREISIGKE, *Namenbuch*, Heidelberg, 1922. For 'Ἰάσων see col. 146; for 'Ἰησοῦς col. 148.

[21] DEISSMANN, (n. 17), pp. 15 ff., following TH. ZAHN, *Einleitung in das Neue Testament*, vol. I, Leipzig, 1906, p. 321, illustrated this development in the transmission of the New Testament text itself.

found in the grave chambers of Talpioth, it becomes plain that the names
of the dead buried in the ossuaries are inscribed. This is the normal custom
as it is also known to us from the necropolis of Jerusalem.

The word αλωϑ is difficult. Sukenik points out that in the Hebrew text of
the Song of Solomon (4: 14) we find the | word אהלות which is translated in
the Septuagint with αλωϑ, and designates the aloes plant. Sukenik excludes
the possibility of a transference of the plant name as a "nickname" for people
– something which was occasionally done. Had this been the case here,
Sukenik would have expected the customary Greek form of the word,
namely, ἀλόη and not αλωϑ. With great reservations he offers as a tentative
solution the interpretation that the word αλωϑ might perhaps have its root
in the Hebrew or Aramaic אלה, which among other things can mean
"wail."[22] In this way, he thinks it possible to regard αλωϑ as an expression
of sorrow and grief.

However, this interpretation is supported by and even based upon his
translation of the inscription Ιησους ιου. Sukenik proceeds by stating that
he could not find a personal name corresponding to ιου which would
signify the father of the Jesus buried here.[23] He therefore refers to the
Greek interjection ἰού, which in classical Greek, however, is found only in
repetition.[24] The interjection ἰού ἰού is known as an exclamation of pain –
ouch, ouch! or woe, woe! – but it is also known as an exclamation of
surprise. Sukenik believes that the single occurrence of this word can be
explained by a "diagonal stroke to the right (which) may have been intended to indicate the repetition of the word" (op. cit., p. 363). He therefore
suggests the translation "Jesus – woe," in the sense of an exclamation of
sorrow. It is an acclamation which is directed to *the* Jesus, Jesus of Nazareth.
This interpretation, of course, determines to a large extent his understanding of αλωϑ. Both ossuary inscriptions are regarded by Sukenik as the oldest
known archaeological evidence of Christianity.

However, objections which render this interpretation invalid can be
brought forth. For the decisive words αλωϑ and ιου can be explained as
personal names and are verifiable as such. Αλωϑ is substantiated through
a papyrus of Fayum from 158 A. D. in which an *Aloth* received a customs
receipt for his camel caravan at the gateway to Dionysias.[25] If αλωϑ is

---

[22] Cf. L. KOEHLER, *Lexicon in Veteris Testamenti Libros*, Leiden, 1951, vol.
I, p. 49.

[23] SUKENIK, (n. 8), p. 363, wrote, "If this inscription recorded the name of the
person buried in the ossuary, we should expect after the name of Jesus the name of
the father, but I cannot find any name corresponding to the form *IOY*."

[24] E.g. Plato, *Gorgias*, 499b: ἰού ἰού, ὦ Καλλίκλεις, ὡς πανοῦργος εἶ. Further
examples in LIDDELL-SCOTT, *Greek-English Lexicon*, Oxford, 9 th. edition, 1940,
vol. I, p. 832.

verified beyond doubt as a name, then nothing hinders the acknowledg-
ment of this word as a name also in the Talpioth inscription. | Thus we
reach the normal and easiest reading, namely that the buried man was
Jesus, Son of Aloth, and we have escaped the philological difficulty, also
sufficiently emphasized by Sukenik, of taking the word back to the root
of אלה.

But ιου also is verifiable as a personal name, since we may regard it as
the genetive of 'Ιάς, a name found in an Egyptian papyrus [26] of the fourth
century A. D., which speaks of a 'Ιὰς Σιλβανοῦ. Littmann, with reservations, refers this word to the Hebrew name Ḥijā.[27] For this identification we have an Aramaic-Greek inscription which confirms this equation [28]
and makes it clear beyond doubt that our inscription refers to *Jesus, Son of
Eias*, buried in this ossuary.

Even though we have only one example for Aloth and two for Eias or
Ias as names, they are methodologically sufficient, since through them we
merely confirm the *normal* interpretation of these inscriptions as referring
to the name of the dead buried in the ossuary. Thus any possibility of a
reference to Jesus of Nazareth in these inscriptions must be discarded.
Since two persons with the name Jesus were buried in the same loculus, it
is very likely that they were grandfather and grandson, for, as Sukenik
emphasized, usually members of *one* family were buried in such a chamber
tomb.

Our *result so far* is that the Jesus inscriptions of Talpioth contain the
names of those buried in the ossuaries. A reference to Jesus of Nazareth
does not exist. These inscriptions add to the number of the known Jesus
inscriptions on ossuaries.[29]

---

[25] PREISIGKE, (n. 20), col. 21, refers to GRENFELL-HUNT-HOGARTH, *Fayum Towns
and Their Papyri*, London, 1900. The text of papyrus 68, printed on p. 200, reads,
τετέλ⟨εσται⟩ δι⟨ὰ⟩ πύλ⟨ης⟩ Διονυ⟨σιάδος⟩ ἐρη⟨μοφυλακίας⟩ Αλωθ⟨ις⟩ ἐξ⟨άγων⟩
εἰς Βυστ⟨   ⟩ καμ⟨ήλους⟩ τέσσαρες... ⟨δραχμὰς⟩ ὀκτώ... followed by the
date. The restorations are indicated by ⟨   ⟩.

[26] PREISIGKE, (n. 20), col. 146, refers to G. VITELLI, *Papiri Fiorentini*, Milan,
vol. I, 1906, 71, 273.

[27] E. LITTMANN in the appendix to PREISIGKE, (n. 20), col. 522.

[28] Cf. M. LIDZBARSKI, *Ephemeris für Semitische Epigraphik*, I, Gießen: A. Toepel-
mann, 1902, p. 189, where we read, הייא בן אלעזר   EIAC YIOC ΛAZAPOY (also
found in: KLEIN [n. 16], p. 42f., No. 117).

[29] Making use of information supplied by VINCENT, (n. 15), pp. 221 f., and FOERSTER,
(n. 17), pp. 285f., on the occurrence of the name Jesus on ossuaries, I am able to
compile the following list:

a) ישוע בר מתי Jesus son of Mattai. Place of find: southwest part of Jerusalem.
CLERMONT-GANNEAU, *Archives des Mss. scientif. et littér.* IIIᵉ serie XI, 1884, p. 99,
No. 26; The same inscription in: KLEIN, (n. 16), p. 24, No. 45.

| III. The Cross Markings

Has it then already been proved that the crosses on the ossuaries also have no relation to the Christian faith? By no means – they *could* still be the first appearances of the Christian sign or symbol in a Jewish family which was converted to Christianity. However, this meaning would have to be established by the presence of similar signs of crosses in definitely Christian monuments. For the present the question remains open as to whether one should then speak of the cross as a symbol, or as Sukenik does of a presymbolic sign which expresses no more than, "He was crucified."[30]

According to the dating proposed by Sukenik, the chamber tomb of Talpioth was in use from the first century B. C. till 50 A. D. He places the Jesus inscriptions and crosses at the end of this period. If this thesis could be proven it would indeed be gratifying for New Testament scholarship to have an inscribed monument witnessing to a pre-Pauline *theologia crucis*, no matter how this would have to be qualified. It would also be revolutionary for Christian archaeology. For, until now, in the field of archaeology it has been an absolute dogma that the symbol of the cross makes its first appearance in the age of Constantine,[31] and that this appearance is directly connected with the finding of the relic of the cross ascribed to the Empress Mother Helena.[32] Does this common opinion now | have to be corrected by taking cognizance of the fact that the sign of the cross was already

---

b) שמעון בר ישוע Simeon son of Jesus. Place of find: southwest part of Jerusalem. CLERMONT-GANNEAU, *Archaeological Researches in Palestine*, (n. 14), I, 1899, p. 394, No. 5; KLEIN, p. 27, No. 67.

c) ישוע Jesus. Place of find: Jerusalem. CLERMONT-GANNEAU, *Archaeological Researches*, p. 437, No. 1; KLEIN, p. 24, No. 44.

d) Ιεσους Ιεσους. Place of find as in b. CLERMONT-GANNEAU, Archaeological Researches, p. 409, No. 22; KLEIN, p. 24, No. 46; Cf. DEISSMANN, (n. 17), pp. 18f.

e) *IHCOYC* Place of find: north of Jerusalem. *Revue Bibl.*, 22, 1913, p. 270, No. 11

f) ישוע בר יהוסף Jesus son of Joseph. Place of find unknown. VINCENT (n. 15), p. 221.

g) ישו Jesus. Place of find unknown. SUKENIK, *Jüdische Gräber in Jerusalem um Christi Geburt*, 1931, p. 19.

h) *IHCOYC ΑΛΩΘ* Jesus Aloth. Place of find: south of Jerusalem. SUKENIK, AJA 51, 1947 (n. 8), p. 358, No. 4.

i) *IHCOYC IOY* Jesus Iou. Place of find: same as h. SUKENIK, *ibid.*, p. 358, No. 3.

[30] SUKENIK, *ibid.*, p. 365.

[31] Cf. G. DE JERPHANION, *Orientalia Christiana Periodica*, 7, 1941, p. 17. He writes, "It is indeed known that historians and theologians as well as archaeologists affirm that the representation and above all the veneration of the cross had not been introduced among Christians until a relatively late period – probably not before Constantine..." The same view is expressed by M. SULZBERGER, *Byzantion*, 2, 1925, p. 386.

[32] Cf. E. SCHÄFER, "Die Heiligen mit dem Kreuz in der altchristlichen Kunst," *Römische Quartalschrift*, 44, 1936, p. 48. For the legend itself see J. STRAUBINGER, *Die Kreuzauffindungslegende* (Forschungen zur christlichen Literatur- und Dogmengeschichte XI, 3), Paderborn, 1912.

affixed to graves of Christians prior to the time of the Pauline epistles?
Would this sign then have fallen again into oblivion, or would it have been
eradicated as a "pagan custom" only to make its resurgence again during
the age of Constantine? Why, among the paintings of the catacombs of the
third century, can no sign of the cross be found? Why does it not appear
until late in the fourth century? Are these views of Christian archaeology
merely constructions, *argumenta e silentio?*

For a time it indeed appeared that we would have basically to rethink
this matter. The *'Cross of Herculaneum'* which, after its excavation in
1938 in the so-called Casa del Bicentenario, was interpreted[33] as a Christian
symbol of the middle of the first century A. D. gave such an impression,
and Sukenik too makes use of it in support of his thesis that in the ossuaries
of Talpioth we have archaeological evidence of primitive Christianity.[34]
The so-called *'Cross of Herculaneum'* concerns a find which has been

Illustration 4: Herculaneum –
Stucco surface with a cross formed recess and nail markings

[33] A. MAIURI, "La Croce di Ercolano," *Rendiconti, Atti della Pontificia Accademia
Romana di Archeologia*, XV, 1939, pp. 193 ff.
[34] Cf. SUKENIK, (n. 8), pp. 364 f.

repeatedly debated in the meantime (See Fig. 4). In the upper floor of an ancient house, | opposite the entrance at head height, a stucco surface measuring approximately 0.65 by 0.82 meters was found and in it a recess which was thought to have been inlaid with a cross in Latin form. A piece of furniture in this room which is more like a small cabinet than a table and in which dice were found was interpreted as being a τράπεζα and the room was thought to be an early Christian sanctuary[35] with the symbol of the cross. However, a more detailed examination of the stucco surface and its cross-formed recess speaks against the presence of a liturgical cross. First of all, the measurements of the horizontal arms are unequal. Secondly, on the vertical bar the top piece does not run in a straight extension from the base. Furthermore, the different nail imprints on the stucco also indicate that the recess was rather used for a practical object. Probably a wall cabinet was once anchored in the recess on the wall.[36] Since the investigation of De Bruyne the 'Cross of Herculaneum' can no longer be considered a cross. With this, however, any support for an earlier dating of the cross used as a sign, emblem, or symbol by Christians has been removed. We have no other archaeological evidence from the first or second centuries of a cross which had definitely been made by Christians permitting us to interpret other signs of crosses of that period as Christian crosses. This means that also the cross markings on the ossuaries of Talpioth cannot be related to the crucifixion of Christ.

But then, what other explanation can be given for these signs? Sukenik rightly recalls the observations of Clermont-Ganneau, which, in Sukenik's opinion, had not received sufficient attention.[37] Clermont-Ganneau in the fall of 1873 inspected the burial chamber of a Jewish family, made notes about more than thirty ossuaries and copies of inscriptions. On four ossuaries he noted the presence of a sign of a cross[38] and already then posed the question of whether the chronology of Christian archaeology should not be basically revised.[39]

However, the number of such cross-signs on Jewish monuments is so large as to void the thesis that every cross | is either purely ornamental or an evidence of a conversion to Christianity. On the basis of the monuments, we must rather reckon with *Jewish cross signs* and seriously pursue this problem.

---

[35] MAIURI, (n. 33), p. 217. Cf. the report of H. FUHRMANN, *Archäologischer Anzeiger*, 55, 1940, pp. 504 ff.

[36] For a critique of MAIURI's statements see the detailed essay of G. DE JERPHANION, "La Croix d'Herculaneum?" *Orientalia Christiana Periodica*, 7, 1941, pp. 5 ff., and also L. DE BRUYNE, "La 'crux interpretum' di Ercolano," *Rivista di Archeologia Christiana*, 21, 1945, pp. 281 ff.

[37] SUKENIK, (n. 8), pp. 359 ff. Prior to SUKENIK with reference to the Talpioth find KRAELING, (n. 8), p. 18.

[38] CLERMONT-GANNEAU, (n. 29b), pp. 381 ff.   [39] *Ibid.*, p. 404.

An examination of the published material on Jewish inscriptions and ossuaries is subject to the difficulty that, with the exception of those investigated by Clermont-Ganneau, the crosses which may have been present were generally not carefully noted and that often on photogaphs the inscriptions were retouched but not the crosses which were regarded as insignificant. Nevertheless the monuments are sufficient for us to gain a clear picture. In the following we will give only a few examples of a larger stock of available material.[40]

1. Jerusalem, Nicanor Ossuary with bi-lingual inscription on the narrow side and reclining cross scratched in. Cf. Clermont-Ganneau, Recueil d'archéologie orientale, 5, 1902, pp. 334ff., and Illustration Plate VII; furthermore: Palestine Exploration Fund, Quarterly Statement, 1903, p. 125, with illustration. For the inscription see S. Klein (above, n. 16), pp. 17f., 89.

2. Jerusalem, Collection Notre Dame de France, ossuary with inscription יהודה on the front side and under it apparently by the same hand an incised standing equilateral cross. Cf. facsimile in Clermont-Ganneau, Archaeological Researches in Palestine, Vol. I, 1899, p. 403, No. 11. Sukenik (AJA 51, 1947, p. 361) does not exclude the possibility that the cross was added later, but gives no reason for this assumption.

3. Jerusalem, like No. 2 found on the Mount of Olives; its present location unknown; ossuary with inscription Ιεσους Ιεσους. In front of this inscription is a cross with the vertical arm slanting down to the right side. Facsimile in Clermont-Ganneau, Archeological Researches in Palestine, Vol. I, 1899, p. 409, No. 22.

4. Jerusalem, ossuary with Hebrew inscription 'Jesus, Son of Joseph.' In the center of the front side between two ornamental rosettes is a standing cross roughly scratched in. Illustration by Vincent (above, n. 15), p. 225.

5. Jerusalem, Nicanor tomb, presence of a cross on two entrances to burial chambers.[41] A photograph | is unknown to me. Cf. the report of the

---

[40] I intend to present the whole body of material in a book about the history of the symbol of the cross and I hope that by then I shall have gained clarity about those monuments which are still doubtful on the basis of their photographs or facsimiles. The beginnings of the Christian symbol of the cross will then be treated by taking archaeological and literary sources into consideration.

[41] Cf. L. H. VINCENT about similar cross markings on Jewish tombs, Revue Biblique, 8, 1899, p. 303. He too interprets these crosses as being later additions made by Christians. Cf. H. INGHOLT, "Inscriptions and sculptures from Palmyra II," in: Berytus 5, 1938, pp. 106ff.; also plates XL, 1 and 2. For Palmyra cf. furthermore the inscription published by DE VOGÜÉ, Syrie Centrale, Inscriptions Semitiques, 1868, p. 55, No. 76. These inscriptions of Palmyra are beyond doubt neither Jewish nor Christian. They were on hellenistic-aramaic tombs. However in my opinion it is not impossible that older Jewish cross signs survived and continued to be used here as apotropaic signs.

find: G. Dicksen, Palestine Exploration Fund, Quarterly Statement, 1903, p. 331: "There are two plain crosses, one cut over the inside of the entrance to chamber group II and the other over the doorway b in the same group. These possibly indicate that the tomb was continued in use by the family after its conversion to Christianity."

6. Beth Shearim, Jewish tomb with standing cross surrounded by a circle appears as scribbles on the wall. Cf. Illustration by A. Reifenberg, Ancient Hebrew Arts (n. 7), p. 131.

7. Rome, Catacomb Vigna Randanini, loculus slabstone with a Greek inscription and two or possibly three reclining crosses on the upper right next to the inscription. Cf. Illustration by J.B. Frey, Corpus Inscriptionum Judaicorum, 1936, vol. I, p. 106, No. 149.

8. Rome (the same as 7), fragment of a loculus slabstone with Greek inscription and deeply incised reclining crosses in the middle above the inscription. Cf. Illustration in Frey, p. 124f., No. 173.

9. Rome (the same as 7), fragment of a loculus slabstone with Greek inscription and three reclining crosses below the inscription. Cf. Illustration in Frey, p. 141f., No. 203.

10. Rome (The same as 7), loculus slabstone with Latin inscription and three reclining crosses scratched to the right of the inscription. Cf. Frey, p. 162f , No. 229.

This selection of monuments of Judaism in Jerusalem and Rome may be regarded as sufficient to be placed beside the crosses of the Talpioth ossuaries.

The material here compiled already permits us to recognize what can be confirmed by still more finds, namely that both the standing and the reclining form of the cross are interchanged. The number of crosses on loculi slabstones varies. At times several are scratched on the surface. While the inscriptions are carefully executed throughout, the crosses, however, frequently show another hand and impress us a having been affixed *ad hoc*. Any ornamental significance of these crosses is eliminated because of their roughness, shapelessness and inaccuracy. For some of the crosses a Jewish origin is beyond doubt. For others, a Jewish origin is probable on the basis of the location of the find and/or the text of the inscriptions.

| The dating of the monuments poses some difficulties. A part of the archaeological evidence has been lost. Its only record are the field notes and the copies made by Clermont-Ganneau. Thus we have no indication for determining the date through the location of the find. Furthermore, the chronology of the ossuaries is just as uncertain as the chronology of semitic palaeography.[42] The period in question for the ossuaries lies between 100

---

[42] Since SUKENIK is preparing a corpus of Jewish ossuaries, an improvement in this matter is soon to be expected. – How uncertain dating on the basis of palaeo-

B. C. and 100 A. D. For the loculi inscriptions the period must be extended to the third century A. D.

The scope of monuments of antiquity bearing signs of crosses could be extended without difficulty if coins, lamps, manuscripts, or even the ornamental heads on scepters and staffs were included here, or if we attempted to sift and classify historically the manifold forms of the cross in the Near East.[43] But in view of the multiplicity and the many strata of hellenistic and oriental monuments with crosses, we want consciously to limit the range of the archaeological material in this essay, in order that the problem here presented may not lose its distinctiveness by being connected with entirely different questions. We will now ask what interpretation can be given to the Jewish cross markings through consideration of literary sources.

IV. The Interpretation of Jewish Cross Markings

So far we have seen that a "Christian" interpretation of the cross sign on the Talpioth ossuaries is not possible. The other possibility which is frequently taken into account, that such signs may be the result of a later "Christianization" of the monuments by means of adding crosses to them, or that the crosses might represent oriental forgeries,[44] does not apply, at least with respect to the Talpioth ossuaries published by Sukenik. Here we have positive evidence for the occurrence of such signs and, here at least, the problem is posed most clearly.

| The simplest explanation would be if the sign could be proved to be a technical marking. This thesis was first advocated by Gladys Dicksen with respect to the cross sign of the Nicanor ossuary (See above catalog, no. 1). She linked it to a similar sign on the lid of this ossuary.[45] However, on the opposite side of the lid there are small indentations to mark its correct placing and these were apparently intended for this purpose. Dicksen's explanation could at most be applied to the cross on the Nicanor ossuary, but not to the crosses, sometimes numbering three, on the loculus slabstones. Furthermore, the question could be raised whether the standing crosses (for instance, of the Talpioth ossuary) had been drawn for the purpose of

graphy still remains is illustrated by the controversy about the dating of the Dead Sea Scrolls. Cf. W. BAUMGARTNER, *Theologische Rundschau*, 15, 1949, pp. 345 f.

[43] For material on the cross relevant to comparative religion cf. V. GARDT-HAUSEN, *Das alte Monogramm*, Leipzig, 1924, pp. 73 ff. and the article 'Cross' in: *Encyclopaedia of Religion and Ethics*, ed. by J. HASTINGS, New York, IV, 1912, pp. 324 ff.

[44] Cf. CLERMONT-GANNEAU, *Palestine Exploration Fund, Quarterly Statement*, IV, 1873, p. 7–10; *idem, Archaeological Researhes*, (n. 14), pp. 403 ff.; VINCENT (n. 15), pp. 226 ff.

[45] *Palestine Exploration Fund, Quarterly Statement*, 1903, p. 331.

dividing the surface so that at some later time rosettes or other ornaments could be worked in. But against this view stands, I believe, the carelessness of these drawings, which, being without any exact measurements, give the impression of an *ad hoc* affixing. We are therefore forced to seek another explanation.

The sign of the cross, standing *or* reclining, is the sign of the last letter of the Hebrew alphabet, Tau. It is remarkable that both in the north semitic and the old Hebrew as well as in the Phoenician and the Aramaic script the same letters + or × are generally found for Tau.[46] Furthermore, Tau (תָו) has the meaning of "sign" and "sign of a cross" and *can*[47] also be translated as cross. Therefore we begin with *Ezekiel 9 : 4 ff.*, where תָו as a word appears in an important connection. In the context of the first temple vision, Yahweh speaks to the messenger who is clothed in linen and who has "the writing case at his side." "Go through the city, through Jerusalem, and put a mark (תָו) upon the foreheads of the men who sigh and groan over all the abominations that are committed in it. And to the others he said in my hearing, 'Pass through the city after him and smite; your eyes shall not spare and you shall show no pity; slay old men outright, young men and maidens, little children and women, but touch no one upon whom is the mark'" (RSV). As far as I can see it is recognized everywhere[48] that in this passage the sign on the forehead must be thought of as the sign of the cross and it should be visualized as + or × | corresponding to the letter Tau. Thus, in this passage we have a sacral marking. The sign is given on the basis of repentance to those who "sigh and groan over all the abominations," who acknowledge the law of Yahweh and do not submit to the sin of the world. It is given as *the protective sign* for salvation at the coming day of judgment. The motif of repentance is connected with the motif of protection. The commentaries correctly point to the frequently found property markings, the branding of slaves and cattle[49] common in antiquity. This idea stands, of course, behind our passage. The cross on the forehead indicates that the person marked with the sign of Yahweh is Yahweh's property and therefore stands under his protection.[50]

---

[46] Cf. D. DIRINGER, "Early Hebrew Writing," *Biblical Archaeologist*, 13, 1950, pp. 74 ff.; IDEM, *The Alphabet*, New York, 1949 ². – For the significance of Tau in rabbinic letter symbolism see G. KITTEL, *Theological Dictionary of the New Testament*, Grand Rapids, I, 1964, p. 2, and M. JASTROW, *A Dictionary of the Targumim* etc., 2nd ed., II, repinted 1943, on תָו, p. 1663.

[47] Cf. e.g. B. DUHM, *Das Buch Hiob*, Leipzig, 1897, p. 151.

[48] Cf. R. KRAETZSCHMAR, *Das Buch Ezechiel*, Göttingen, 1900, p. 101; A. BERTHOLET, *Hesekiel*, Tübingen, 1936, p. 37; G. A. COOKE, *The Book of Ezechiel*, (ICC), New York, I, 1937, p. 106; NILS MESSEL, *Ezechielfragen*, Oslo, 1945, p. 16 and 55; *et al.*

[49] Cf. F. DÖLGER, *Sphragis*, Paderborn, 1911, pp. 18 ff., and H. LILLIEBJÖRN, *Über religiöse Signierung in der Antike*, Uppsala, 1933, pp. 1–9. For sources and other literature cf. also H. SCHLIER, *Der Brief an die Galater*, Göttingen, 1949, p. 210 f. (on Gal. 6. 17).

[50] Cf. W. HEITMÜLLER, *Im Namen Jesu*, Göttingen, 1903, p. 174, as well as the

As B. Stade has already shown,[51] this idea is much more widespread in
the Old Testament than appears at first. The picture of sacral marking
often becomes apparent in the biblical texts and the notion of a crude
custom of religious stigmatization is supported by many passages, even
though it is often methodologically difficult to draw the line between real
sacral marking and symbolic manner of speech. To begin with, we recall
Gen. 4: 15 – the mark of Cain. That this is also a mark of protection and
not a mark of infamy is certain on the basis of the context. The sign by
which Cain is marked and protected is called אות and we should probably
visualize it as a sign on the forehead.[52] Furthermore, it should be taken
into account that Cain is here regarded not primarily as an individual but
as the representative of a tribe and that therefore allusion is made to a
tribal sign.[53] But the | basic notion cannot be the idea of a tribal sign,
because the Ezekiel passage already emphasizes the selection of those who
belong to Yahweh. *Isa. 44: 5* also refers to this: "This one will say, 'I am
the Lord's,' another will call himself by the name of Jacob, and another
will write on his hand, 'The Lord's' and surname himself by the name of
Israel" (RSV). This verse still presupposes, at least for the time of the
exile, the custom of stigmatization even if the hand is now mentioned in
place of the forehead.[54] In view of the fact that Lev. 19: 28; 21: 5f. and
Deut. 14: 1f. contain not only a prohibition against tatooing with the
signs of other gods, but rather also express a general criticism of all sacral
markings, it is significant that in Deutero-Isaiah the stigmatization of the
hand in no wise appears to be offensive. The motif of the criticism of those
passages is the endangering of Israel's relationship to Yahweh as his property. The custom of a marking on the forehead also lies behind *I Kings 20:
41* in which the prophet of Yahweh becomes recognizable to King Ahab
as a prophet by taking off a blindfold.[55]

As in any sacral marking, so likewise in this custom as it is known in
Israel, use and misuse cannot always be clearly distinguished. The sign of
Yahweh can have the character of a true confession, but it can also be used
in a crude apotropaic manner. It depends on whether the motif of repent-

interesting and, for our subject, valuable contribution of D. DAUBE, "Über die Um-
bildung biblischen Rechtsgutes," in: *Symbolae Friburgenses in honorem Ottonis Lenel*,
Leipzig, 1935, pp. 245 ff.

[51] B. STADE, "Beiträge zur Pentateuchkritik I: Das Kainszeichen," *Zeitschrift
für die Alttestamentliche Wissenschaft*, 14, 1894, pp. 250 ff.

[52] Cf. STADE, p. 315; also R. EISLER, "Das Qainszeichen und die Qeniter," *Le
Monde Oriental*, 23, 1929, pp. 48 ff.

[53] Cf. STADE, p. 307; J. SKINNER, *Genesis*, Edinburgh, 1930, p. 110.

[54] STADE, pp. 313 f., wrote, "In all probablity the sign of Cain is identical with one
of the two Yahweh signs mentioned in the Old Testament. We have to look for it on
the hand or the forehead."

[55] Cf. STADE, pp. 314 ff., and his remarks on p. 310 with reference to Zechariah
13: 6.

ance and of being Yahweh's property stands in the foreground and places
the bearer of these signs under obligation, or whether the motif of protection, the quest for security through magical signs is the determining
factor. Ezek. 9, where the Tau protects against the angel of judgment, shows
that a more apotropaic understanding of the Yahweh sign can also be
substantiated. Likewise in Exod. 12: 22ff., the Angel of Death in the
Passover night passes by the doors of the Israelites which are marked with
blood.[56] In this instance also we find a protective sign affixed by Yahweh's
command. Yet the motif of confession was also present at the Passover
celebration. This is indicated by the passage *Exod. 13 : 9*, probably revised,
which says, concerning the | Passover celebration, "And it shall be to you
as a sign on your hand – לְאוֹת עַל־יָדְךָ – and as a memorial between your
eyes לְזִכָּרוֹן בֵּין עֵינֶיךָ." This shows clearly that the Passover celebration should
have the same significance which otherwise the sacral sign on the hand or the
forehead had, namely, the significance of the obligation to Yahweh and
his commandments. Also in this case, sacral stigmatization is presupposed.

So far, our examination, which has largely followed Stade, has shown the
existence of the custom of a cross-sign tatooed on the forehead or the hand
during the pre-exilic and exilic periods. However, all such customs and
ideas thus far reconstructed and interpreted are able to help us understand
the archaeological monuments only if we can show their existence also
within postexilic Judaism. Only if archaeology and the history of art rely
on *contemporary* sources can they successfully disclose the meaning of
monuments and especially of symbols which frequently change their
meaning. If we keep this methodological principle in mind, then the passages thus far investigated give us various valuable indications and hints,
but they cannot furnish evidence for those Jewish signs of crosses of the
first centuries B. C. and A. D.

However, the idea of a property and protection sign does not disappear in the
postexilic period. Let us take as first witness the Psalms of Solomon 15: 6–9:

"For the mark of God is upon the righteous that they may be saved.
Famine and sword and pestilence (shall be) far from the righteous
For they shall flee away from the pious as men pursued in war,
But they shall pursue sinners and overtake (them),
And they that do lawlessness shall not escape the judgment of God,
As by enemies experienced (in war) shall they be overtaken
For the mark of destruction is on their forehead."[57]

---

[56] It is interesting, even though for our problem unimportant, that the typology
expressed in the arts of the 12th and 13th century took up the Exodus passage and
used the sign Tau of the Passover as a prefiguration of the Christian sign of the cross.
Cf. H. CORNELL, *Biblia Pauperum*, Stockholm, 1925, pp. 129, 144, 148.

[57] Translation of G.B. GRAY, in: R. H. CHARLES, *Apocrypha and Pseudepigrapha
of the Old Testament*, Oxford, vol. II, 1913, p. 646.

A thought identical to Ezek. 9: 4 and Exod. 12: 22ff. is expressed here. To be sure in the Ezekiel and Exodus passages we do not find an explicit confrontation of the σημεῖον τοῦ θεοῦ with the σημεῖον τῆς ἀπωλείας, but this confrontation is implicit because the absence of the sign of Yahweh is the sign of destruction. The *haggadic interpretation* of Ezek. 9 reads like a commentary on this subject: "God said to Gabriel, 'Go and set a Tau of ink upon the foreheads of the righteous that the destroying angels may have no power over them; and a Tau of blood upon the foreheads of the wicked that the destroying angels may have power over | them.'" [58] Furthermore the *Damascus Document* indicates that the protective sign was an apparently widespread notion within the context of Jewish eschatology. The Damascus Document takes up the prophecy of Ezekiel and brings this passage into the eschatology of "the congregation of the new covenant." "When the Messiah (משיח) comes from Aaron and Israel," [59] then the prophecy of Ezekiel will be fulfilled; then the sign on the forehead will deliver the holy remnant. "Just as it was during the period of the first visitation, concerning which He spake through Ezekiel 'to set a mark (Tau) upon the foreheads of them that sigh and cry,' but the rest were delivered to 'the sword that avenges with the vengeance of the covenant.'"

These passages indicate that the idea of a sign of Yahweh as a protective sign remained alive in certain circles, and that now within the context of Jewish eschatology it received a new accent. It becomes the sign of the messianic deliverance. Naturally it is not clearly recognizable whether the sacral stigmatization was really still practiced in the form of tatooing or whether a spiritualization of this idea took place. On the basis of a polemical passage in Philo, one can reach the conclusion that religious tatooing was still in use at times among Jews. Otherwise his statement that sacral stigmatization is indelible and blocks the road to repentance (εἰς μετάνοιαν) would be meaningless. [60]

It is surely no accident that in primitive Christian literature the pictures

---

[58] *Bab. Shabbath* 55a (Translation of: *The Babylonian Talmud*, ed. by I. EPSTEIN, London, 1938); Cf. F. PERLES, *Orientalistische Literaturzeitung*, 5, 1902, col. 365; M. JASTROW, (n. 46), p. 1663b. On the survival of this idea cf. DAUBE, (n. 50), and his reference to the anointing in the form of a χ according to *Bab. Horajot* 12a, "Our teachers taught, 'How does one anoint? ...The priests in the form of a chi.'"

[59] Text by L. ROST, *Die Damaskusschrift*, (Kleine Texte 167), 1933, p. 29; B-Text 9, 10–12; Translation of R.H. CHARLES, *Apocrypha and Pseudepigrapha of the Old Testament*, Oxford, vol. II, 1913, pp. 816f.

[60] Philo, *De specialibus legibus* I. 58. Translation of F.H. COLSON, *Philo*, in: *Loeb Classical Library*, vol. VII, 1937, p. 133. "But some labor under a madness carried to such an extravagant extent that they do not leave themselves any means of escape to repentance, but press to enter into bondage to the works of men and acknowledge it by indentures not written on pieces of parchment, but, as is the custom of slaves, branded on their bodies with red hot iron. And there they remain indelibly, for no lapse of time can make them fade."

of the "sealing" and of the "protective sign" are numerous in precisely those places where the use of Jewish antecedents must be assumed. Therefore we may draw for interpretation on these sources also inasmuch as only the existence of the idea is to be attested. W. Bousset in his commentary on the Book of Revelation already ventured the opinion that the frequent occurrence of the "sealing" | may perhaps prove that "also among Christians at the time of the Apocalypse, the custom was still in use now and then to protect oneself against all kinds of danger by cutting the names of God or Jesus" into the skin.[61] The idea of Ezek. 9: 4 or rather its further development in the Psalms of Solomon is clearly present in the Revelation of John. On the one hand, those who will be or who have been saved bear the name of the Lamb or of the Father on the forehead; they are branded as δοῦλοι τοῦ θεοῦ (Rev. 7: 3; 9: 4; 14: 1; 22: 4). On the other hand, the followers of the Beast, the subjects of the world, are sealed on the forehead or the right hand with a χάραγμα τοῦ θηρίου (13: 16f.; 14: 9; 16: 2; 20: 4). The same idea of a "sealing" of the eschatological remnant is found in the Apocalypse of Elijah;[62] the identical concepts are present in the Odes of Solomon.[63]

It is unimportant for our problem whether in Judaism an actual sacral stigmatization was practised or whether this concept was more spiritualized. It is essential only that the Yahweh signs found in Israel remained alive as ideas of sealing and now also received new meaning in the context of Jewish eschatology.[64] Furthermore, the two-fold significance of the signs was retained. On the one hand, they expressed an obligation to the will of Yahweh, to be his property, a confession to be his slave, and, on the other, they expressed the idea that as Yahweh's marked property one stood under his protection.

Of course, all these sources speak only of a marking on the hand or on the forehead, but not of some kind of burial symbolism. This objection, it appears to me, carries no weight. It is easily understandable that when the idea of the final judgment and of the resurrection of the dead became at home in Judaism, then such markings would be especially taken up in order to protect the dead against the angels of destruction, to mark them as the property of Yahweh, and to confess with the sign of the cross that the one buried here had been a follower of Yahweh's commandments; he had been taken by Yahweh as his property; he is not subject to condemnation! The crosses, reclining or standing, have the same meaning. They are

---

[61] W. BOUSSET, *Die Offenbarung Johannis*, Göttingen, 1906, p. 281.

[62] G. STEINDORFF, *Die Apokalypse des Elias* (Texte und Untersuchungen zur Geschichte der altchristlichen Literatur, N. F. II. 3a), Berlin, 1899, pp. 156 and 166.

[63] Cf. Odes 8: 15; 4: 5–8 etc. Cf. DÖLGER, (n. 49), pp. 59f.

[64] P. VOLZ, *Die Eschatologie der Jüdischen Gemeinde im neutestamentlichen Zeitalter*, Tübingen, 2nd ed., 1934, p. 304.

nothing else but the Tau. Also the plurality of crosses | and finally their careless execution in distinction to the carefully engraved inscriptions become understandable. The opinion may perhaps be ventured that these signs which "seal the dead" were often drawn only with charcoal, such as those on the one Talpioth ossuary, and this is the reason why they are not still more frequently found on Jewish ossuaries. And when these crosses appear on doorposts or even on the walls of Jewish chamber graves, then the ideas of Ezek. 9 as well as Exod. 12 have been taken up and the same thought of protection and of confession is expressed. Naturally, we do not and cannot limit the interpretation of the Jewish cross markings. They may often have been meant in a crudely apotropaic sense. They may have been misused as a kind of amulet, and then again they may have expressed a deeper hope rooted in the confession of life eternal. To differentiate between these alternatives is impossible and unnecessary. [65]

V. The Result

The ossuary find at Talpioth gave rise to this investigation which, through the process of interrogation of available sources, led to the following results:

1. The Jesus inscriptions on the two Talpioth ossuaries have no reference to Jesus of Nazareth. Instead they contain the names of those whose bones are buried there, and thus they completely agree with Jewish burial customs. As soon as these Jesus inscriptions lose their reference to Jesus of Nazareth as suggested by Sukenik, then a "Christian" interpretation of the cross markings drawn in charcoal is also without any foundation and the problem of a different understanding of these signs is posed. |

2. Those monuments with cross markings which have been discovered at excavations of Jewish burial places during the past eighty years and which have been interpreted until now either on the basis of a later conversion to Christianity of some family members or on the basis of a later Chris-

---

[65] What this essay endeavored to substantiate has, in my opinion, already twice before been suggested as a possible solution. 1) M. SULZBERGER wrote in: *Byzantion*, 2, 1925, p. 447, "It is evidently necessary to give a great deal of importance to the fact that the letter T was sacred among the Hebrews, and that is was marked on the forehead of the priests; it is the origin not only of the sign of the cross, but perhaps of this idea that the form of the cross had a magical or divine meaning." 2) C. H. KRAELING wrote in: *Biblical Archaeologist*, 9, 1946, p. 20, "Again it would be possible to suppose that the crosses had apotropaic significance being intended to guard the bones against evil demonic powers that might disturb the repose of the deceased." – The graffito published by E. LITTMANN in: *The Muslim World*, 40, 1950, pp. 16 ff., serves as a Christian analogy to the Talpioth ossuary. A cross in a circle is connected with an inscription obviously referring to Jesus Christ, and takes the form of a 'magical' circle. LITTMANN believes this Thamudic inscription to be the oldest monument of Christianity in northern Arabia.

tianization of the monuments, must be understood as Jewish cross markings in the light of the Talpioth finds. They can be explained neither as ornaments nor as technical markings. Nor have these crosses yet become stylized symbols of art, as otherwise found in Jewish art. Rather, they show a careless execution, changing in form between the standing and the reclining cross ($+$ and $\times$) and are comparable to scribbles.

3. The standing or reclining cross is the last letter of the semitic alphabet, Tau. This Tau can be verified as a sign for sacral markings on the forehead and the hand for the pre-exilic and exilic periods. Passages like Gen. 4: 15; Ezek. 9: 4; I Kings 20: 41; and Isa. 44: 5 had already been interpreted by Old Testament scholarship as meaning that a stigmatization in the form of $+$ or $\times$ has to be taken into account. The meaning of such cross markings was to confess oneself to be Yahweh's property and at the same time to postulate the protection of the property holder over his property. This sacral practice which, since Stade's work, has been accepted as a custom in Israel, the extension of which cannot be determined, has, however, its parallels also in Jewish postexilic literature, as shown directly by the 15th Psalm of Solomon and the Damascus Document, as well as indirectly by the Christian apocalypses and the Odes of Solomon, which make use of Jewish sources. Thus the literary sources of Judaism confirm and interpret that which is illustrated by archaeological evidence. If cognizance is taken of the fact that the ideas of the sacral seal, which go back to Ezekiel 9 and Isaiah 44: 5 and probably also to the Passover Feast interpretation of Exodus 13, reappear in Jewish literature within the context of the eschatological drama, then the application of crosses, especially in graves, becomes clearly understandable. For the explanation offered here it is unimportant whether the Israelite custom of stigmatization on the forehead or the hand actually still persisted – as it appears to have done – or whether the idea was preserved in a more spiritualized sense.

4. Our conclusion that the Jews knew and employed the sign of the cross as an expression of a confession to be Yahweh's property and as an eschatological protective sign needs to be stated more precisely.

First of all, in view of the archaeological material and of the peculiar character of the contemporary literary sources quoted here, | it is not possible to attribute the cross sign to Judaism in general. The silence of the rabbinical literature, for instance, concerning the cross sign cannot simply be ignored. Just as Philo is not representative of the *whole* of Judaism and just as the synagogue paintings of Dura were not characteristic of third century Judaism in general, so likewise here we are forced to differentiate: *In certain circles of Judaism*, be they sectarian or monastic, the sign of the cross was known.

Till now we have intentionally spoken only of a Jewish cross sign, avoiding the word symbol. As we stated before, archaeological evidence of such monuments must be interpreted on the basis of literary sources. In the light of our interpretation of these signs, I now do not hesitate to designate them as *symbols*. That means that a sign of definite form, in this case the letter Tau in the form of ✕ or +, signifies something holy for the viewer or participant; that in the sign a complex of ideas is summed up, and that at the same time the sign as a symbol is not here an indicator, but the container and bestower of magical power. The Jewish cross sign is not a sign which adequately renders a definite concept, as for instance in Egyptian writing ☥ is the sign for life. Furthermore, it represents not only the word Tau. Rather, a total context of faith is summed up in *one* sign. Realities believed and hoped for are read into a visible picture. This picture, however, is more than merely a mirror. It is a picture from which saving power is expected. For this, no concept other than symbol is applicable.

At the beginning we spoke of the connection between Judaism and Christianity. The course of our investigation has already illustrated the proximity of both through the question of whether the frequently found cross signs are Jewish or Christian. But nevertheless, it must now be stated that our assertion of the existence of a Jewish cross symbol does *not* imply that the *origin of the Christian cross symbol* has been disclosed. There is no direct continuity between the two symbols. Only *indirect connections* can be shown to exist.[66] The statement of Franz Cumont, the master of the interpretation of monumental art in late antiquity has validity: "A well-known phenomenon in the transmission of symbols is the change which their significance undergoes in the course of time and this is why, strictly speaking, one may only | interpret this type of monument with the assistance of contemporary evidence."[67] The migration and transformation of symbols and myths from one religion to another is a hermeneutical problem not only for theology but also for archaeology and the history of art. Continual reciprocal interpretation of literary and of monumental evidence is necessary in order clearly to distinguish that which is constant from that which is variable in the migration and changes of symbols and myths. As far as the Jewish and the Christian symbol of the cross is concerned, there is no mere acceptance, no simple migration of the symbol. The Christian symbol of the cross is a new beginning, the source of which is not the Jewish σημείωσις τοῦ θαῦ,[68] but the Pauline λόγος τοῦ σταυροῦ.*

---

[66] The relationship is much more complicated than is the case with the symbol of the crown of victory investigated by GOODENOUGH (n. 6).

[67] F. CUMONT, *Recherches sur le symbolisme funéraire des Romains*, Paris, 1942, p. 25.

[68] Cf. Origen, *Selecta in Ezechielem* IX, J.P. MIGNE, *Patrologiae cursus completus, series Graeca*, vol. XIII, p. 800.

* [Translator's postscript: For additional literature see: B. GUSTAFSSON, "The Oldest Graffiti in the History of the Church?" New Testament Studies, 3, 1956–1957, pp. 65–69; D. FISHWICK, "The Talpioth Ossuaries Again," New Testament

Studies, 10, 1963, pp. 49–61. FISHWICK interprets ιου and αλωθ as Jewish magical
incantations, ιου being an abbreviation of Jahweh and αλωθ an abbreviation of Sab-
baoth, while Iησους, far from identifying the man whose bones were interred in the
ossuary, also "forms part of the magical inscription" and provides "the earliest
evidence of Christian influences within Jewish syncretic magic" (pp. 60 f.). FISH-
WICK, however, is unable to give evidence of other magical incantations on *ossuaries*
which would refute the normal interpretation of such inscriptions as referring to
the names of the dead.]

Must One Believe in Jesus if He Wants to Believe in God?

Preliminary reflections on the interpretation of I Cor. 15:1–11*

by

Ernst Fuchs

Translated by Irvin W. Batdorf

The question whether one must believe in Jesus if he wants to believe in God is not as modern as it sounds. Implicitly at first and then soon explicitly primitive Christianity recognized that belief in Jesus was the decisive factor for the formation of belief in God. A very old formula runs: God has made Jesus both Lord and Christ (Acts 2:36). Thus every man must believe in Jesus if belief in God is to be taken seriously (Rom. 10:9f.). Since and after God had done something so decisive, an earnest faith in God could not possibly ignore this deed of God. The fact that the Jewish community did not then follow suit, although the actual fact of Jesus' crucifixion was set over against the message of his resurrection, was reckoned with from the outset. The problem of *true* faith in God (Jn. 14:6) was therefore provoked precisely by belief in Jesus. Not only do believers quarrel with unbelievers about true faith at this point, but also believers with believers. Christian faith thus appears from the beginning to be destined to be an orthodox faith. As a matter of fact, the phenomenon of orthodoxy always stood in the center of Christian declarations of faith. Christian faith could no longer allow another faith to pass as true faith. This intolerance, required by logic, was misunderstood by theological liberalism. Upon this fact rest its defeats, while all the movements which in their turn have come forward and do come forward as intolerant, have a support or a predecessor in the essence of Christianity, so that they sooner or later had to fight with Christianity, if this was not initially their will and declared intention.

Thus we are asking a relevant question when we ask about the relation of belief in Jesus to belief in God: But we are surely doing this also | in a critical spirit. To be sure, the theological explication of Christian faith wishes simply to repeat what Christian faith believes. But this repetition must run the risk of not succeeding. It might indeed be that Christian

---

* "Muß man an Jesus glauben, wenn man an Gott glauben will?," ZThK, 58, 1961, pp. 45–67. – Guest lecture given at the Kirchliche Hochschule in Wuppertal on January 27, 1961.

faith has brought forth results by which it has outdone itself. Why should not that which God once allowed to happen in Jesus have been only the beginning of a deed of God which continues to unfold? Such a point of view in no way as yet subjects our examination to a general law of the development of intellectual processes. Thus when philosophers today ask for a philosophic faith in God, this demand need not necessarily comprise a curtailment of the Christian faith. It could be that the philosophers only draw the consequences out of a development introduced by God himself, so that it would not be necessary to relinquish the dialogue with the philosophers only to representatives of the Jewish faith in God. But it could also be that even the representatives of modern unbelief deceive themselves concerning their unbelief, to the extent that they are prepared to discuss belief in God. If it is our point of departure that Christian faith is orthodox and therefore intolerant, this does not rule out the fact that a dialogue must be carried on also with the representatives of unbelief over the question whether even they, perhaps very unwillingly, are not really conditioned by some kind of faith. And this perspective need not be based merely on the consideration that today everyone has come under the influence of the Christian tradition. On the other hand, it can be that this tradition nevertheless permits a clearer view of the human situation than is possible for those who want vehemently to close their minds to the influence of the Christian tradition. Intolerance belongs not only to the realm of Christian faith. Intolerance is innate already in man's history itself, since, for example, no one can evade the truth that his birth has already decreed to what family and to what nation he belongs, even if he wants to separate himself from his origin, or fancies that he is able to break with it. By the same token the natural conditions of human existence are intolerant. Whoever does not submit to them dies; he can increase the danger of death for other men, seldom decrease it. We have no reason to lay aside the question put to us simply on the ground that it draws us into the realm of a necessarily intolerant way of thinking. However, we must take care that we not only do not lose sight of the phenomenon of intolerance, but clarify it more precisely. To be sure, we do not wish in any way to deny the fact that the intolerance of Christian faith can be misused in the most egregious way. The glib adoption of Christian intolerance by non-Christian and anti-Christian movements shows, anyway, | that Christian faith must assume the obligation of protecting the intolerance peculiar to it against confusion. This obligation prompts the suspicion that Christian intolerance is being fought out within the Christian camp itself only for the reason that Christendom itself is generally exposed to the misuse of the intolerance constitutive for it. To Christian faith obviously belongs the very misunderstanding of itself from the start.

Now, if Christian faith is initially threatened by misunderstanding, it stands in need of a criterion also for the question to be considered by us. Quite obviously, we do not dispose with certainty of the orthodoxy maintained by Christian faith, but we could be deluding ourselves precisely concerning the innermost reality of Christian faith. However that may be, is it not to be expected that Christian faith must prove its worth above every thing else as *proclamation*, if it desires to be a message concerning the ways in which God has acted? Would it not first of all wish to make this message understandable to the one who could not yet know about it? Then the criterion for our deliberation will need to be sought at the place where Christian faith intends to become address, thus in its confrontation with the man who does not yet believe, with the non-Christian. He is the one who would most likely raise a question such as ours, namely, whether one must believe in Jesus if he wishes to believe in God, – in case he wishes to enter into a dialogue concerning faith at all. Thus it will be possible to speak about faith as something that one has a right to expect from man. And so the question raised by our topic has the prospect of itself being a criterion for the self-understanding of Christian faith. In this sense we can now start over again from the beginning as is fitting for a way of thinking that is scientific, i. e. open to general discussion.

I

I will not now enter upon an all too easily disputed argument about what presuppositions a phrase like "faith in" entails with respect to its structure, and thus formally. It is better to proceed in a practical way and presuppose simply that some one or other wants to believe in God and indicates this desire as one in other respects also indicates that he wishes or desires something. There is then somebody who wants to believe in God. In this case he normally says that beyond nature and above (perhaps also within) history, he cares to worship a power by comparison with which every other power, even life and death, is inferior. And he will on this account consider it good and appropriate when man calls upon this power while giving thanks to it, and when he endeavors to discover | what God requires of man. Perhaps God wills that man should ask of him. At any rate, God would desire that man order his life according to His will. To believe in God thus normally means to let oneself be concerned with the will of God, at least to ask about it. In this case I confess that I will the will of God, even though this will may be only partly known to me or even now and again entirely unknown. Perhaps God is a "hidden" God for the world and not only for me. Or is God only hidden for sinners, thus for those men who do not believe in him, who do not want to let themselves be concerned with his will, since for them even the idea that God has a will is not acceptable? On the other hand, faith seems to say that God in reality is so manifest a God that everybody should be able to lay his hands on God's existence if he only wanted to, since God is unmistakably active, while man does not accomplish very much. This was the understanding of the apostle Paul (Rom. 1:20). Of Jesus likewise (Mt. 5:45). Then sin would certainly be tantamount to guilt, and consequently failure in the light of God's manifest existence. Is it already pedantic to distinguish between a "hidden" and a "revealed" God? May one *think* at all if he wishes to believe? One *must* obviously think as soon as he wishes to believe. That is simply the case since faith itself raises *questions*! As soon as one speaks of a will of God, the question of what God wills arises entirely of its own accord. It is precisely talk about a revealed God that raises such questions, just as genuine love raises questions, since in the case of genuine love it is always important to us what the *other* wills. But even what we say about a hidden God raises questions. If we have described it correctly, faith is perhaps or probably not everybody's cup of tea. In spite of this fact, faith deals with a truth which seems to apply to everyman, at least insofar as the question is certain to arise why one believes and the other does not. Faith leads to questions in this sense also. Where there are questions there must consequently be the act of thinking. Questions never stop with what is self-evident although they presuppose it. And questions expect answers, supposing that the answers have not been given with the question itself. We wish to guard ourselves against questions that are merely rhetorical.

In spite of what was said at the beginning about orthodoxy, it will be worth while to ponder more exactly why the thematic question we are discussing is not to be taken as a rhetorical question. According to the text of the New Testament, it actually appears as though our thematic question already poses not only a rhetorical but even a forbidden question, which perhaps does not always oppose the practice of proclamation but certainly denies its essential nature, since God is not | required to justify himself to man. In the New Testament faith in God so completely embraces faith in Jesus that faith in Jesus has become the essential content of faith in God. To be sure, Jn. 14:1, for example, says this though still in a reserved fashion: "Believe in God and believe in me!" Yet a few verses later, Jn. 14:6 expresses it unambiguously: "No one comes to the father but by me." The relation between God and Jesus is certainly not so unambiguously formulated in the New Testament as is the significance of Jesus for faith. The titles of honor attributed to Jesus already demonstrate this. If God is often called father, Jesus is not only called the son but even more emphatically the Lord, a name which in the Old Testament belongs only to God. The confession of faith recorded in I Cor. 8:6 is interesting: "There is one God, the Father, from whom all things (are) and we through him, and there is one Lord, Jesus Christ, through whom all things (are)

and we through him." The parallelism could be mitigated even more by
supplying varying predicates. Measured by the standards of the Old
Testament, God and Jesus nevertheless appear here as two competing Lords.
It is in this way, at any rate, that a Jew must have thought who would
daily and most emphatically confess God in his prayer as the one and only
Lord: "Hear, Israel, the Lord our God is one Lord" (Deut. 6:4). And a
heathen Stoic could hardly understand Christianity otherwise than as a
return to an unphilosophical polytheism, especially when next to God and
Jesus the Holy Spirit was also taken up into the Christian confession of
faith. This was done in a baptismal formula still familiar to us, the so-called
apostolic but in fact quite post-apostolic creed, when Christians in Rome
around 135 A. D. supplied as a creed for faith one or rather three denomi-
nators. This trinity in the strongest, most decisive Christian confessional
formula corresponds to the fact that the New Testament can actually
name alongside each other not only God and Jesus, but also God and the
Spirit, as well as Jesus and the Spirit. The Roman formula of faith and
confession thus sought, in a canonical way so to speak, to put an end to
this lack of symmetry.

Even here, however, one question remained. As its name "theo-logy"
implies, Christian theology has to do with thinking concerning God. But
this theology developed beyond the Roman formula into a trinitarian theology, a doctrine of the triune God. In theology faith engages in thinking
in such a way that it reflects upon the essence of God precisely with reference to the *distinctions* among God, Jesus and the Spirit. These distinctions thus are not denied in any way.

If we now ask about the necessity of combining faith in God | with faith
in Jesus, our question itself appears to lag behind the basic position of
Christian trinitarian theology. For this reason we could not carry on a
relevant discussion of our question within Christian theology at all, so
long as we let the question stand as it is. Nevertheless I do not care to
abandon our thematic question. I intend to treat it first of all in a *pre*-theo-
logical way, so to speak. This appears to be possible if, in a provisional
way, we enter upon a middle course, just as within a sermon there might
be an element which simply suspends the decision between belief and
unbelief in order that neither false delusions nor false haste may intervene.
With this purpose in mind, we want to risk a comparison between the New
Testament and the question of God as we know it, more in the neighborhood
of proclamation than theology, much as, scientifically speaking, the
phenomenologist of religion might draw such a parallel in his field. With
this experiment I certainly expose myself to the reproach that I introduce
into the process of thinking a neutrality which could never do justice to
the decisional character of faith itself. However, inasmuch as we have to
do in the New Testament with texts for which thinking about faith would

be more familiar than for any contemporary discussion partner, we will simply let it depend upon how the texts correct us. At the same time that is a procedure not unknown to theology itself.

II

The comparison between the New Testament and our customary question concerning God is connected with variously oriented religious attitudes. I say intentionally "attitudes" *(Einstellungen)* and not "conceptions" *(Vorstellungen)*. Conceptions can be shared and thus held in common, even where the attitude of one person has nothing in common with that of another person, who need by no means be an opponent. What is without doubt true of every item of daily need, which, although referring to the same conception, nevertheless calls forth quite different attitudes – one thinks only of the difference between the merchant and the housewife who makes a purchase – is even more true in the religious realm. It is not the conception but the attitude that is decisive.

A religious attitude that is widespread today (and not only today) holds that every man can seek and perhaps also find a *contact* of sorts with the divine. The divine is thereby understood by conscious or unconscious analogy with the erotic, since it is considered self-evident that the erotic, as an | experiential faculty that exercises crucial influence over man and therefore is not to be separated from religion, is a contact phenomenon. On this basis one no longer asks whether something like 'contact' is at all suitable for the essence of the relation to God, but one simply continues to search for the contact and analyzes accordingly the unconscious and even the subconscious, for example by dream analysis.

The exchange of subject and object in a dream already appears to support the test. This procedure, therefore, is only interesting for us when it is clear from the very beginning that the contact is really a matter of a *relation (Bezug)*, which, strictly speaking, means that our relation is with *somebody withdrawn (entzogen)* from us. Here, too, the analogy with the erotic remains clear. For in spite of every contact, the erotic experience does not bring satisfaction so long as it does not respect the mode of existence of the person who is withdrawn precisely in the erotic experience, who is really not at one's disposal – and precisely therefore provokes and entices the exercise of erotic skill. A merely erotic experience is, strictly speaking, nothing, as is shown by the drive to repeat it as frequently as possible. Thus a strange disjuncture between willing and achieving exhibits itself in the misuse of the erotic: the erotic expert does not accomplish what he wishes. He rather destroys the unity of his self.

This remarkable disjuncture, which in no way needs to be brought to consciousness, but on the contrary is hidden from its own consciousness as carefully as possible, also characterizes religiosity which seeks contact. Its problem remains the distance or distinction of man from the divine. We do not even need to deny that there is genuine contact between God and man. But these contacts would confirm the *distinction* between God and man, if everything goes right. Usually it happens in the opposite way. The difference between God and man is denied so long as an attempt is made to prompt, and in this manner to establish contact. However, every attempt to put at our disposal what lies beyond our disposal strikes and hurts *us*, not that which we do not have at our disposal as such. Whoever imagines that he is able to exercise control at least over himself, since he has a body contradicts the New Testament in any case. Nothing is more hateful to Paul than sin against one's own body (I Cor. 6:18; Rom. 1:24). Paul sees rather that man is beyond his own grasp precisely because he has a body to which 'everybody' is bound. As one grows older, the more readily he understands this point of view. It is then one realises how hard we find it.

If divinity is that which is essentially and completely withdrawn from us, how then can one wish to be united with it?

Even a fleeting review of ancient pre-Christian and non-Christian religious piety reveals the same problem, only that in antiquity the | *ecstatic element* seems to play a still greater role than with us. In the mystery religions, in gnosis, and in Jewish apocalypticism there are enough examples of this which are so well known that I need not go into them in detail. The analogy in antiquity that suggests itself is less the erotic than *magic*. It is not a question of charming, as is the case with the erotic, but of bewitching and being bewitched, as Paul censures the Galatians (Gal. 3:1). This is true whether one is a mystic like Apuleius, a wandering soul lost in the world, who has lost his head through intoxication, like the soul in the Hymn of the Pearl in the Acts of Thomas and in the Naassene Hymn; or only a visionary like the prophet and the glossolalist, the speaker in tongues, in the Christian community at Corinth (I Cor. 14).

The example of the glossolalist at Corinth is perhaps the most instructive for our question. Paul says in I Cor. 14:20ff. that a general speaking with tongues in the gathering of the community would give to unbelievers the impression of frenzy (v. 23). On the other hand, prophetic speech as something meaningful brings them under conviction for their heart's aspiration (v. 24f.). Paul gives the preference to prophetic speech since it is directly understandable (v. 29). Speaking with tongues, on the contrary, needs an interpreter (v. 27). Why? Since the contrast in the entire chapter, strictly speaking, is only between understandability and non-understandability, there scarcely exists a substantial difference between the experience of the prophet and that of the glossolalist. Even the ecstasy of the one who speaks in tongues, in spite of what cannot be uttered, presupposes the knowledge of the ecstatic realm. Otherwise the apostle's desire that an interpreter should attend the glossolalist (in case this person does not himself interpret what he experiences) would be senseless. Even speaking in tongues had thus in principle a content capable of being understood. According to II Cor. 12:1–5, which is a self-confession of the apostle, who had himself at least experienced glossolalia (cf. I Cor. 14:18), it is to be assumed that in this ecstatic realm several heavens or heavenly districts separated from one another by terror and joy are traversed one after another. By the groaning and the eruption of joy on the part of the glossolalist, it would be clear to the (obviously prophetic) expert where precisely the ecstatic visionary feels himself to be, whether in the blaze of a consuming fire or rather in a state of refreshment. This the interpreter then conveys to the community. Paul the visionary cannot tell whether he was in the body or outside the body (II Cor. 12:2f.). He holds these experiences of pure ecstasy to be unedifying for all others. The pentecostal pattern of speaking in tongues pictured in Acts 2:3f. is misleading, or has at least been reworked, as is suggested by the ensuing interpretation of Peter and its alleged understandability (vs. 8).

| But even the tendency so clear in I Cor. 14 toward an edifying rationalization of the ecstatic phenomenon ought not to keep us from seeing the strangeness of ecstasy. We have here an opportunity to discover the decisive phenomenon which has put its mark upon Pauline theology. The decisive phenomenon already in Paul's own religion is this, that Paul has not let the revelatory event remain in the ecstatic sphere of a miraculous seeing or appearing, to which the early Christian tradition could have led him on the basis of the appearances of the Risen One (I Cor. 9:1; 15:5–8). Paul has rather transformed the ecstatic-prophetic domain into the everyday sphere of our tangible existence. As it seems to me, he has done the same thing as the historical Jesus, who indeed likewise, particularly in his parables, exalted everyday life as the "stuff" of the revelatory event. This is true although Jesus was quite likely not less charismatically gifted than, for example, his disciple Simon Peter – they both came from John the Baptist – or the apostle Paul. Jesus' transformation of the ecstatic – apocalyptic realm into the everyday might have been endangered through the Easter visions. However it was not annulled; but, as the example of Paul shows, it became the decisive impulse for a new theological way of thinking. While the ecstasy of the Christian gnostics who soon emerged led to false religious self-assertion, and therefore made necessary new barriers and practically a re-establishment of the law that had been overtaken by faith, as the Galatian example shows, Paul followed the tendency that issued from Jesus himself and bound faith and thought together *in the realm of everyday life*.

In accomplishing this Paul certainly stood in need of help. But the help had already been provided. For Paul himself it consisted not in the *words* of the historical Jesus, else he would have cited them; Paul, however, cites as "words of the Lord" only words of Jesus that already bore a liturgical stamp. He even repels ideas that were certainly central in the early church like that of the kingdom of God, which actually is an apocalyptic conception. Paul sees that here where we are in this everyday world weakness rules (II Cor. 12:5 and other passages). One is persecuted, for example, as a Christian (II Cor. 11:23ff.). Thus the innerworldly realm that lies before the eyes of every man is characterized not by apocalyptic powers but by weakness, certainly not simply by impotence but also not by might. This situation is not simply the consequence of the passing lust of the flesh which oppresses every man. It is the same situation where faith has become alive in man. Every man sighs under an existence characterized by the body of death (Rom. 7:24). And precisely here in this realm of weakness | in which we have our existence God's strength has appeared. It is not as though we were to become strong men, religious heroes so to speak, out of our weakness. On the contrary, the strength of God strove to join itself to the weakness characteristic of our human existence, as the strength of God and not of man, so that the treasure remains what it is, undiluted, in earthen vessels: God's being and not ours (cf. II Cor. 4:7ff.). For this reason alone Paul carries on missionary work. On this account he founds communities, not conventicles. The strength appearing in the communities is not the power of ecstatic vision but rather the community itself as power, which is active in every single individual not only as charisma but primarily as *faith*. This faith has the power to love (Gal. 5:6). It is therefore never intent upon itself. Faith much rather has the power to say: When I am weak, then I am strong! (II Cor. 12:10). Faith never relates itself to powers that may be experienced individually, nor is it a charisma (in spite of I Cor. 12:9). It is rather always related, at least for Paul, to the strength of another, to Christ (II Cor. 12:9). And Christ is the crucified Jesus. Paul preaches him as "the word of the cross" (Gal. 3:1; I Cor. 1:17f.). No one less than Jesus should and would live in the believer by the power of God (Gal. 2:20; II Cor. 13:4).

What the Christian gnostic professes to attain by identifying himself with Christ, a Pneuma-Christ, this Paul professes to attain through faith alone. Faith does not identify us with a Pneuma-Christ, but faith joins us with the crucified Jesus. The question which now remains is whether faith says or brings to us too little. At *this* point orthodoxy distinguished itself from sectarian fanaticism. We let this distinction stand as an exegetically legitimate one, but we test further whether orthodoxy does not now in its own way fall into the danger of perverting faith into the acceptance of a kind of professorial or administrative statutes, the acceptance of a redemptive history which could be officially decreed and the beginnings of which seem to show through as early as in Paul, for example, at I Cor.

15:3–8, so that already the primitive Christian kerygma would have to be understood as a "Kerygma-dogma," as Heinrich Schlier suggests.

What then does the name of Jesus the Crucified mean for Paul? According to what has been said, i. e. in view of the transformation of the ecstatic realm into the sphere of everyday life, the name of the crucified Jesus signifies first of all the *place* of the revelation of God. In the first place Jesus' name is a designation of place: precisely the encounter between God and man remains for Paul located in our everyday world. But yet it is not the world but precisely the Crucified One who is the place of encounter, so that Paul can say: through Christ the world is crucified to me | and I am crucified to the world (Gal. 6:14). The apostle of Jesus appears in the world as a man who "is nothing," as his opponents say ironically (II Cor. 12:11). However, Paul knows that exactly in this form, in view of his being nothing, one has to deal with God himself, when and since one has to deal with this man Paul. Paul is weak and appears as weak, without strength of his own, which lies alone with the one who has given him his commission (II Cor. 13:3f.). But the one who has given the commission is strong. He is the God who makes the dead alive, the Almighty (Rom. 4:17).

Thus faith places all power, even that of wordly authority (Rom. 13:1 to 7), upon the side of God, not because faith proceeds from the proposition that weak man is generally impotent, but because faith proceeds from the proposition that God is about to reveal himself as almighty in and through man amidst the need of the world, indeed that God already has so revealed himself in Jesus. That is the meaning of the Pauline reference to the crucified Jesus. Accordingly, to believe in Jesus means to believe in the revelation of the almighty God in a world otherwise hostile to God and on that account so much in need, to believe that with Jesus the *time* of his revelation has come and that no one can any longer withdraw himself from the time of this revelation. If the crucified Jesus is the mark of the *place* where God wished to reveal himself, namely, nowhere else than in our world marked by death, then the preaching of the resurrection or the glory of this Crucified One is nothing other than the proclamation of the *time* of God's revelation as our time (Rom. 1:4). *Faith in Jesus is faith in the revelation of God in our time and in our sphere of existence*, no matter what our eyes otherwise might see or what our inner ear might otherwise hear. If that is true, then one *must* believe in Jesus if he wants to believe in God, since this faith claims to have become an event in our time and in our sphere of existence (Jn. 1:14). For this reason Paul speaks of a "law of faith" (Rom. 3:27). By this he means the gospel which God has established through the Crucified One as the office of proclamation for the reconciliation of the world (II Cor. 5:19).

III

For the sake of needed clarity we must now add to these observations on the Pauline heritage a reflection which ought to clear up certain confusions within the *theological* debates of the present time. The whole matter could indeed be entirely different. It could be that we actually say too little when we claim Jesus Christ only as the place and for the time of revelation. | Must one not ask further whether this place then does not claim to extend itself, and even does extend itself to the entire "body of Christ," which certainly includes in itself not only heaven but heaven and earth? Must one not ask also whether the time of Jesus Christ does not claim to *consummate* itself as the time of the revelation of Jesus Christ after God the Father had revealed himself in Jesus at that time? Why should not such thoughts retain their right as "thoughts of faith"? Is not this pattern of thought also widely accepted in the New Testament? And does not such a way of thinking relatively easily agree with certain constructive features of the Old Testament? Have we the right to deny God a "plan," as though God could not plan? Or are such thoughts not compatible with faith?

In order to be able to make decisions in what is perhaps a pious debate, we must retrace our steps. We have asked whether faith in Jesus were necessary if anyone wished to believe in God. Our exegetical result consisted in the statement that faith in God is dependent on the revelation of God, and that this revelation points to its place and its time in Jesus. Nevertheless, we must now also say something about what the situation is with respect to that intention, which affirms its desire to believe initially in God without Jesus, as, for example, is the case with the Jews and many philosophers.

If we follow Paul, then the world that is hostile to God does not at all wish to believe sincerely in God. Or if one concedes that it has this intention, – it simply cannot believe in God. According to Rom. 1:18 – 3:20 it is too late for that. The world wishes rather, with or without ecstasy, to believe in itself. That is the meaning of that boasting which is displayed by those who brag about their good works, as Rom. 3:21ff. and Rom. 4 show. But now such boasting is not a special case confined to Jews. The ecstatics or their gnostic counterparts, to be sure, boast less in their works. It may be precisely good works they despise. But they boast all the more in their religious powers, their charisma. Their relation to Christ misses faith, since, for example, it turns out to be lovelessness toward the community (I Cor. 11:21).

At this point a word can now be said concerning the expansion or extension of the "body of Christ." Such extension of the body of Christ takes place only and exclusively as the expansion of true love in the world. In heaven all things have in effect already been settled (I Cor. 15:20-28;

Phil. 2:9–11). On earth it holds true: he who believes loves; he who cannot love does not believe. To be sure, one does not recognize faith simply on the basis of love – for in the realm of love many things remain silent and | inconspicuous –, but faith is recognized in the capacity to love, in that selflessness which indeed may also appear as demand but which is really the gift of God's grace. What characterizes the world is not simply a lack of love in the world, but the acute incapacity to love at a time when this by all means ought to have absolute priority, for example, in the relation between slave and master (I Cor. 7:20ff. etc.), and also in the intercourse of the sexes. Ever and again man in the world is pulled into the realm of things upon which he is dependent, of the "flesh," as Paul says, of the "visible," of the "perishable." If he wishes to overcome this he stands in need of the spirit of God, of the help of God (Gal. 5:16ff.; Rom. 8:26: the spirit helps our weakness!). But God does not allow himself to be mocked. If the time of this forbearance is past, the time for decision has come for all. As a result, faith has gained its antithesis in faith directed toward ourselves: the new freedom for faith in God now stands over against the *compulsion towards faith in oneself*. True Christian faith frees from this compulsion in which God's will had embroiled sinful man (Rom. 7:5f.). And for that very reason the movement of the revelation of God is not away from the existence of man in the world, but toward the existence of man within the world. He who wishes to escape this movement still stands under the old compulsion and not in the new freedom. Paul understands Christ not as the beginning of heavenly excursions but as the end of the law (Rom. 10:4; II Cor. 3:13). As a result, he holds fast to this end as the beginning in time, in the world, at the cross of Jesus (II Cor. 4:6). And as a result, he names the crucified as the one through whom God had reconciled the world to himself (II Cor. 5:18f.; Rom. 5:19). Now peace rules in the believer (Rom. 5:1), now love begins its activity in our hearts (Rom. 5:5), now one knows what holy spirit means, since one experiences its fruit (Gal. 5:22). Faith is thus indeed well grounded, grounded in Jesus Christ (I Cor. 1:30). It needs no substantiation or extensions since it *has been* grounded.

It seems now as if new questions were beginning to arise. What is the situation with reference to the subjective side of faith? Faith, to be sure, allows itself to accede to the time and the place of the revelation of God as our time and our place, if there is true faith at all. And this permitting oneself to accede is certainly an interpretation of the cross of Jesus. But what this cross says to faith remains a word that is proclaimed. Faith thus remains my *own* decision!

Nevertheless, faith has its mark, its characteristic, on the basis of which it is certain of itself. This mark is not love, although faith leads to love without fail. But while faith is certain of itself, | love remains open-ended and in need of hope to the extent that love cannot always see its result. To say the least, we are hindered at this point by the fact that we mourn people who have passed away. Love dismisses no one from its realm. Love remains dependent upon futurity precisely for the sake of the dead. But that does not hold in the same way for faith, so far as faith is to be distinguished from love and from hope.

What now is the mark by which faith becomes certain of itself? This mark can only lie in me myself. Luther has taken conscience as the basis of its designation. Paul did that only occasionally in this form. It was enough for him to point to the *freedom* bound up with faith. In this respect, the apostle again follows Jesus, who in his parables likewise called man to freedom. But now, what sort of freedom ought this to be? Certainly a freedom which, for example, may be able to treat the hard pressed neighbor with consideration, i. e. which does not put him in the shade in a fanatical or gnostic way. Paul developes this question with reference to the problem of how one ought to behave toward the phenomenon of meats consecrated to idols. I do not need to discuss these texts further here. For one fact is clear without further ado: when there are strong and weak ones in the congregation, as Paul says, then these groups are not differentiated in that some believe and others do not; surely they all belong to the congregation and are not to be expelled. However, no one ought to bring any compulsion to bear on his neighbor, so that this neighbor falls from the protection of his faith since he makes himself stronger than he is. Weakness and strength are distinguished in the realm of faith exclusively by whether and how far he who believes has the power of Christ at his side when he falls into a disquieting situation, which puts his faith in question. There surely are great differences here which reflect the reality of our personal disposition, just as not every one has the same charismata at his disposal as his fellow Christian. But if faith endures in all these circumstances, that can only mean that at all points that old compulsion to believe in one's own self has disappeared. Faith thus has its inner mark simply in the fact that the believer is no more compelled to believe in himself. On the basis of this new freedom he recognizes whether he is really able to accede to the proclamation of the word of the cross. Therefore, faith is *certain* of itself when it believes in Jesus Christ. It then freely believes in God's revelation in our time and in our sphere in that it believes concretely in the help of God.

IV

| If now it is to be a valid statement that faith becomes conscious of this certainly on the basis of freedom, that the believer since Jesus no longer need believe in himself, because he rejoices in the *help* of God, – how then

can those kerygmatic formulations be explained, which according to their form seem to establish something like a "kerygma-dogma"? How shall we explain, for example, the obviously pre-Pauline text in I Cor. 15:3–8, which even begins solemnly with this phrase, "that Christ died for our sins according to the scriptures and that he was buried and that he arose on the third day according to the scriptures and that he appeared to Cephas" etc.? What can be said about the "historical exclamation mark" (*notabene*) (Kierkegaard) implied in this formula? The sentences of the formula must be considered as having at least been influenced by apocalypticism, not only by reason of the phrase, "he appeared," but probably also by the phrase, "on the third day." What happened in those days is certainly underscored in the formula as a historical occurrence – in addition, those continuing appearances before others up to Paul are meant to bear further witness to that. But this historical occurrence is an event "according to the scriptures" and thus scriptural, and to that degree is bound to the scripture or to its interpretation from scripture. It happened, since it had to happen, as is the case with all apocalyptic events (cf. the phrase, "it must take place," from Mark 13:7). It cannot be said of faith that it must take place. Indeed, that is not said. Faith, however, since it must be certain of itself, surely depends upon that premise which we understood as freedom from the compulsion of the necessity to believe in one's own self. If now it were required that faith in Jesus should mean believing in a kerygma-dogma, even if it were one lifted bodily from the scripture, then faith would consist, as in Rome, precisely in the recognition of this kerygma-dogma. Paul even says in I Cor. 15:11, "so we preach and so you received the faith." Likewise, a few sentences later he makes everything depend on the *fact* of the resurrection of Jesus (I Cor. 15:17): otherwise "your faith" is "in vain." If these *sentences* be valid, is not faith then a new compulsion, although it is to mean freedom from the old compulsion of a faith directed to ourselves? And if, for example, we are even to prove the Easter event according to the scripture or are to regard it as a scriptural fact, as a fact that is to be proved and has been proved from the scripture, then does not our faith depend basically on that same compulsion from which it ought to free us – from a belief in our exegetical insight or from the exegetical insight of that so-called apostolic council at Jerusalem, which the text in I Cor. 15:3ff. appears to have in mind?

Now we can hardly on principle exclude the possibility that | Paul can also contradict himself. The purity of faith need not necessarily coincide with the purity of statements arising out of subsequent reflection on faith. Already the fact that there are many credal formulations precisely in Paul shows that the declarations were not formally leveled and did not arise out of the same occasion or at the same time, but were dependent upon the terminology used in them.

The only important thing is that at that time in the realm of the apostolic proclamation the obligation was seen to express the authoritative and demanding nature of the proclamation in terms of *content*. But this authoritative demand in the proclamation must not be mistaken for that compulsion from which faith sets free. It is therefore false to equate the form with the content of proclamation. Precisely the fact that this content was expressed not in a single formula but in a variety of ways and with the help of very diverse ideas, for example, very different titles of honor for Christ, in always new approaches, demonstrates that the content of faith as the content of proclamation was basically subject to theological reflection; such theological reflection is to be understood as an act of freedom and not as an act of compulsion. What is compulsory here admittedly goes together with the old compulsion from which faith wishes to set free. If the liberation from the old compulsion of faith in ourselves was to be understood as an act of God – and of this no formula leaves any doubt – then the new content of faith, the message, *must* be designated and understood as a message of *God*. On the other hand, this message of God claimed indeed to be an event in our time and in our sphere. Just on that account it had its content in the historical Jesus and in the result of his historical appearance and of his destiny. There was thus the necessity of maintaining this event-character of the message under all circumstances. *Faith was directed to the event that was here proclaimed*, and to nothing else. The message belonged substantially to the event itself since it had to announce the event as the event that makes faith possible anew, as word from God (cf. II Cor. 2:17). The message did not make God and man one, but it mediated between God and man as Jesus himself had done, and it specified for its mediation that same Jesus, in whose name it spoke. Jesus himself became the word that he proclaimed, not the symbol for, but the actual occurrence of this word, since it now, after his death, was carried on in his name. *Jesus had to become this word since through his crucifixion the fact that he had spoken in the name of God was contested.* It is *this* necessity, the decision that must be demanded in view of the personal destiny of Jesus, | that Paul intends when he speaks of the resurrection of Jesus, that is, of Jesus' dignity as the representative of God (II Cor. 4:4). Had he said less, had he only repeated words of Jesus, then Paul would have eliminated precisely the event-character of the claim of Jesus which became historical – the claim to have spoken in the name of God. Since the important thing in this connection was faith and not visions, Paul had in other passages, for example, Rom. 4:25 and 3:25f., defined Jesus' death on the cross as the word of God (cf. I Cor. 1:17). The death and resurrection of Jesus only supply content for faith so far as they maintain the connection between word and faith, that is, the perpetual event-character of the *proclamation* of the freedom of the children of God.

The faith that was certain of itself was in need of theological reflection since it was to *remain* certain of itself, i. e. of the event of freedom from the necessity of having to believe in one's own self; and to remain certain of it *as* an event, *as* a deed of God, and therewith *as* a word from God.

To talk about a kerygma-dogma, however, is to stabilize the articulations of the content of faith in terms of the oldest statements. This goes together with the misguided conviction that the meaning of what is historically first must also have been exhausted in the formulations that were historically first. Here it is forgotten that what is left unsaid, since it is self-evident in a word, is generally much more important for the meaning that what is expressed, which depends upon the situation. If faith is to retain its character as event and thus its relation to God, it must be constantly formulated anew, and the specific mark of faith must lie *in the proclamation itself*, which for its part wishes to be pure event.

But where does this leave the "historical exclamation mark" *(notabene)*? It stays put. For now it becomes clear that faith, precisely because as event it does not hang in the air but occurs in the name of Jesus, must always anew master and overcome the earlier and earliest formulations of faith, and to be sure even the best, in order that faith does not solidify into a formula, but remain event.

In that case, our theology would be obliged to revise the apocalyptically influenced understanding of history, which was behind that text in I Cor. 15, if the proclamation today is to express the same event and lead to the same faith which has *generated* those oldest formulations. Whoever makes such texts into a kerygma-dogma confuses cause and effect. For those formulations were the effect. The cause remains the event that has made Jesus the word of faith for us. Is this event identical with the resurrection of Jesus? Can it be identical with it? It is only identical with it when we ourselves *shall* share in the resurrection of Jesus. | Of this love knows. It should never be too early to speak of love for a faith that is certain of itself. As a matter of fact, however, when the New Testament attempted to give expression to the resurrection of Jesus by itself, it has constantly left this event in its concealment. In this sense, only Jesus himself, and not his resurrection, is a historically available fact. That must be said against I Cor. 15:17f. Historically available is also the other fact that henceforth the proclamation called man into the freedom of faith in the name of Jesus. The effect thus permits us to think back upon the cause, upon Jesus himself, as the word of God, in that we seek to retranslate for ourselves the texts which speak of the cause, into the event that has generated the text. The sole criterion for this can only be the understanding of *faith* at work in the texts themselves, a faith which, as our thematic question shows, has its sole inner characteristic in the fact that it is certain of itself.

V

To believe in Jesus means to let oneself accede to Jesus as God's work and thereby to be free from the compulsion of having to believe in oneself. To believe in oneself consequently means to permit oneself to accede to oneself. Yet does not faith also do this? Faith wants indeed to be *my* faith. But the question is whether I let myself accede to myself under compulsion or whether I have the *freedom* to do it. When true faith is certain of itself then I let myself accede to myself in freedom. Can I deceive myself concerning this freedom? If *only* a subjective freedom were intended, then the objection could scarcely be averted that freedom of faith as a subjective act is liable to self-deception. But the freedom of faith is not limited by the defects of subjectivity. The defects of human subjectivity are certainly not denied by faith. But faith is certain of the help of God. If the believer is in error, he can only be in error about the fact that behind the dependency which characterizes the circumstances of his life, another existence is being prepared which he was not able to see. The same is true with regard to other men. No one can know what blessing, for example, death veils, since otherwise the blessing would perhaps be lost for us. The example of the "laughing heirs" is not completely inappropriate. Loving testators wish their heirs to rejoice. They do not wish their heirs to be drowned in sadness. Last wills and testaments can speak with love simply by surprising one.

God thus speaks to us not only through Jesus. Will the statement suffice that God nevertheless, in any event, and under all circumstances, *has* spoken to us in Jesus? So that for the fact that God speaks, and thus for the question | whether God speaks to us at all, we have a "support" in the historical Jesus? So that we also were finally discharged of the question whether God spoke with men only at just that time? For this much is clear: Man can only enjoy the certainty that he is discharged of himself when he is allowed to understand the help of God not only as a supplementation of human effort, not only as a prolongation of our activity, but also as a correction of our activity, indeed as a necessary correction, perhaps, of nature and history. As a believer I am withdrawn from myself precisely in my concrete existence exactly in the same way God is withdrawn from me, and only in this certainty am I free from myself. To faith thus belongs also the independence of love from my loving, the independence of hope from my hoping. As the presuppositions of my personal ability to believe, these independencies depend, however, on their part upon whether I can for that very reason let myself accede to faith. If I can do this, then all things can become for me a word of God, on account of the independence of love and of hope. Thus, I can, for example, wait and exhort to forbearance when outward appearance aligns itself against us (Rom. 5:3–5). I must be able to let myself *and others* be comforted by the strength of God. For this occasion, often encountered in faith, my personal faith requires a base. When I now know that Jesus wanted such faith, when I hear that he believed that the time for this faith had come, then I am constantly asked whether I let myself accede to this time for believing, which has already been declared ours in the name of Jesus, viz. by the will of Jesus in the name of God. Therefore to believe in Jesus means to let oneself accede in the name of God to our time and our sphere, as to the time for believing and the place for believing, and to hold fast this call.

In I Cor. 15, too, the Christian message consists in the call that for us all this time, the time for faith, has already come, in this place, namely in the world into which the call to faith entered. Man is then no longer only a doer but first of all a hearer, and all existence now would depend on whether we are able to hear. Not something absurd, but the relation between a call, a word and our hearing thus becomes a mode of being in which we are encountered not as doers but first of all as persons, since we are being addressed. Thus, with respect to our acting, God would be a God often hidden, but in the realm of our hearing he would be quite manifest. And the sin of man would consist in the confusion of the person with the work, of hearing with acting. But the sin is forgiven, God himself corrects its results when we allow ourselves through Jesus to be called back into the realm of hearing (Psalm 37:5).

| Whether faith in God believes in Jesus depends thus also upon how we evaluate the sin of man one way or the other, how far we are prepared to own up to our sin and to take upon ourselves its consequences, since we expect correction from God alone. In this practical and final sense, I must admit, our thematic question has undergone a transformation. The insight into the necessity of faith in Jesus, and thus of the fact that our faith stands in need of a base in Jesus, depends upon whether we are prepared to recognize our sin and with this to see through the *compulsion* to believe in ourselves as a result of *sin*. Then we shall understand that faith in Jesus implies that God *has* already corrected the most terrible consequence of sin, the compulsion to believe in ourselves, by making Jesus for us the word of freedom from ourselves. On this basis the New Testament has "historicized" the mythical account concerning a son of God sent down into the darkness of the world, and has used it for the interpretation of the historical existence of Jesus.

To the *inner* mark of faith, freedom from ourselves, there is joined now an *outer* mark. This outer mark consists not simply in the formulated creed, but generally in the limitation of our action to that which is possible for us in love, that is, for the sake of neighbor within the limits of hope, that is, within the limits of our time and our sphere, and thus in the forbearance of faith. On the strength of that, Christian orthodoxy must prove its identity by the right understanding of *works*. Instead of making faith itself into a work, instead of warping it under given propositions, Christian orthodoxy must always learn anew to distinguish works from faith. The danger for us theologians is greatest at the point where we overvalue our thinking as a work. On this account we as theologians shall probably have only to reflect *(nachdenken)*, without being able to establish beforehand the limits of this reflection, since the truth of which we would like to speak remains dependent entirely upon its taking place *(Ereignis)*.

VI

Since Bultmann's protest against Barth's exegesis of I Cor. 15, the theological discussion of the present time turns, not accidentally or just tenaciously ever and again around vss. 1–11. The text speaks in an extraordinarily definite tone that brooks no contradiction, although it is by no means immediately transparent; some of the things which Paul still knew, so that they were self-evident for him, we no longer know. We simply do not know, for example, at | what places and at what time the "appearances" of the Resurrected One took place. We therefore correlate them naturally with the Easter accounts of the Gospels. The Easter accounts tempt us to understand the statement concerning the "third day" as a simple counting of days, while it probably belongs more to the category of an apocalyptic, and thus for us enciphered, statement, which has to do with the meaning of the enthronement of the Crucified. But what is this meaning? Concerning this, the text, to be sure, has something to say. Hence the silence about details proves to be appropriate.

First of all, Paul recites the One gospel which is characterized by a quite specific, official version, and had to be accepted in faith by every one who wished to be saved (from the wrath of God). From the outset, in the statement about Christ's death quoted at the beginning, this apostle likewise takes his stand in the kerygmatic tradition – the tradition even of the 'apostles,' although he who had formerly been a persecutor of the community, measures up to everybody with respect to his office, as he emphasizes in his letter to the Galatians. The apostles are the proclaimers of the *logos* here cited and nothing else. By the word *logos* Paul means not the Johannine *logos*, but the kerygma to which he can also point in an emphatic way as his own kerygma (compare 15:14 with 2:4; compare further Rom. 16:25; II Tim. 4:17; Tit. 1:3; in Mt. 12:41, with its parallel, Lk. 11:32, the proclamation of judgment by the prophet Jonah is limited temporally: it can no longer be put in the same category with a word of Jesus).

The list of witnesses in verses 5–8 is by no means confined to apostles. Thus a Cephas is placed in I Cor. 9:5 next to the brothers of the Lord and is not enumerated among the apostles. The apostolic message does not coincide with the fact of that appearance for which the witnesses vouch; it says more. Faith is, however, faith in the message. To this degree those witnesses to a specific occurrence, which even repeated itself, conflict with faith, and what they have seen conflicts with the message that is to be believed. The text, I Cor. 15:3ff., is thus not precisely balanced and betrays this also through the loosely constructed additions in the enumeration of the witnesses for the appearances. The creed obviously suppresses older statements such as Peter might have made. Likewise James has obviously forced Peter into the background.

The message in its nucleus is formulated in parallel clauses like similar credal expressions, for example, Rom. 4:25. The scheme, to be sure, is not strictly adhered to throughout. The statements in vs. 3 and vs. 4b set forth a parallel: "that Christ died for our sins according to the scriptures" and "that he has been raised on the third day according to the scriptures." Both clauses beginning with "that" | correspond formally in synonymous parallelism and therefore also with respect to content; by which arrangement what follows each time explains what precedes in the clause introduced by "that": Christ is Christ because he died and was raised (cf. Rom. 8:34). He died because the time had come for God to establish propitiation or an 'offering' for our sin, as Paul understands it (Rom. 3:24–26; 4:25;8:3, 32; II Cor. 5:18–21 etc.). This deed of God, in view of its meaning, and particularly in view of its time as the time of an eschatological event, is endorsed by the "scriptures" and therefore subject to exegetical proof. In particular the (third) day of resurrection guarantees the eschatological meaning of the death of Christ as an act of propitiation, of the "grace" of God, as it says afterwards in the autobiographical sentences, verses 9f. Hence that list of witnesses in verses 5–8 is to be understood equally as an attestation of the eschatological time, as Paul enjoins in II Cor. 6:2 on the basis of Isa. 49:8. According to Paul, the last witness, there is no other Gospel of the end of the law than this (Rom. 10:4).

The statements concerning Christ's being buried and his having appeared first of all to Peter seem likewise to correspond with one another. But by this correspondence the synonymous parallelism of the 'that'-clauses, vss. 3 and 4a, would be broken. The being buried is the transition from the first 'that'-clause to the second. The appearing before Peter corroborates, however, the scriptural proof by a new occurrence followed by others, since the appearance to Peter is not endorsed by scriptural proof. The weakest point of the message is the statement concerning the entombment, which today is looked upon as self-evident. Actually it only has an inner logical meaning as an analytical assertion in the light of the resurrection, and is thus perhaps only inferred. We do not know exactly what was done with the corpses of executed persons, but we usually refer this statement again to the Easter accounts.

Now verse 3 doubtless recalls Isaiah 53:9. The LXX writes with the Vulgate: *et dabit (δώσω) impios pro sepultura, et divitem pro morte sua.* But instead of the retaliation of God there has appeared now the grace of God (cf. Isa. 53:6; Rom. 3:25; 8:3). The "logic" of this new creed localizes Christ in heaven (Rom. 8:34; 1:4) and our sins in the past of Christ's grave, exactly like Rom. 6:4. Thus the apostolic message has probably found its precise formulation not at all through Peter or those witnesses, but in the realm of the pre-Pauline yet Hellenistic community, within the scriptural purview of the LXX.

What had been seen was intended for the sake of *faith*. Faith must not be confused with this having seen. The true rivalry exists not between faith and seeing, but | between Jesus' death and our sins, between God's grace and our guilt-laden history, between the word of God and the law, that nails us down in our sins, as verses 17 f. know; cf. verse 56.

Paul can be of the opinion that those appearances do not conflict with faith only because he already understands the cross of Christ as a word of grace. On that account he says elsewhere that Christ "gave" himself "for us" (Gal. 1:4; 2:20). Christ's cross in its finality simply belongs no longer in the context of the old history (Rom. 7:4). Not the law that rules that history (Rom. 7:1 f.) but really only Christ is God's word. And only with this word the time for believing has come, the time which was promised with Abraham (Gal. 3:23). The word of God was formerly hidden (II Cor. 3:12–18). By the same token faith was hidden (Rom. 11:4). But now the time for faith has definitely come. That is the meaning of the scriptural proof in I Cor. 15:3 f. And the apostle is the herald of this time (II Cor. 6:2). His gospel is quite simply the time announcement of the time of grace, without spatial boundaries (Rom. 1:14 f.). The creed brings with it the eschatological reconciliation of God with sinners.

The profundity of faith thus depends, as was said, upon how one evaluates the power of sin brought to naught by God. If this is the power of death, then the time of grace means our life (II Cor. 2:16). And this means that all believers exactly like the apostle open their mouths at that point where death says scornfully to the survivor: Now speak. The death of Jesus is so little an objection that faith rather can allow Jesus himself in the place of death to speak to the world as Lord (II Cor. 5:20). The test of faith is thus exactly the word that faith is able to speak in a situation in which the sinner must fall silent if he lacks faith. For faith comes from the word. The word of faith (Rom. 10:7) is not the servant of any history, but the preaching of this word shows through its very occurrence that history has been subjected to the word (I Cor. 15:57). The nature of the word *is* precisely proclamation, just as faith is one mode of word. Christ is thus Lord *because* it is proclaimed that the time for faith has come. The crucified Jesus became the all-governing word of the cross (I Cor. 1:17). That is the wonder of his resurrection. Jesus and faith in him do not conflict at all, but are one and the same: the event of the coming of God into a world hostile to God. One must not believe in Jesus if he wants to believe in God, but one is invited to believe in him, since God speaks with us in the person of Jesus, in that he also makes us persons and thus keeps us by his side. Then our life is not idle talk but a conversation with God.

The Problem of a New Testament Theology*

by

Herbert Braun

Translated by Jack Sanders

The problem of a theology of the New Testament has a double aspect. If one takes "theology" in the broader, customary sense he must define the problem in this way: The authors of the New Testament make statements dealing with man's salvation and with his relation to God which cannot be brought into harmony with one another, and which prove by their disparateness that their subject matter is not what they state, *expressis verbis*, in mutual contradiction. On the other hand, if one conceives of theology in the narrower sense – as doctrine concerning the deity – it is clearly seen that the New Testament reckons naively with the existence of a deity, just as do Old Testament and Jewish literature and a good part of Hellenistic literature as well. The New Testament is thus alienated from us who are no longer able to make such a presupposition. Both types of problems hang closely together in point of view of their essence; here, however, they shall be dealt with separately. Only then, in a third section of this essay, can the effort be made to break through this two-fold problem.

I

The New Testament makes divergent statements about central theological subjects. We shall ponder one after another christology, soteriology, relation to the Torah, eschatology, and doctrine of the sacraments.

a) The whole New Testament, of course, agrees that Jesus teaches. The preaching of the Synoptic Jesus (where, I am still convinced, one is more likely to find fragments from the preaching of the historical Jesus) demands from man radical obedience to God and standing up unconditionally for his neighbor. This preacher of unconditional obedience thereby takes sides precisely with the religiously out | cast among his contemporaries. The person of this preacher, on the other hand – apart from his demand and apart from his friendship with tax-collectors and sinners – appears to have been of no interest during the period of the public ministry.

* "Die Problematik einer Theologie des Neuen Testaments," ZThK, Beiheft 2, September 1961, pp. 3–18.

The same would also be true if one wished to suppose that the historical Jesus considered himself to be the Messiah. He evidently did not himself demand such an acknowledgement from those around him. It is with the Easter faith that the earliest community confesses Jesus to be the Messiah who is shortly to come. Christology thus becomes central. Jewish, Hellenistic, and gnostic honorific titles are now applied to Jesus and are recast, step by step, back into Jesus' life. The Fourth Gospel is an end point of such development. Here Jesus speaks exclusively of the necessity of knowing and acknowledging him as the bearer of salvation. It is in keeping with this that the call which the historical Jesus addresses to men is repressed by the growth of christology. The Pauline Christ effects salvation by dying and rising; his exhortation, however, does not play a central role. The Johannine Jesus, finally, does not make a general call for obedience to God's commands and for love of neighbor in general; he calls for acknowledgment of himself. The New Testament picture of Jesus cannot on the surface be reduced to a common denominator.

b) The New Testament as a whole looks toward the final salvation that man is to gain before God. Man gains this final salvation, according to the preaching of Jesus, through obeying the instruction of Jesus and through allowing, in this obedience, all his claims before God to be shattered. A specific view about Jesus' dignity is not here demanded of the one who obeys. Beginning with the rise of the earliest community, the Yes to Jesus as the bringer of salvation serves as the condition for the attaining of salvation. This Yes simply goes alongside the demanded ethos, without an organic bond being established between the Yes to the bringer of salvation and the ethos that is demanded. This is the case in parts of the Catholic Epistles, and also in Acts. The Yes to Jesus as the bringer of salvation can, however, also be interpreted in a very sharply defined way: as renunciation of fame; as being sustained by God's miraculous action $(\pi\nu\varepsilon\tilde{\upsilon}\mu\alpha)$, out of which the responsibility for right conduct grows (so Paul); as Yes to the true reality, measured by which what is materially or religiously pregiven becomes unreal, Yes to the reality in which the obedient one first learns the proper understanding of himself (so John). In the Synoptic pattern, the problem of gaining final salvation is indeed sighted, but the final salvation is considered to be endangered by the disobedience of man; the obedient one, on the other hand, will be saved. There is no mention yet of a *christological* overcoming of this danger. | The naive juxtaposition of christology and conduct signals, to be sure, the basic impossibility of man's gaining salvation, but does not make this impossibility very evident. Paul and John, on the other hand, underscore salvation as a human impossibility. Here Christ becomes the cipher for the organic abrogation of this impossibility by means of the divine miracle. The soteriological question, viewed from the surface, does not receive an unequivocal answer in the New Testament.

c) The same is true of the relation of the New Testament to the Torah, to the law of the Old Testament and Judaism. Various aspects come into play here, and we must consider them one after the other. There is first the question of the content of the specific instructions. As the Synoptics show, Jesus basically viewed the contents of the Torah as entirely binding. Jesus even sharpened the Torah. Existence for one's neighbor is meant more seriously than the contemporary interpretation of the Torah and even the wording of the Torah itself advise. It is precisely the radicalizing of the Torah which leads, of course, to its concrete break-up. Cultic purity is made altogether unimportant by Jesus. He appears to have broken the Sabbath provocatively by his healings. This concrete freedom over against the Torah does not remove for Jesus, however, the basic Yes to the contents of the Torah. Whoever keeps the Ten Commandments will obtain life. This attitude, which is in itself not unequivocal, is now subsequently modified. A severely Jewish-Christian point of view sees in Jesus the one who requires observance of the Torah to the last letter (Mt. 5: 17–19). Jewish food and marriage laws even become important in certain circles of Hellenistic Christianity (Acts 15: 28f.). Other circles of Hellenistic Christianity display a certain freedom, but also a conscientious obligation to the food laws (I Cor. 8:10; Rom. 14 and 15), whose content, however, is now mixed with aspects of Hellenistic oriental asceticism. In the post-Pauline period (John, James, the Pastoral Epistles) the ritual content of the Torah has become irrelevant. Only the command of love and its concrete, paraenetic application were held onto through the whole development covering the period of the composition of the New Testament writings.

From the question concerning the content of the Torah is to be separated the question concerning the Torah as the way of salvation. In this regard, Jesus does not dispute the basic statement that right doing results in life. To be sure, he seems to see that precisely the obedience of the Torah can become spiritually dangerous for man. Thus, the son of Luke 15 who behaves legally is the one who is really lost, and the calculating claim of the twelve-hour workers misunderstands God's goodness that gives sovereignly (Mt. 20). But neither with Jesus nor with the earliest community does that lead to a fundamental renunciation of | the Torah as way of salvation. That occurs first with Paul. Here the Torah as way of salvation is forbidden because it necessarily leads man into self-praise. This wrong way is inherent, according to Paul, in every legal way. Thus the non-Jew also has an ethical observance similar to the Torah, and boasting in it too must be excluded by faith. Law may not be used as a way of salvation. From here derive the harsh words that the Torah comes from the demons (Gal. 3 and 4).

This extreme position, faith *or* (exclusively) legal works as way of salvation, is soon given up. The Deutero-Pauline and Pastoral Epistles still reproduce the formulas; but the emphasis now lies on faith as the way of salvation, while the warding off of the legal way becomes irrelevant. The law is considered now as an unbearable yoke (Acts 15: 10), no longer as a dangerous inducement to self-praise. One sees only its ethical contents, purified of ritual observances. Thus there comes into use the slogan, considered to be Pauline, "Law *and* Faith" (Acts 13: 38 f.; James 2; cf. I Clem. 31: 2). There are even whole bodies of literature that are no longer interested at all in the question of the Torah as way of salvation (Johannine literature, Catholic Epistles).

Even where the New Testament understands the law as oracular text which looks forward to the messianic period and the Messiah and thus confirms the present Christ event – and hence ignoring the demands of its contents, ignoring its use as a means of attaining salvation –, even there no unanimity prevails. The Old Testament and the Torah, to be sure, are cited throughout the New Testament as authority. But the use of this authority is of quite varying intensity. Along side of Paul, Hebrews, and Matthew, with their repeated scriptural proofs, stands the more cautious use of the Old Testament in John, in the Pastoral Epistles with their quotations (πιστὸς ὁ λόγος) of *Christian* formulations, and in Acts, where partly formulated *topoi* of the diatribe are used alongside the Old Testament.

The attitude of the New Testament to the Torah is an oscillating color chart.

d) The movement around Jesus is rooted in Jewish apocalypticism. Like the Qumran community, Jesus expected the end of the world as being very near. Resurrection of the dead and general judgment are essential pieces of this expected final drama. Jesus' exorcisms signalize the immediate nearness of the moment in which God will begin his reign, and Jesus' preaching wishes to prepare the hearer for the proper endurance of the threatening judgment. Since with the Easter faith Jesus is considered to be the Messiah, this belief in the near end is preserved both in the earliest Jewish-Christian community and in the Hellenistic community. Now, however, it is Jesus' coming | as Messiah that lies ahead. His earthly life likewise receives in retrospect, at first by degrees, a messianic character. Thus Paul (Rom. 13: 11; Phil. 4: 5) and his congregations (I Thess. 4) still expect the parousia in their lifetime, even though they now consider the final salvation as present and, accordingly, the present time as end time.

This expectation is given up in the rest of the New Testament in a double way. First, the date of the parousia is extended. This occurs in a hesitant way in Mark and Matthew (some will experience the end, Mk. 9: 1); more decidedly with the third evangelist (for whom the Son of Man sits at the right hand, without saying anything about his coming within the limits of time; Lk. 22:69 compared with the parallels), for whom the apostolic age has become historical; in II Thessalonians ("the day of the Lord is at hand" is a false slogan); and in II Peter 3 ("a thousand years as one day"). Alongside this way of extending the date stands the resolute absorption of the end into the present in such a way that the temporal future falls out, and judgment, life, and resurrection occur in the present stance of the hearer toward the message of Jesus. That is the way in which the Fourth Gospel interprets eschatology. This consistent eschatologizing of the present which renounces the temporal future did not succeed, however. Some glosses reintroduce the temporal future into the Fourth Gospel, and now make it just barely possible to understand the Johannine text in the sense of the extended eschatology. The eschatological views of the New Testament are, in any case, full of strong tensions.

e) For the entire development of the history of dogma and of piety during the first Christian centuries, it is no doubt valid to say that the intensifying of what is sacramental corresponds to the subsiding of the eschatological tension. In the New Testament itself, to be sure, imminent eschatology and sacrament still overlap at least partially. Jesus let himself be baptized with the baptism of John as though it were the eschatological sign, and it is possible that he himself baptized. We possess, however, no word from him which indicates to what extent the baptism of John was meaningful for him or for his adherents. Baptism in the name of Jesus is then practiced in the earliest community as placing one under Jesus' protection, as cleansing from previous sins, and, perhaps not immediately from the beginning, as bestowing the spirit – that is, placing one under God's action upon man to effect his final salvation. The Hellenistic community interpreted baptism, furthermore, in analogy to the mysteries as the *neophytes* taking part in the fate of the cult hero. Paul, to be sure, then applies the brake to the aspect of pure naturalism connected with this view in order to emphasize the character of the new life as obligation. He does this without breaking through the frame of nature categories in his own thinking, not to speak of later theology. The sacrament is there.

Something similar holds true for the Lord's Supper. I am still unable, in spite of attempts to link Qumran to the Lord's Supper, to regard Mark 14 and parallels even partially as an authentic report of the Last Supper. I consider rather that the tradition about the *last* Supper, together with the words of institution, is of Hellenistic origin. But even if the saying about the bread, for example, were authentic, precisely Qumran would show that the eschatological meal is no more a sacrament than the regular meal of the daily breaking of bread in Acts is sacrament. Here also that which is really sacramental begins with the Hellenistic community. In this community, participation in the elements means taking part in the blood and body of Christ, and an improper use of this holy matter brings about, so

one supposes, illness and death, i. e. the opposite of *the* life which is expected from the sacrament. Paul can use these magical trains of thought; he
merely stresses that the sacrament does not produce life if one's conduct is
bad. A massive, sacramental doctrine of the Lord's Supper is unorganically
inserted into the Fourth Gospel. There thus follows upon the unsacramen-
tal attitude of the Jewish Christian beginning a more or less marked
sacramentalizing on the soil of Hellenistic Christianity. In keeping with
this the cult in which the Jewish Christian community at first also took
part – the Temple and sacrificial cult in Jerusalem – becomes unimportant
for the further development on the way into the Hellenistic world; it
makes room for a Hellenistic Christian cult. Thus, alongside the Jewish
calendar of festivals still used in Acts, there comes in the ἡμέρα κυρίου, the
first day of the week, which is influenced by Hellenistic oriental religion.

The New Testament does not have a uniform doctrine of sacrament and
cult.

II

We escape the perplexity and the problems indicated by this disparateness of New Testament theological views too cheaply and too simply if we
merely state that these differences must be neutralized in a higher unity.
This is certainly the case. But we must be cautious lest we locate the
point of coincidence, the higher unity, as too close at hand, shortsightedly
and over-hastedly. To this end, a deepening of the problems just pointed
out is required.

The situation with regard to the disparate standpoints which are advocated in the New │ Testament is by no means such that we should simply have
to choose between the two or more advocated positions and should in this
choice have to decide for one of them. Each of the positions, including the
point of departure of the whole, i. e. that which can be made out about the
views of Jesus of Nazareth, appears in problematical light and brings up a
number of questions which we ought not to suppress if we are interested in
finding out what the statements of the New Testament may have to say to
us today. I shall now discuss such questions in the same order as the five
groups of theological statements dealt with above.

a) All the designations of dignity which the community applied to Jesus
in confessions – Messiah, Son of Man, Kyrios, Sōtēr, Logos – fit for the
Jew of that time as well as for the religious person in Hellenism into a
firmly outlined system of coordinates. That there is such a figure as the
Messiah or the Kyrios is beyond discussion for the man of that time; it is
rather an obvious presupposition everywhere. This prerequisite which the
man of antiquity meets in his religious world view without being expressly conscious of it is not diminished in its character as prerequisite by
the fact that the contents of these titles are modified by what the com-

munity brings in as peculiar and independent, e. g. the Messiah dies as the atoner, something which is not originally contained in the concept of the Messiah. We today with our world view are not able to meet this prerequisite, namely that there is a Messiah, a Kyrios. Thus, the New Testament question, "Do you hold Jesus to be the Messiah, to be the Kyrios?" becomes a problem for us in the sense that neither our Yes nor our No can have as an answer the meaning which is, on the surface, attached to it in the New Testament.

b) Final salvation is gained, according to the assertion of the New Testament, through an obedience which makes no claim before God, or through belief in Jesus. Let us put aside for the present the christological side of the problem. Final salvation is conceived either in a Jewish way, as life free from toil upon the renewed earth, or dualistically, as an unearthly, otherworldly condition in the place where God and the heavenly beings are. Both ways of thinking are foreign to us. One should not object that their foreignness is merely a question of a different way of viewing things. Such a prolonged earthly-thisworldly or heavenly-otherworldly form of what we here call life is in its naiveté neither believable for us nor worth striving for. Final salvation as an extension of life or living on upon an otherworldly plane, which is in the final analysis again thought of as thisworldly, is problematical for us.

c) The colored scale which is reproduced above of New Testament atti- | tudes toward the Torah is governed by a pervading presupposition. That is, that God has decreed binding orders which man is to accept. This acceptance occurs first naively and heteronomously. Old instructions, to be sure, are broken through and replaced by new contents; the Jewish ritual elements as divinely willed content gradually vanish from the New Testament. Such vanishing is again, however, at least as it looks on the surface, legitimized by a heteronomous authority. Authentic sayings of Jesus or sayings of the exalted one in the mouth of the apostles now give the modified order. Casuistry, which lays down God's will precisely, is lacking, to be sure, in the oldest layer with Jesus himself. But the on-going paraenesis of the community in the form of secondary sayings of Jesus, the concrete admonitions of Paul in spite of the ground rule that it is love which fulfills the law — all make clear that the theonomy as heteronomy is not fundamentally overcome. Even Paul's replacing of the law as way of salvation with faith, even the proclamation that everything that does not proceed from faith is sin (Rom. 14: 23), does not change the fact that the orders given by God stand firm with regard to content. The law is holy and the commandment is holy, right, and good. The dulling, following upon Paul, of the exclusive antithesis between legal works and faith is the very return to the heteronomy of the content imposed by God upon man. Precisely this presupposition, however, that God has proclaimed in an authoritarian way instructions of a definite content which are therefore, i. e. heteronomously, binding, is not within our reach and is unattainable in its naive heteronomy. Thus we are also able to grasp the oracular character of the Torah only as a phenomenon of the history of religion; for the concept of God which lies behind it, (that there are holy texts full of profound divine meaning), is unattainable for us.

d) Of the three forms of New Testament eschatology the oldest, the consistent imminent expectation, is obviously an error and is accordingly, for all practical purposes, no longer advocated today at all – irrespective of peripheral instances in Christianity. The form of extending the time limit, on the other hand, which dominates in the later New Testament and which also overlies the original form of the Gospel of John, still has numerous advocates. This is due to the fact that we do not make clear to ourselves what kind of a concept of God is active in each temporal conception of eschatology, be it near expectation or extended eschatology. It is the deity existing in itself, which directs the course of history, which establishes beginning and end. Is God not here, however, naively taken as given? And is it not this naive acquiescence which brings it about that the hearer plunges into the desperate adventure – desperate in terms of our world view – of extending the time limit, | after the near expectation has proved to be error? The genuine Johannine renunciation of the temporal future of the final drama is, to be sure, not affected by this reproach. And yet it is difficult to see how it is fitting to call the eschatological terms now actualized in John – judgment, life, resurrection, damnation – eschatology. They are called that in the Fourth Gospel with the historical justification that they originated in the discussion with the temporal eschatology of that day. But precisely this presupposition is not valid for us when we read the Fourth Gospel. The interpretation of temporal eschatology which the Fourth Gospel undertakes is for us merely beating the air.

e) There is no doubt that Paul resists the materializing of salvation; baptism and Lord's Supper offer no guaranty of salvation. But this resistance occurs nevertheless against the background of a basic Yes, which is able to acknowledge that baptism incorporates one into the σῶμα of Christ, that chalice and bread unite with Christ's blood and body. Salvation is palpable; the sacrament attaches the receiver to the sphere of the deity. But even the old regular meal, in which the near final salvation is anticipated with rejoicing, as well as baptism understood unmysteriously, which takes away previous sins in view of the near judgment, even these older, not specifically sacramental concepts remain within the sphere of a way of thinking in which the coming of the deity is taken temporally and objectively – that is, in the area of a naive concept of God.

If one takes all these aspects of the deepened problems together, one

arrives at the following statement. Each of the groups of concepts which
has been mentioned has a considerable sector within which an objectifying
thinking takes place which, in its statements concerning the deity, disregards man. The world of God is thought here to be a reality existing in
itself, in a definite place, present or to be present at a definite time. Thus
God too is, in this view, a quantity existing in and for himself. Here faith
means to reckon with the fact that God *exists* and rewards those who seek
him (Heb. 11: 6). And this prerequisite which man meets reigns to
a great extent in the New Testament. For this God who exists in himself
makes his will public, which is then to be accepted by man heteronomously.
He sets up the variously named bringer of salvation; he prepares the final
salvation in his world; he establishes the moments and the end of the
course of time; he, with his transcendent world, becomes concretely palpable in the sacrament. To realize all this means at the same time to recog-
nize the impossibility of this view and of this concept of God. |

III

The New Testament itself, of course, has enough statements on the
basis of which even this, its own conception, is broken open. Thus we
stand now before the final step, in which an effort will be made to overcome the problems which have been presented up to now. One should
be able to break through these problems of New Testament theologizing,
previously set out, in such a way that he overcomes the disparateness of
New Testament statements with the same step that also leaves behind
the objectifying thinking about God and his world permeating the New
Testament. We shall now attempt to think through again, from this point
of view, the five groups of New Testament statements we have been dealing with.

a) We recognized that, upon an old non-christological stage, the life of
Jesus, there follows, after the formation of the community, the christological epoch. In this epoch the meaningfulness of Jesus is expressed with
Jewish, then with Hellenistic titles, in the form of the Easter faith, which
itself often varies in individual details. The old stage, the preaching Jesus,
puts man under radical obligation ("Why do you call me 'Lord, Lord,' and
do not do what I tell you," Lk. 6: 46) and brings him under the sovereignly
giving God ("Do you begrudge my generosity?" Mt. 20: 15). Precisely
this, however, is also the meaning of the explicit Pauline christology.
Faith in Jesus means to renounce boasting (Rom. 3: 27), to obey the God
who gives and commands ("You present yourselves as slaves to obedience,"
Rom. 6: 16). With John, however, faith knows that man can truly live
only by the miracle of the radical renewing of existence, the new birth
(3: 5); the new birth is attached to man's experiencing the critical love

that uncovers him (3: 16–21). In the last analysis, the pre-christological and the christological epochs are one in the interrelationship of "I may" and "I ought." The "I may" is obviously attached in the beginning of the whole development to an experience that men had in encounter with Jesus of Nazareth. Where this "I may" and "I ought" again become event – in the community by means of the proclamation – there is Jesus; Jesus now, to be sure, in christologized form, now as Christ, as Kyrios. Jesus is therefore not simply there – the Messiah, Kyrios is not simply there – although this naive givenness, this naive objectivity is not excluded in the New Testament. The fact of a pre-christological *and* a christological stage in the New Testament, and again the disparateness of the statements even within the christological stage show rather that Jesus always occurs in my "I may" and | "I ought" – in the realm of the relation with one's fellow man. And such occurrence breaks down the objectivity of the given.

b) We recognized that the preaching of Jesus demands obedience and renunciation of any claim before God as a way to final salvation, and that the preaching of the community and of the apostles demands faith in Jesus and right conduct. Faith and conduct can thereby stand unorganically alongside each other; they can also, however, be organically combined. Insofar as faith in Jesus and conduct stand unorganically alongside each other, Jesus becomes – contrary to the proper sense of christology just explicated – an object, and christology becomes naive, more or less massive metaphysics. Where, however, conduct arises from the "I may" as something experienced, or in christological terms from faith in Jesus, there Jesus is understood as "I may" and "I ought," there he is an event analogous to what occurred historically with regard to Jesus of Nazareth. To that extent the New Testament soteriological teaching is, however, *in the last analysis* uniform if one has in view the interpreted version of christology. Only where Christology stands uninterpreted *alongside* conduct, would one have to speak of two ways of salvation within the New Testament: Of obedience and renunciation of all claims in the teaching of the Synoptic Jesus on one hand, and on the other hand the combination of faith in Jesus and conduct, in the texts which have an uninterpreted christology. In the latter, final salvation would then also have no inner connection with the way of salvation.

For we further recognized that the New Testament understands the final salvation to a considerable extent naïvely as thisworldly, prolonged life or as continued life upon an otherworldly plane, which is in the last analysis, however, also thought of in thisworldly terms. Now, beside this naïveté which is foreign to us today, we find precisely in the texts that do not show the naïve coexistence of faith in Jesus and conduct just discussed – i.e. in some Synoptic, Pauline, and Johannine sayings – a way of viewing things for which final salvation and the way of salvation hang together in an organic and suitable way. This way of viewing things does not oppose the naïve, metaphysical expression of final salvation *explicitly*. The breaking up of the naïve lengthening of life or continuation of life ensues instead as a natural consequence, from the logic of the subject matter, when e. g. according to Jesus the obedient one is only like a slave who is never entitled to recompense for his fulfilling of his obligation (Lk. 17: 7–10); when the reward that Paul expects consists in his preaching without remuneration (I Cor. 9: 18); or when life according to John is not something that is coming, but something that the one who believes in Jesus has, i. e. deciphered, the one who allows his worldly and religious standards to be shattered (Jn. 17: 3; 9: 39). Thus | final salvation is brought down from the heights of a metaphysical so-called world of God onto the profane floor of the true relation with one's fellow man. *Here* then might the salvation of God be found. This is of course, as has been said, a consequence – a justified consequence, to be sure – alongside of which final salvation conceived in a naïvely objective way continues to exist in the New Testament.

c) We recognized that the contents of the New Testament instruction fluctuate because the ritual element of the Torah slowly retreats into the background and finally disappears, having become irrelevant, while the command of love holds throughout the entire New Testament. This clear tune at the basis of all variations of paraenesis is particularly underscored in its unity – a unity that holds everything together – in that love toward God is interpreted as love toward one's neighbor. The help and kindness demonstrated or not demonstrated to the oppressed neighbor is in fact demonstrated or not demonstrated to Jesus (Mt. 25: 31 ff.). Ἀγάπη for Paul is directed toward the neighbor (I Cor. 13). Love toward God is actualized concretely in the demonstration of love toward one's neighbor (I Jn. 4 : 20). The true relation with one's fellow man is *the* often varied content of New Testament instruction. Thus the paraenetic materials of the diatribe appear alongside the Torah, whose ritual content one soon no longer accepts as source of command. The paraenetic materials have in certain circumstances passed through the filter of Hellenistic Judaism, which had already used these contents in its own service. Thus there is present here a far-reaching unity in the New Testament. The problems set in with the question of the basis. I do not mean now the basis of conduct, of the "I ought" in the non-christological or christologically coded "I may," which we have just considered in the passage on soteriology. Rather we wish to investigate who gives the authorized contents of the instruction – the previous contents, the contents radicalized by Jesus, those de-ritualized more and more strongly by Jesus and the later development?

We recognized above that God is widely understood as the giver of the Torah; then it is Jesus and the Spirit speaking in the apostle that are the stages which legitimize the radicalizing and the de-ritualizing. Theono-

my is therefore widely taken as heteronomy. Now the New Testament
also, to be sure, makes considerable beginnings which break through this
heteronomy. Man is lord of the cultic day, which is subordinated to man
(Mk. 2: 27–28). This is perhaps an authentic saying of the Lord and not a
christologizing saying formed by the community. What defiles comes not
from without, but from the heart (Mk. 7: 15). Such words of Jesus certainly
do not mean that their contents are valid because of Jesus' authority;
rather they count on the conscientious Yes of the hearer simply on the
basis of their content. In fact, therefore, we have theonomy as autonomy,
not | as heteronomy. Thus Paul too is of the opinion that the pagan knows
about the proper norm (Rom. 2: 14) and is therefore, just as the Jewish
student of the Torah, properly informed. Thus Paul renounces casuistry and
binds the norm for right doing to the conscience of the believer (Rom. 14:
23). The reflection of the believer upon what is right to do in the given
case is meaningful (Phil. 4: 8–9). With John, the unquestionable certainty
of believing existence is promised to the believer (Jn. 16: 23). All that
means that it is not God or Jesus as outside authority who legitimizes,
heteronomously, the content of an order. Rather it must read the other
way; to be able to act in this way or that with a conviction, with confidence,
conscientiously, means to act upon God's order, according to God.
Theonomy and autonomy coincide. God is thus the expression for the
phenomenon of being able to act conscientiously, confidently, and with
conviction. Of course, as has been said, these are only beginnings. They are
not thought through in the New Testament. The New Testament as a
whole is ambivalent at this point, and herein lie its inner problems.

The ground for this ambivalence becomes clear when we remember that
the spiritual danger of the Torah as the way to salvation, and thus the
Pauline exclusiveness of faith or works, is not at all unanimously accepted in
the New Testament. There is also in the New Testament a soteriology in
which uninterpreted faith in Jesus and conduct stand unorganically alongside one another. Precisely in the non-Pauline and non-Johannine passages
with an uninterpreted christology the "I ought" does not grow organically
from the "I may." If then even Paul, who relates conduct strictly to salvation and leaves the knowledge of the norm to the conscience of the believer
(Rom. 14: 23), designates the content of the law as holy and good (Rom.
7: 12) and consequently still remains bound to the theonomous heteronomy,
how could this heteronomy not become completely active at those points
in the New Testament where, contemporary with and after Paul, faith in
Jesus and conduct stand again unconnectedly alongside one another? The
measure in which theonomy becomes autonomy or heteronomy in the
New Testament therefore corresponds to the interpreted or uninterpreted
christology and to the available or not available interrelatedness of faith
and works.

The Torah as prophetic text is widely used in the New Testament, but in subsiding intensity, as we established. Christian and also profane quotations take the place of the Torah. The concept of God connected to this view, however, that God speaks full of profound meaning in holy texts, is foreign to us. But this static concept of God is nevertheless broken through, at least to the extent that it is now assumed that even people | outside the Old Testament know something of the proper meaning of faith. Theonomy, in this widening of the quoted texts to include profane writings, is at least faintly perceived as human autonomy.

d) We recognized that the imminent eschatology is an error of the first generation, which the prolonged eschatology seeks to correct in an inconsistent and implausible way, while both forms presuppose the deity existing in itself and appointing beginning and end. The intention of these eschatological statements however, as it imposes itself upon us, becomes comprehensible when one lets go of the conception of the deity existing in itself and of the conception of the temporal periods fixed by this deity. Precisely the near expectation conceals, in the lap of this objectifying thinking, something which in fact breaks through all these objectivisms. For the man of the near expectation is *now* to repent (Mk. 1: 15), *now* to treat properly his fellow human beings entrusted to him (Mt. 24: 43–51 and parallels), *now* to build the house with right conduct upon the rock instead of sand (Mt. 7: 24–27), *now* to watch (I Thess. 5: 1–11). Here in the near expectation it is not therefore a matter, properly understood, of the calculating of an objective course of time which an objective deity fixed; here it is a matter of perceiving the proper καιρός (Rom. 13: 11). Καιρός, to be sure, not understood in the sense of the imminent end taken literally, not in the sense of the calculation which all too obviously has been proved to be a miscalculation. Rather imminent eschatology signalizes the filledness, the irretrievable once-and-for-all-ness, and the inevitable urgency of my being addressed, challenged, and sustained in the sense of final validity. Thus extended eschatology would be proved to be precisely a pronounced misinterpretation of imminent eschatology, by the fact that it takes the temporal character of near eschatology, its objectifying scheme, seriously, and disregards what is really intended in imminent eschatology, the urgency of the now. What is really intended does become active in John in an excellent way – but only as interpretation of the *topoi* of the apocalyptic world view that is lost to us. Imminent eschatology however, properly understood, leads us to the decision here and now – *hic Rhodos, hic salta*. God would then be where the moment is received and lived in its filledness.

e) We recognized that a sacramental, material thinking with regard to baptism and the Lord's Supper grew up in the New Testament out of older, not specifically sacramental ideas in the course of the development of the first and second generations. Pre-sacramental and sacramental stages, however, take the presence of the deity, either expected or believed at hand, objectively and materially. Now this objective | thinking, as had also become clear to us, is not at all the only dominant way of thinking. Jesus let himself be baptized and perhaps himself baptized; but from none of his words can we infer that baptism as such possessed central significance for him and his. What is now stressed in the Christian presentation of the Baptist will have also been Jesus' opinion. Repentance cannot be ritually compensated for by baptism (Mt. 3: 7–10 and parallels); the Yes to the baptism of John presupposes obedience to the Baptist's preaching (Mk. 11: 30–31). And with Paul the life mediated in baptism and in the Lord's Supper is not primarily a gift *(Gabe)*; it is rather at the same moment a task *(Aufgabe)* to be carried out in one's conduct (Rom. 6: 4; I Cor. 10: 1–13). The Fourth Gospel mentions baptismal water when speaking of the new birth that establishes Christian existence only *en passant*, if the mention belongs to the original text at all. Over against this, the miracle of God and the descent and ascent of Jesus the Son of Man stand in a central position (Jn. 3: 5–13). Briefly, the palpable character of participation in salvation is broken through in the New Testament in many places; God is understood not as a holy given, but in the system of the coordinates "I may" and "I ought." The ambiguity, the ambivalence of the New Testament teaching regarding the sacrament is certainly to be conceded. It is an act of venturous interpretation when we state that the sacramentalizing which is indeed noticeable in the New Testament opposes the personal "I may" and "I ought," opposes the nonobjective concept of God in which the New Testament, according to its own statements, is so decisively interested.

We stand at the end and draw the conclusion. The New Testament conceals within itself disparate ideas; we have made them clear for ourselves in terms of christology, soteriology, attitude toward the Torah, eschatology, and doctrine of the sacraments. These diversities refer, for their part, to a still deeper problem within the New Testament statements, God as palpable and given and God as not palpable and not given. What is finally God in the New Testament sense? Here the knot of the several problems is tied, and here the breakthrough of the problems, which we attempted in this last part, must prove successful. That God and his world are *also* considered as object, as thing, in the New Testament cannot be disputed. We think we have pointed out, however, in the case of the five areas mentioned, that such objectifying does not correspond to the real trend of the New Testament. As what, however, would God then be understood?

At any rate, God would not be understood as the one existing for himself, as a species which | would only be comprehensible under this word.

God then means much rather the whence of my being agitated. My being agitated, however, is determined by the "I may" and "I ought"; determined by being taken care of and by obligation. Being taken care of and obligation, however, do not approach me from the universe, but from another, from my fellow man. The word of proclamation and the act of love reach me – if they really do reach me – from my fellow man. God is the whence of my being taken care of and of my being obliged, which comes to me from my fellow man. To abide in God would therefore mean to abide in the concrete act of devoting oneself to the other; whoever abides in ἀγαπᾶν abides in God (I Jn. 4: 16). I can speak of God only where I speak of man, and hence anthropologically. I can speak of God only where my "I ought" is counterpointed by "I may," and hence soteriologically. For even according to the New Testament, God in the final analysis, i.e. the inadequate objectifying of the doctrine of God set aside, is where I am placed under obligation, where I am engaged; engaged in unconditional "I may" and "I ought." That would mean then, however, that man as man, man in relation with his fellow man, implies God. That would always have to be dis-covered anew from the New Testament. God would then be a definite type of relation with one's fellow man. The atheist misses *man*. One may even ask, Is there really such a thing as an atheist? For does not every instance of a relation with one's fellow man already contain something of the intimate connection between the "I may" and 'I ought" that is so close to the heart of the New Testament?

Revised October 31, 1965

harper ✦ torchbooks

HUMANITIES AND SOCIAL SCIENCES

American Studies: General

American Studies: Colonial

American Studies: From the Revolution to the Civil War

---

† The New American Nation Series, edited by Henry Steele Commager and Richard B. Morris.

‡ American Perspectives series, edited by Bernard Wishy and William E. Leuchtenburg.

* The Rise of Modern Europe series, edited by William L. Langer.

‖ Researches in the Social, Cultural, and Behavioral Sciences, edited by Benjamin Nelson.

§ The Library of Religion and Culture, edited by Benjamin Nelson.

ᵒ Not for sale in Canada.

Σ Harper Modern Science Series, edited by James R. Newman.

FRANK THISTLETHWAITE: America and the Atlantic Community: *Anglo-American Aspects, 1790-1850* TB/1107

A. F. TYLER: Freedom's Ferment: *Phases of American Social History from the Revolution to the Outbreak of the Civil War. 31 illus.* TB/1074

GLYNDON G. VAN DEUSEN: The Jacksonian Era: 1828-1848. † *Illus.* TB/3028

LOUIS B. WRIGHT: Culture on the Moving Frontier TB/1053

American Studies: Since the Civil War

RAY STANNARD BAKER: Following the Color Line: *American Negro Citizenship in Progressive Era. ‡ Illus. Edited by Dewey W. Grantham, Jr* TB/3053

RANDOLPH S. BOURNE: War and the Intellectuals: *Collected Essays, 1915-1919. ‡ Ed. by Carl Resek* TB/3043

A. RUSSELL BUCHANAN: The United States and World War II. † *Illus.* Vol. I TB/3044; Vol. II TB/3045

ABRAHAM CAHAN: The Rise of David Levinsky: *a documentary novel of social mobility in early twentieth century America. Intro. by John Higham* TB/1028

THOMAS C. COCHRAN: The American Business System: *A Historical Perspective, 1900-1955* TB/1080

THOMAS C. COCHRAN & WILLIAM MILLER: The Age of Enterprise: *A Social History of Industrial America* TB/1054

FOSTER RHEA DULLES: America's Rise to World Power: 1898-1954. † *Illus.* TB/3021

W. A. DUNNING: Essays on the Civil War and Reconstruction. *Introduction by David Donald* TB/1181

W. A. DUNNING: Reconstruction, Political and Economic: 1865-1877 TB/1073

HAROLD U. FAULKNER: Politics, Reform and Expansion: 1890-1900. † *Illus.* TB/3020

JOHN D. HICKS: Republican Ascendancy: 1921-1933. † *Illus.* TB/3041

ROBERT HUNTER: Poverty: *Social Conscience in the Progressive Era. ‡ Edited by Peter d'A. Jones* TB/3065

HELEN HUNT JACKSON: A Century of Dishonor: *The Early Crusade for Indian Reform. ‡ Edited by Andrew F. Rolle* TB/3063

ALBERT D. KIRWAN: Revolt of the Rednecks: *Mississippi Politics, 1876-1925* TB/1199

WILLIAM L. LANGER & S. EVERETT GLEASON: The Challenge to Isolation: *The World Crisis of 1937-1940 and American Foreign Policy* Vol. I TB/3054; Vol. II TB/3055

WILLIAM E. LEUCHTENBURG: Franklin D. Roosevelt and the New Deal: 1932-1940. † *Illus.* TB/3025

ARTHUR S. LINK: Woodrow Wilson and the Progressive Era: 1910-1917. † *Illus.* TB/3023

ROBERT GREEN MCCLOSKEY: American Conservatism in the Age of Enterprise: 1865-1910 TB/1137

GEORGE E. MOWRY: The Era of Theodore Roosevelt and the Birth of Modern America: 1900-1912. † *Illus.* TB/3022

RUSSEL B. NYE: Midwestern Progressive Politics: *A Historical Study of its Origins and Development, 1870-1958* TB/1202

WALTER RAUSCHENBUSCH: Christianity and the Social Crisis. ‡ *Edited by Robert D. Cross* TB/3059

WHITELAW REID: After the War: *A Tour of the Southern States, 1865-1866. ‡ Edited by C. Vann Woodward* TB/3066

CHARLES H. SHINN: Mining Camps: *A Study in American Frontier Government. ‡ Edited by Rodman W. Paul* TB/3062

TWELVE SOUTHERNERS: I'll Take My Stand: *The South and the Agrarian Tradition. Intro. by Louis D. Rubin, Jr.; Biographical Essays by Virginia Rock* TB/1072

WALTER E. WEYL: The New Democracy: *An Essay on Certain Political Tendencies in the United States. ‡ Edited by Charles B. Forcey* TB/3042

VERNON LANE WHARTON: The Negro in Mississippi: 1865-1890 TB/1178

Anthropology

JACQUES BARZUN: Race: *A Study in Superstition. Revised Edition* TB/1172

JOSEPH B. CASAGRANDE, Ed.: In the Company of Man: *Twenty Portraits of Anthropological Informants. Illus.* TB/3047

W. E. LE GROS CLARK: The Antecedents of Man: *Intro. to Evolution of the Primates.* º *Illus.* TB/559

CORA DU BOIS: The People of Alor. *New Preface by the author. Illus.* Vol. I TB/1042; Vol. II TB/1043

RAYMOND FIRTH, Ed.: Man and Culture: *An Evaluation of the Work of Bronislaw Malinowski* ‖ º TB/1133

L. S. B. LEAKEY: Adam's Ancestors: *The Evolution of Man and His Culture. Illus.* TB/1019

ROBERT H. LOWIE: Primitive Society. *Introduction by Fred Eggan* TB/1056

SIR EDWARD TYLOR: The Origins of Culture. *Part I of "Primitive Culture." § Intro. by Paul Radin* TB/33

SIR EDWARD TYLOR: Religion in Primitive Culture. *Part II of "Primitive Culture." § Intro. by Paul Radin* TB/34

W. LLOYD WARNER: A Black Civilization: *A Study of an Australian Tribe.* ‖ *Illus.* TB/3056

Art and Art History

WALTER LOWRIE: Art in the Early Church. *Revised Edition. 452 illus.* TB/124

EMILE MÂLE: The Gothic Image: *Religious Art in France of the Thirteenth Century.* § *190 illus.* TB/44

MILLARD MEISS: Painting in Florence and Siena after the Black Death: *The Arts, Religion and Society in the Mid-Fourteenth Century. 169 illus.* TB/1148

ERICH NEUMANN: The Archetypal World of Henry Moore. *107 illus.* TB/2020

DORA & ERWIN PANOFSKY: Pandora's Box: *The Changing Aspects of a Mythical Symbol. Revised Edition. Illus.* TB/2021

ERWIN PANOFSKY: Studies in Iconology: *Humanistic Themes in the Art of the Renaissance. 180 illustrations* TB/1077

ALEXANDRE PIANKOFF: The Shrines of Tut-Ankh-Amon. *Edited by N. Rambova. 117 illus.* TB/2011

JEAN SEZNEC: The Survival of the Pagan Gods: *The Mythological Tradition and Its Place in Renaissance Humanism and Art. 108 illustrations* TB/2004

OTTO VON SIMSON: The Gothic Cathedral: *Origins of Gothic Architecture and the Medieval Concept of Order. 58 illus.* TB/2018

HEINRICH ZIMMER: Myth and Symbols in Indian Art and Civilization. *70 illustrations* TB/2005

Business, Economics & Economic History

REINHARD BENDIX: Work and Authority in Industry: *Ideologies of Management in the Course of Industrialization* TB/3035

GILBERT BURCK & EDITORS OF FORTUNE: The Computer Age: *And Its Potential for Management* TB/1179

THOMAS C. COCHRAN: The American Business System: *A Historical Perspective, 1900-1955* TB/1080

THOMAS C. COCHRAN: The Inner Revolution: *Essays on the Social Sciences in History* TB/1140

THOMAS C. COCHRAN & WILLIAM MILLER: The Age of Enterprise: A Social History of Industrial America TB/1054

ROBERT DAHL & CHARLES E. LINDBLOM: Politics, Economics, and Welfare: Planning & Politico-Economic Systems Resolved into Basic Social Processes TB/3037

PETER F. DRUCKER: The New Society: The Anatomy of Industrial Order TB/1082

EDITORS OF FORTUNE: America in the Sixties: The Economy and the Society TB/1015

ROBERT L. HEILBRONER: The Great Ascent: The Struggle for Economic Development in Our Time TB/3030

FRANK H. KNIGHT: The Economic Organization TB/1214

FRANK H. KNIGHT: Risk, Uncertainty and Profit TB/1215

ABBA P. LERNER: Everybody's Business: Current Assumptions in Economics and Public Policy TB/3051

ROBERT GREEN MCCLOSKEY: American Conservatism in the Age of Enterprise, 1865-1910 TB/1137

PAUL MANTOUX: The Industrial Revolution in the Eighteenth Century: The Beginnings of the Modern Factory System in England ° TB/1079

WILLIAM MILLER, Ed.: Men in Business: Essays on the Historical Role of the Entrepreneur TB/1081

PERRIN STRYKER: The Character of the Executive: Eleven Studies in Managerial Qualities TB/1041

PIERRE URI: Partnership for Progress: A Program for Transatlantic Action TB/3036

Contemporary Culture

JACQUES BARZUN: The House of Intellect TB/1051

JOHN U. NEF: Cultural Foundations of Industrial Civilization TB/1024

NATHAN M. PUSEY: The Age of the Scholar: Observations on Education in a Troubled Decade TB/1157

PAUL VALÉRY: The Outlook for Intelligence TB/2016

Historiography & Philosophy of History

SIR ISAIAH BERLIN et al.: History and Theory: Studies in the Philosophy of History. Edited by George H. Nadel TB/1208

JACOB BURCKHARDT: On History and Historians. Intro. by H. R. Trevor-Roper TB/1216

WILHELM DILTHEY: Pattern and Meaning in History: Thoughts on History and Society. ° Edited with an Introduction by H. P. Rickman TB/1075

H. STUART HUGHES: History as Art and as Science: Twin Vistas on the Past TB/1207

RAYMOND KLIBANSKY & H. J. PATON, Eds.: Philosophy and History: The Ernst Cassirer Festschrift. Illus. TB/1115

JOSE ORTEGA Y GASSET: The Modern Theme. Introduction by Jose Ferrater Mora TB/1038

SIR KARL POPPER: The Open Society and Its Enemies
Vol. I: The Spell of Plato TB/1101
Vol. II: The High Tide of Prophecy: Hegel, Marx and the Aftermath TB/1102

SIR KARL POPPER: The Poverty of Historicism ° TB/1126

G. J. RENIER: History: Its Purpose and Method TB/1209

W. H. WALSH: Philosophy of History: An Introduction TB/1020

History: General

L. CARRINGTON GOODRICH: A Short History of the Chinese People. Illus. TB/3015

DAN N. JACOBS & HANS H. BAERWALD: Chinese Communism: Selected Documents TB/3031

BERNARD LEWIS: The Arabs in History TB/1029

SIR PERCY SYKES: A History of Exploration. ° Introduction by John K. Wright TB/1046

History: Ancient and Medieval

A. ANDREWES: The Greek Tyrants TB/1103

P. BOISSONNADE: Life and Work in Medieval Europe: The Evolution of the Medieval Economy, the 5th to the 15th Century. ° Preface by Lynn White, Jr. TB/1141

HELEN CAM: England before Elizabeth TB/1026

NORMAN COHN: The Pursuit of the Millennium: Revolutionary Messianism in Medieval and Reformation Europe TB/1037

G. G. COULTON: Medieval Village, Manor, and Monastery TB/1022

HEINRICH FICHTENAU: The Carolingian Empire: The Age of Charlemagne TB/1142

F. L. GANSHOF: Feudalism TB/1058

EDWARD GIBBON: The Triumph of Christendom in the Roman Empire (Chaps. XV-XX of "Decline and Fall," J. B. Bury edition). § Illus. TB/46

MICHAEL GRANT: Ancient History ° TB/1190

W. O. HASSALL, Ed.: Medieval England: As Viewed by Contemporaries TB/1205

DENYS HAY: The Medieval Centuries ° TB/1192

J. M. HUSSEY: The Byzantine World TB/1057

SAMUEL NOAH KRAMER: Sumerian Mythology TB/1055

FERDINAND LOT: The End of the Ancient World and the Beginnings of the Middle Ages. Introduction by Glanville Downey TB/1044

G. MOLLATT: The Popes at Avignon: 1305-1378 TB/308

CHARLES PETIT-DUTAILLIS: The Feudal Monarchy in France and England: From the Tenth to the Thirteenth Century ° TB/1165

HENRI PIRENNE: Early Democracies in the Low Countries: Urban Society and Political Conflict in the Middle Ages and the Renaissance. Introduction by John H. Mundy TB/1110

STEVEN RUNCIMAN: A History of the Crusades. Volume I: The First Crusade and the Foundation of the Kingdom of Jerusalem. Illus. TB/1143

FERDINAND SCHEVILL: Siena: The History of a Medieval Commune. Intro. by William M. Bowsky TB/1164

SULPICIUS SEVERUS et al.: The Western Fathers: Being the Lives of Martin of Tours, Ambrose, Augustine of Hippo, Honoratus of Arles and Germanus of Auxerre. Edited and translated by F. R. Hoare TB/309

HENRY OSBORN TAYLOR: The Classical Heritage of the Middle Ages. Foreword and Biblio. by Kenneth M. Setton TB/1117

F. VAN DER MEER: Augustine The Bishop: Church and Society at the Dawn of the Middle Ages TB/304

J. M. WALLACE-HADRILL: The Barbarian West: The Early Middle Ages, A.D. 400-1000 TB/1061

History: Renaissance & Reformation

JACOB BURCKHARDT: The Civilization of the Renaissance in Italy. Intro. by Benjamin Nelson & Charles Trinkaus. Illus. Vol. I TB/40; Vol. II TB/41

ERNST CASSIRER: The Individual and the Cosmos in Renaissance Philosophy. Translated with an Introduction by Mario Domandi TB/1097

FEDERICO CHABOD: Machiavelli and the Renaissance TB/1193

EDWARD P. CHEYNEY: The Dawn of a New Era, 1250-1453. * Illus. TB/3002

R. TREVOR DAVIES: The Golden Century of Spain, 1501-1621 ° TB/1194

DESIDERIUS ERASMUS: Christian Humanism and the Reformation: Selected Writings. Edited and translated by John C. Olin TB/1166

WALLACE K. FERGUSON et al.: Facets of the Renaissance
TB/1098

WALLACE K. FERGUSON et al.: The Renaissance: Six Essays. Illus.
TB/1084

JOHN NEVILLE FIGGIS: The Divine Right of Kings. Introduction by G. R. Elton
TB/1191

JOHN NEVILLE FIGGIS: Political Thought from Gerson to Grotius: 1414-1625: Seven Studies. Introduction by Garrett Mattingly
TB/1032

MYRON P. GILMORE: The World of Humanism, 1453-1517.* Illus.
TB/3003

FRANCESCO GUICCIARDINI: Maxims and Reflections of a Renaissance Statesman (Ricordi). Trans. by Mario Domandi. Intro. by Nicolai Rubinstein
TB/1160

J. H. HEXTER: More's Utopia: The Biography of an Idea New Epilogue by the Author
TB/1195

JOHAN HUIZINGA: Erasmus and the Age of Reformation. Illus.
TB/19

ULRICH VON HUTTEN et al.: On the Eve of the Reformation: "Letters of Obscure Men." Introduction by Hajo Holborn
TB/1124

PAUL O. KRISTELLER: Renaissance Thought: The Classic, Scholastic, and Humanist Strains
TB/1048

PAUL O. KRISTELLER: Renaissance Thought II: Papers on Humanism and the Arts
TB/1163

NICCOLO MACHIAVELLI: History of Florence and of the Affairs of Italy: from the earliest times to the death of Lorenzo the Magnificent. Introduction by Felix Gilbert
TB/1027

ALFRED VON MARTIN: Sociology of the Renaissance. Introduction by Wallace K. Ferguson
TB/1099

GARRETT MATTINGLY et al.: Renaissance Profiles. Edited by J. H. Plumb
TB/1162

MILLARD MEISS: Painting in Florence and Siena after the Black Death: The Arts, Religion and Society in the Mid-Fourteenth Century. 169 illus.
TB/1148

J. E. NEALE: The Age of Catherine de Medici °
TB/1085

ERWIN PANOFSKY: Studies in Iconology: Humanistic Themes in the Art of the Renaissance. 180 illustrations
TB/1077

J. H. PARRY: The Establishment of the European Hegemony: 1415-1715: Trade and Exploration in the Age of the Renaissance
TB/1045

J. H. PLUMB: The Italian Renaissance: A Concise Survey of Its History and Culture
TB/1161

CECIL ROTH: The Jews in the Renaissance. Illus.
TB/834

GORDON RUPP: Luther's Progress to the Diet of Worms °
TB/120

FERDINAND SCHEVILL: The Medici. Illus.
TB/1010

FERDINAND SCHEVILL: Medieval and Renaissance Florence. Illus.   Volume I: Medieval Florence
TB/1090
Volume II: The Coming of Humanism and the Age of the Medici
TB/1091

G. M. TREVELYAN: England in the Age of Wycliffe, 1368-1520 °
TB/1112

VESPASIANO: Renaissance Princes, Popes, and Prelates: The Vespasiano Memoirs: Lives of Illustrious Men of the XVth Century. Intro. by Myron P. Gilmore
TB/1111

History: Modern European

FREDERICK B. ARTZ: Reaction and Revolution, 1815-1832. * Illus.
TB/3034

MAX BELOFF: The Age of Absolutism, 1660-1815
TB/1062

ROBERT C. BINKLEY: Realism and Nationalism, 1852-1871. * Illus.
TB/3038

ASA BRIGGS: The Making of Modern England, 1784-1867: The Age of Improvement °
TB/1203

CRANE BRINTON: A Decade of Revolution, 1789-1799. * Illus.
TB/3018

J. BRONOWSKI & BRUCE MAZLISH: The Western Intellectual Tradition: From Leonardo to Hegel
TB/3001

GEOFFREY BRUUN: Europe and the French Imperium, 1799-1814. * Illus.
TB/3033

ALAN BULLOCK: Hitler, A Study in Tyranny. ° Illus.
TB/1123

E. H. CARR: The Twenty Years' Crisis, 1919-1939: An Introduction to the Study of International Relations °
TB/1122

GORDON A. CRAIG: From Bismarck to Adenauer: Aspects of German Statecraft. Revised Edition
TB/1171

WALTER L. DORN: Competition for Empire, 1740-1763. * Illus.
TB/3032

CARL J. FRIEDRICH: The Age of the Baroque, 1610-1660. * Illus.
TB/3004

RENÉ FUELOEP-MILLER: The Mind and Face of Bolshevism: An Examination of Cultural Life in Soviet Russia. New Epilogue by the Author
TB/1188

M. DOROTHY GEORGE: London Life in the Eighteenth Century
TB/1182

LEO GERSHOY: From Despotism to Revolution, 1763-1789. * Illus.
TB/3017

C. C. GILLISPIE: Genesis and Geology: The Decades before Darwin §
TB/51

ALBERT GOODWIN: The French Revolution
TB/1064

ALBERT GUERARD: France in the Classical Age: The Life and Death of an Ideal
TB/1183

CARLTON J. H. HAYES: A Generation of Materialism, 1871-1900. * Illus.
TB/3039

J. H. HEXTER: Reappraisals in History: New Views on History & Society in Early Modern Europe
TB/1100

A. R. HUMPHREYS: The Augustan World: Society, Thought, and Letters in 18th Century England °
TB/1105

ALDOUS HUXLEY: The Devils of Loudun: A Study in the Psychology of Power Politics and Mystical Religion in the France of Cardinal Richelieu § °
TB/60

DAN N. JACOBS, Ed.: The New Communist Manifesto & Related Documents. Third edition, revised
TB/1078

HANS KOHN: The Mind of Germany: The Education of a Nation
TB/1204

HANS KOHN, Ed.: The Mind of Modern Russia: Historical and Political Thought of Russia's Great Age
TB/1065

KINGSLEY MARTIN: French Liberal Thought in the Eighteenth Century: A Study of Political Ideas from Bayle to Condorcet
TB/1114

SIR LEWIS NAMIER: Personalities and Powers: Selected Essays
TB/1186

SIR LEWIS NAMIER: Vanished Supremacies: Essays on European History, 1812-1918 °
TB/1088

JOHN U. NEF: Western Civilization Since the Renaissance: Peace, War, Industry, and the Arts
TB/1113

FREDERICK L. NUSSBAUM: The Triumph of Science and Reason, 1660-1685. * Illus.
TB/3009

JOHN PLAMENATZ: German Marxism and Russian Communism. ° New Preface by the Author
TB/1189

RAYMOND W. POSTGATE, Ed.: Revolution from 1789 to 1906: Selected Documents
TB/1063

PENFIELD ROBERTS: The Quest for Security, 1715-1740. * Illus.
TB/3016

PRISCILLA ROBERTSON: Revolutions of 1848: A Social History
TB/1025

ALBERT SOREL: Europe Under the Old Regime. Translated by Francis H. Herrick
TB/1121

N. N. SUKHANOV: The Russian Revolution, 1917: Eyewitness Account. Edited by Joel Carmichael
Vol. I TB/1066; Vol. II TB/1067

A. J. P. TAYLOR: The Habsburg Monarch, 1809-1918: A History of the Austrian Empire and Austria-Hungary °
TB/1187

Political Science & Government

Psychology

6

Christianity: General

Christianity: Origins & Early Development

Christianity: The Middle Ages and The Reformation

Christianity: The Protestant Tradition